❖❖❖❖❖❖❖❖❖❖❖❖❖❖❖❖❖❖❖❖❖❖❖❖❖❖❖❖❖❖❖❖❖❖❖❖❖❖❖❖❖❖❖❖

# OPEN YOUR OWN
# BED & BREAKFAST

### Third Edition

❖❖❖❖❖❖❖❖❖❖❖❖❖❖❖❖❖❖❖❖❖❖❖❖❖❖❖❖❖❖❖❖❖❖❖❖❖❖❖❖❖❖❖❖

# OPEN YOUR OWN BED & BREAKFAST

## Third Edition

# Barbara Notarius

## Gail Sforza Brewer

**JOHN WILEY & SONS, INC.**

*New York • Chichester • Brisbane • Toronto • Singapore*

This text is printed on acid-free paper.

Copyright © 1987, 1992, 1996 by Barbara Notarius
Published by John Wiley & Sons, Inc.

All rights reserved. Published simultaneously in Canada.

*Library of Congress Cataloging-in-Publication Data:*
Notarius, Barbara.
    Open your own bed & breakfast / [Barbara Notarius, Gail Sforza
Brewer.] — 3rd ed.
       p.    cm.
    Includes index.
    ISBN 0-471-13044-3 (acid-free)
    1. Bed and breakfast accommodations.  2. Hotel management.
I. Brewer, Gail Sforza.  II. Title
TX911.2.N68 1996
647.94' 068—dc20
                                                                        95-23952

Printed in the United States of America

10 9 8 7 6

# Acknowledgments

Thanks for assistance and support for this book project go to:

- Cydney Notarius-Klein, my daughter, who has shouldered many of my responsibilities at the B&B while I devoted my attention to this book.

- Pat Wilson and Sarah Sonke of the American Bed and Breakfast Association, a clearinghouse for B&B information.

- The late Betty Rundback, author of one of the first B&B guides, who testified at my zoning trial and helped make it possible to establish a legal precedent for a Bed and Breakfast in residential neighborhoods.

- Arthur D. Levy, CPA, for information about the tax consequences of operating a Bed and Breakfast in your home.

- Cheryl Woods and Joseph Schilling of the New York State Department of Commerce.

- Janice Archbold of Guesthouses, Inc., Susan and Richard Kreibech of American Family Inn Bed & Breakfast, Susan Morris and Helen Heath of Southern Comfort Bed & Breakfast, Aster Mould of Bed & Breakfast Adventures, Ruth Young of Mi Casa Su Casa, and all the other members of Bed

& Breakfast Reservation Services Worldwide, without whom our trade association would not be possible.

- Gary Craig, who introduced me to John Wiley & Sons Publishers.

- PJ Dempsey, our editor.

- Brenda Barta, my partner at the inn who edited the text and contributed a myriad of her own ideas, facts, and information gleaned from telephone canvassing across the country. I also want to thank her for putting up with my behavior and shortness during the last very stressful weeks of getting this book finished.

- All the small innkeepers who have been so generous with  their time and experience.

- All the hosts, who have taught me as much as I have taught them and without whom Bed and Breakfast could not exist.

# Contents

# Introduction: America Is Waking Up to Bed and Breakfast

F ifteen years ago in the United States, one could find private-home Bed and Breakfast accommodations in only fifteen locations, primarily in California, with each host functioning as a sole entrepreneur. Today, over 20,000 families open their homes to paying guests, and most are linked coast to coast through state and national associations. Newsletters describing advances in the industry abound. Directories of establishments are published regularly. Major corporations include B&B travel as executive perks and sales incentives. Indeed, the term *Bed and Breakfast* has become so popular that even national hotel chains claim to offer the service.

There has never been a better time to become part of the Bed and Breakfast movement. This book is dedicated to helping you open a B&B in your home—be it a single room in your apartment, a room that is available when your child is away at college, or a multibedroom country mansion you can't wait to restore and fill constantly with guests. This book will assist you in finding out what is unique about your area, your home, and yourself, for it is the personal approach to gracious hospitality that distinguishes B&B hosting from all other types of travel services.

This book is an outgrowth of seminars for prospective hosts that I gave when I was president of Bed & Breakfast U.S.A., Ltd. The seminars presented the basics of starting a B&B. Questions from audience members were encouraged. Some of the most common questions and their answers are included at the end of most chapters.

In this book, I go beyond the introductory seminars and provide very detailed business management information culled from hundreds of owners, reservation services, and professional associations that I work with regularly. All this is offered in the hope that it will increase the joy and ease with which you manage your Bed and Breakfast. For most hosts, it is the pleasure that comes from adding new people to their lives that keeps them involved, not the intricacies of the latest Internal Revenue Service ruling on the tax consequences of home-based businesses. However, I cover that as well.

There have long been country inns, and many of the people attending my seminars think that they will learn how to run a country inn. But as you will see, a private-home B&B is not a country inn on a smaller scale; it is first and foremost a private home. It is a type of accommodation that is new to America, and its development has been very different from that of its precursors in Europe.

What makes me an expert on private-home Bed and Breakfast? Perhaps a brief description of how I became involved fifteen years ago will provide an answer.

## OUR DREAM HOUSE

In 1981, when my ex-husband and I bought our house, we were not looking for a 5,000-square-foot abode, but that's exactly what we fell in love with. My mother, and most of Croton-on-Hudson, New York, looked at the house and saw a white elephant that had been on the market for a year and a half. All they could see was that the house needed massive cosmetic repair, and they were scared off by it. What my ex-husband George and I saw was its potential to be the home of our dreams. I never thought we would be able to afford a house with a river view, an in-ground pool, and space for our family to grow and enjoy our many hobbies.

What we failed to understand was that although we could definitely afford the mortgage, the maintenance costs of such a large house would become our undoing. We had lived in a normal four-bedroom colonial home in lower Westchester, New York, before coming to Croton. The movers laughed as they delivered our furniture. The contents of the entire first floor of our old house barely filled up the thirty-five-foot sun porch of our new one. And our new living room, dining room, and downstairs office and study were pitifully empty.

The first year, I took a part-time job as a psychologist a few hours a week and spent my entire salary on wallpaper, paint, and filling up the many empty rooms with treasures acquired at garage sales, estate sales, and auctions. All my free time (when my little daughter was napping) was spent atop a ladder, scraping off years of accumulated wallpaper, sealing cracks, painting ceilings, and putting up new wallpaper. The house began to look better.

After the first winter, George sat down with me to talk about the cost of making our dream house a reality. Our heating bill the first winter was over $5,000 for 4,300 gallons of fuel oil; and even with oil heat, our electric bill was more than $200 a month. Our property taxes had gone from $4,800 to $6,200 just because the house had changed hands and taxes were based on the new selling price. Every new project seemed to cost twice as much as we expected and took three times as long to complete. For example, when we uncovered the pool, we found ten broken coping-stones (the concrete blocks that rim the pool). Each one had to be cut separately to a paper pattern by hand by a professional stonecutter, a major project—with a price to match.

Although our grand plan had been for me to be an at-home mom until our daughter, Cydney, reached school age, it became quite apparent that this scenario was only a dream. It began to look as though I would have to go back to a full-time job or that we would have to move into a smaller, more affordable home. After all the work I had done on the house, selling it was unthinkable. When I explored the idea of resuming my job in New York City, I realized that although on paper I earned $25,000, after paying taxes ($12,500), a baby-sitter ($7,000), transportation ($2,000), and maintaining a professional wardrobe ($2,000), what I would be earning for being away from my home and child all day would be under $2,000. This was obviously not the solution. I knew I couldn't start a home-based business and expect to earn $25,000, but could I beat $2,000 after taxes? I bet that I could. Having a home-based business that would allow us to write off some of our outrageous maintenance costs looked better and better. Our assets—the spaciousness of the house, many unused bedrooms, our enjoyment of entertaining and offering gracious hospitality—were ripe with possibility.

## OUR FIRST GUEST

I sent press releases to 150 publications throughout the world that were printed in English, had travel sections, and had large circulations. Bill, our very first guest, came to us from Brisbane, Australia, after reading about our place in the newspaper. He was sixty-seven years old and had traveled around the world twice before. On this trip, he had crossed Russia via the Trans-Siberian Railway and visited for a few weeks with his daughter in England. He wanted to break up the twenty-four-hour plane ride home. He decided to stay with us for a week of rest and relaxation and perhaps a little sightseeing in New York City. The day before he arrived, my husband was very worried that Bill would expect us to change our life during his visit. I pooh-poohed this, saying that non-Americans were much more familiar with the B&B concept and would not expect anything of the sort. Of course, secretly I was worried, too—needlessly, it turned out. Bill's stay with us was so enjoyable that the day before he left, George took the day off to spend more time with him. He was a thoroughly delightful guest, full of yarns and humorous stories about a land halfway around the world.

Bill wanted to visit New York City for one or two days, but only if he could see some interesting things that most tourists don't get around to. We put together a list of special places and he had a ball. What he was really interested in was sampling a slice of American life. He asked if he could tag along with me to the local supermarket, nursery school, and town meeting. These trips to places where I normally go without paying attention took on a new interest. Looking through Bill's eyes at what I took for granted made me appreciate my town, my life, and being an American.

The day Bill and I went to the supermarket for groceries, he was as overjoyed as a small child at a toy store. While standing at the deli counter, he told me that in Russia, he had been able to shop at an Intourist store (where the average Russian is not permitted) and there was told that the Russians have the best smoked salmon in the world. But what was being sold at our deli counter, available to anyone who wanted it, was every bit as good. At the poultry counter, he stared at the variety of turkey parts and remarked, "In Brisbane, we don't have to kill the bird ourselves anymore, but we still have to buy a whole bird. Consequently, most single folks only eat turkey in restaurants." I actually felt lucky coming out of the market that day.

In fact, by the time Bill left for home, I felt that Croton had to be one of the best places in the world to live. One of our most enjoyable afternoons together was after a snowfall. Along with my then three-year-old daughter, Bill went sledding down my neighbor's hill. It was the first time he had ever played in the snow.

One evening, we attended a town zoning meeting because our neighbor down the street wanted his next-door neighbor to remove a rotting boat that was blocking his river view. Bill was amazed as various people got up to speak, and he celebrated our friend's victory with us afterward. Over a brandy, Bill remarked that in Australia there is no such forum for neighborhood disputes. "In all likelihood, the boat would have 'caught fire' one night, and that would have been that!" During Bill's visit I called the local newspaper and they sent a reporter out to interview him. When the story appeared, I began receiving more and more calls from people asking how to get into the B&B business. The media coverage from our first guest had a snowball effect.

Bill's visit was an auspicious beginning, and both his and our lives were enriched by the experience. The first year, we earned $1,500. Six years later, we earned $15,000. And we were living a more enjoyable and unpressured life than many couples trying to maintain two full-time jobs and raise their families after hours. In 1989, after getting divorced, I made a five-year plan to expand and improve the B&B from a private-home B&B with five guest rooms sharing two hall baths to a B&B inn with seven guest rooms, all with private baths, five with fireplaces, and two with Jacuzzis. Our sales topped $130,000 in 1994. Today, although divorced, I live a lovely lifestyle with my daughter and live-in assistant—life is never dull, and the B&B guests provide a continuing array of stimulating conversation.

## BED & BREAKFAST U.S.A., LTD

In the beginning, I had hoped that other host homes would join me so that we could share the cost of advertising and the work of answering phones and inquiries and doing promotion.

After the publicity surrounding Bill's visit, a number of people called me, interested in opening their homes but not in the myriad behind-the-scenes tasks needed to promote this new type of travel accommodation. They said they would prefer to pay a commission to an outside service to screen their guests, represent their Bed and Breakfast to the public, collect the money, and leave them free to enjoy their guests. That was how Bed & Breakfast U.S.A., Ltd., a reservation service, was born. It began in a spare room of my house and moved into a storefront with many phone lines and with a staff to answer them, inspect and represent our host homes, and coordinate promotion for our network. We had local as well as national coverage on radio and television and in magazines and newspapers. *Bed and Breakfast* became a household term.

Recently, someone told me that she saw me as a pioneer of the eighties. This was the nicest thing anyone has ever said about me. But I don't think I'm alone in looking for ways to personalize more of my life. Leo Buscaglia, a professor and best-selling author of books about contemporary relationships, commented recently that the reason so many people have responded to his work is that they want to be treated as individuals. People want to be appreciated for themselves. I believe that the growing national interest in traveling in a less anonymous fashion, really coming to know your guests or hosts and sharing some of your life in the process, is a part of this trend. Most of the people I meet who become hosts share these sentiments. In July 1990, I sold Bed & Breakfast U.S.A., Ltd., to a proprietor of a 22-room inn in the Berkshires, leaving me free to write, lecture, and do consultations for B&B owners. Unfortunately, he could not devote enough resources to the service and was forced to close in 1992.

# BED & BREAKFAST RESERVATION SERVICES WORLDWIDE

Bed and Breakfast has been a grass-roots movement. Reservation services have helped people open their homes to guests, and there are currently more than 100 such services around the world. In 1985, Bed & Breakfast Reservation Services Worldwide, a nonprofit trade association, was formed to help its members work together to unify standards and promote private-home accommodations through education, advertising, and public-service announcements. In a few short years, it has been instrumental in opening up communication among reservation services, making Bed and Breakfast more easily available to travelers and travel agents and educating both hosts and guests. If you live in an area where there is no reservation service and you are looking for a full-time job commitment, consider starting one. The financial rewards are not easily won, but the reward of helping hosts open their homes and offering a very special personal service to travelers is very great.

You can get a membership or services that belong to Bed & Breakfast Reservation Services Worldwide by writing to them at PO Box 14841, Baton Rouge, LA 70898, fax: (504) 343-0672. For the latest in B&B information from their members, dial (800) 364-7242 from a touch-tone phone. A guide sheet describing B&Bs in any member region will be faxed to you at a cost from $3.95 to $7.95 per reservation service.

## BECOME PART OF THE INDUSTRY NOW

Since 1990, I have seen the industry mature considerably. In 1985, the U.S. government estimated that less than one-tenth of 1 percent of the American public had ever stayed at a B&B but that a growing interest promised tremendous expansion. By 1995, the number of travelers seeking out a B&B had grown at least a hundredfold. There is room in the industry for all who are sincere and capable.

# 1

# Bed and Breakfast Defined: Basic Principles

**B**ed and Breakfast is a grass-roots movement that has taken off across our country, gaining acceptance in many different kinds of communities and providing accommodations for an ever-increasing number of people who, for one reason or another, don't want or need to stay in the more traditional hotels and motels that dot the countryside. But what is Bed and Breakfast? Where did it come from? How will you know if Bed and Breakfast is for you?

## INTERNATIONAL ORIGINS

*Bed and Breakfast* is a generic term for accommodations offered in private homes rather than commercial facilities such as hotels or motels. It began in Britain after World War II, when American soldiers were waiting for troop carriers to ship them back home. Many waited weeks for their turn to come and chose to use their extended leave to see a little of the country they had just helped. The courageous women who had gone to work in the airplane factories now were called upon to open their homes to these young men because there was far too little hotel space left standing to go around. The soldiers were charmed by these women, who shared with them stories about their locale, steered them to out-of-the-way restaurants and places of interest, and often called on friends or relatives in other parts of England to open their homes to these guests.

The women, in turn, enjoyed befriending these appreciative young men, and the few dollars that they were paid to offer a pleasant guest room and hearty morning meal were a way to buy luxuries long unavailable during wartime. They repaired and spruced up their homes, and many continued to offer B&B long after the soldiers had gone home and were replaced by American tourists. The tourists, who had been unable to travel during the war, flocked to England in large numbers.

Because B&B accommodations were initially made available at the request of the government, regulations were initiated. Once a B&B host was approved, a little sign went up outside the home so that travelers could easily find a place to stay. Not all hosts wished to have strangers ring the bell without warning, however, and many of the finer places became affiliated with booking agencies that matched appropriate guests and hosts and otherwise protected the hosts' privacy.

Even castles are sometimes available through such agencies—taking in B&B guests helps the owners pay their taxes. In Great Britain today, as many as 40 percent of all overnight stays are spent in Bed and Breakfasts. Although literally a cottage industry, this is no small business.

## WHY NOT AMERICAN BED AND BREAKFAST?

Popular plays in London are usually seen on Broadway within two years, and anything Princess Diana wears can be bought at major department stores practically the next day. But the Bed and Breakfast concept took forty years to become popular in America. It spread rapidly as *pensiones* in Italy, *Zimmer frei* in Germany, and under many other names throughout Europe, but not in the United States. Many people ask why. The answer, I believe, lies in the system of supply and demand. In America, there used to be tourist homes in every village, often big old houses where the elderly owner took in boarders or roomers and also let rooms by the night to travelers passing through.

As our modern road system took shape, motor hotels or motels sprang up close to highway exits. Motorists could pull off when they became tired, knowing that they would find a clean, comfortable room at a reasonable price. Over time, the tourist homes deteriorated because fewer patrons drove through on local roads and the owners of tourist homes could no longer afford to keep up their places. The small mom-and-pop motels charged low rates and used the profits to support Mom and Pop rather than reinvest in the maintenance of their structures.

Motel chains sprang up. They promised no surprises, and that's what they gave you. At first, this was good. The American public liked the idea of uniform standards and patronized these motels in huge numbers. By the time most Americans can drive, they can close their eyes and describe the average chain motel, even down to the color of the bedspreads. The chains set up central booking agencies with toll-free 800 telephone numbers and did everything possible to attract the consumer. They were successful, but the ever-rising hotel/motel costs began to turn some patrons away.

## FIGHTING THE PLASTIFICATION OF AMERICA

In the late sixties, many American young people were tremendously dissatisfied with the way our culture was heading. As a reaction to being ove. processed, turned out by machine, and identified by numbers instead of being seen as individuals, people turned to organic foods, homemade meals, and handicrafts, and away from synthetic materials, artificial coloring, and plastic. In the seventies and eighties, as the hippies became the yuppies and the average age of Americans rose, a demand developed for rediscovering the enriching travel that our grandparents enjoyed, travel that allowed you to get to know the people in other parts of our country, not just see the monuments. People who were struggling to restore historic houses yearned to really talk with others who had fought and won many of the same battles against years of past neglect. Those who live most of the year in a high-rise apartment building want to experience life on a farm or a yacht or in an old country house in the mountains; suburban families want to live for a few days in an apartment in a fast-paced city. By the early eighties, these factors combined with the dramatic jump in hotel prices to create the demand for Bed and Breakfast.

## THE COUNTRY INN FANTASY

Country inns have long appealed to the traveler for their old-fashioned hospitality. Think "country inn," and what comes to mind is a sprawling older home in New England set back on a tranquil country lane. Ask any group of six people and you are likely to find that five will admit to fantasies of giving up their present way of life to run a country inn.

But fantasies are not reality. Few people actually relocate to live their idyllic dreams. To begin with, most people are unable to make such a drastic change in lifestyle. Moreover, a country inn is a serious commercial business. Success depends on good organization, substantial capital, publicity, promotion, advertising, and the ability to manage a staff, maintain buildings, and run a restaurant. There is considerable turnover in the country inn business. All too soon it can become apparent to an enthusiastic beginner that keeping the occupancy rate high and the guests and the staff happy leaves little time for personal pursuits. This is certainly not consistent with the fantasy of living a relaxing, and simpler, life in the country.

## THE COMMERCIAL INN

A commercial inn is a place that is open to the public, has a sign outside, may be privately or corporately owned, and usually has more than ten rooms, sometimes more than twenty. It is in an area that is either unzoned or commercially zoned and is usually required to be licensed by the state. A commercial inn must have approval and regular inspection by the health department and is subject to all aspects of the state's fire and safety regulations and restaurant code. It usually has a restaurant that may be open for dinner and lunch as well as breakfast and that takes reservations from people who are not staying at the inn as well as from guests. An inn has a large staff, cleans its rooms and changes its linens on a daily basis, is open day and night to receive guests, and commits large amounts of time and money to promotion and advertising. In order to increase business, many inns also cater parties and weddings and are constantly on the lookout for other ways to keep their occupancy rate as high as possible.

## PRIVATE-HOME BED AND BREAKFAST

Private-home Bed and Breakfasts are very different from commercial inns. Generally, they are located in residentially zoned areas, offer from one to five rooms, and have no sign outside. Usually, they belong to a reservation service through which they find many of their guests. They leave promotion and advertising to their reservation service, along with the screening of the guests and the collecting of deposits. As a rule, there is no staff to manage other than an occasional gardener, housekeeper, or serviceperson. The hosts have very different expectations and much less stress related to carrying on the business. They meet people from many cultures, earn extra income, and enjoy the tax advantages of using their homes for a business, but they do it at their own convenience. They take guests when they want, and although they enjoy the extra income, they don't expect to support themselves from it.

A private-home B&B is primarily a private home. It is a home where some business is done, not a place of business where people live. This may sound like a mere semantic distinction, but think for a moment of the implications. In a private home, the host and hostess are using their assets (extra bedrooms and genial personalities) to meet interesting people and earn some extra money. They can decide which types of guests they will enjoy being around and which they won't. If smokers or toddlers drive a host to distraction, he or she can restrict guests to nonsmokers or children over six. Naturally, such restrictions reduce the pool from which guests come and lower potential volume. But hosts who do not rely on B&B for a living can afford to do this. A commercial inn, which needs a certain occupancy rate to stay alive, cannot afford to be so choosy.

My classic response to those who want to know the difference between a private-home B&B and an inn is that it is similar to the difference between being a gourmet cook and a chef.

## Staff and Overhead

In a commercial inn, the occupancy rate is crucial because a certain amount of business is necessary to show a profit. Overhead is considerable, and there are few ways to lower it in proportion to the decrease in business during seasonally slow periods. Staff laid off may not be available when they are needed again. Training new staff is costly, and most businesses strive to keep turnover as low as possible. The rule of thumb is that for each five rooms one staff member is necessary.

In a private home, little to no staff is necessary. Overhead costs for the family to reside there are raised only slightly by having extra guests. Yet a portion of those costs will be legitimate business expenses.

## Guests' Expectations

In many respects, the difference in service between a B&B and a commercial facility is reflected in the rates charged. If you start charging luxury rates, guests will expect luxury service, too.

In a commercial inn, guests pay luxury prices and expect to be pampered, with telephones and televisions in their rooms and a maid waiting each morning to clean and to make up the bed. No matter when guests arrive, someone is expected to be waiting to greet them. In a private home, guests realize that host families have full and interesting lives outside of the home and that it is necessary to call in advance to arrange a mutually convenient arrival time. If they fail to do this, they may arrive to find a note on the door letting them know that the family is attending a child's soccer game and will return in a few hours.

Guests, too, behave differently toward the staff at a commercial inn and the hosts of a Bed and Breakfast. The less commercial the place, the more the hosts will be treated as new friends. Many times, private-home guests help to clear the breakfast table, share interesting recipes, and send thank-you notes or even presents. I know hosts who have received theater tickets from happy guests who couldn't use their subscription seats, potholders appliqued with the host's name, and a variety of other creative thank-yous for warmth and hospitality.

## Time Commitments

People who run a country inn or hotel know that theirs is a full-time job. Often, it seems like time and a half. B&B hosts commit only as much time to their business as they want to. Some B&Bs are open only during a particular season, on weekends, or for a certain number of days each week or month. Guests don't usually come to sit around the house. They arrive with a list of places they want to see, usually too numerous to cram into the limited time they have. Others are visiting family or hospitalized friends or relatives, attending weddings, or house hunting. Once breakfast is over, guests disappear and may not be seen again until they come back to change for the evening. A few moments of consultation about making dinner reservations and plotting the route to the restaurant and they are off again.

Guests receive a key to the home and come and go at will. No one has to stay around twenty-four hours a day to baby-sit for the house. All guests come by advance reservation, and hosts have the opportunity to make sure that the larder is stocked for the expected arrivals and that the home and guest rooms are sparkling and ready for company. This leaves the hosts free to enjoy the other aspects of their lives.

It certainly helps to be a morning person because morning is the most important time of the day for the hosts. That is when breakfast is prepared and served. And that is usually when guests avail themselves of the hosts' expertise about the area and plan their day. It is up to the host to decide whether breakfast is served at fixed hours or according to when the guests want to eat. But it is fairly safe to assume that by 11:00 A.M. on weekends, and earlier during the week, a host's breakfast responsibilities are over.

## An Opportunity to Get to Know Each Other

In a private-home Bed and Breakfast, interaction with guests varies depending on personal taste. Often, the type of guests who seek out your home have a lot in common with you and have chosen your place because of that. Breakfast style is more varied than in a commercial setting. Sometimes, guests eat in the kitchen while you prepare the meal; other times, they may join you on the porch or alongside the pool. Or if you're in the mood, you may serve breakfast in the dining room on fine china. You have ample opportunity to relax and get to know your guests. Taking care of two couples or even four couples at the breakfast table is relatively easy and is very different from trying to serve different dishes to more than twenty at different times, as the commercial innkeeper must do.

## THE BED AND BREAKFAST INN

So far, I have described differences between a private-home B&B and a commercial inn. In many states, there is something in between: the B&B inn. Usually, this is a place with four to ten rooms, generally in a very tourist-oriented area with few zoning restrictions. It may have a sign outside, and the hosts will often belong to a reservation service but also promote their business themselves. They will serve breakfast, but to their guests only, not to people from the outside. Because of the larger number of rooms, they attempt to keep their occupancy rate high enough to contribute substantially to their income and do regard this as one or both of the hosts' main occupation. It is financially feasible only if the state they are in permits this many rooms without major structural changes to conform to fire and safety codes and the area attracts a high volume of guests with little seasonal variation. Many people who own such inns are retired or semiretired and combine their B&B income earned with pension and investment income.

The following table will give you an idea of the differences between a private-home B&B, a B&B inn, and a commercial inn.

### DIFFERENT TYPES OF FACILITIES

|  | Private-Home B&B | B&B Inn | Commercial Inn |
|---|---|---|---|
| Number of rooms | 1 to 5 | 4 to 10 | Over 10 |
| Open to public | No | Sometimes | Yes |
| Sign outside | No | Sometimes | Yes |
| Commercially zoned | No | Sometimes | Yes |
| Belongs to reservation service | Yes | Yes | Sometimes |
| Restaurant | No | Guests only | Public |
| Serves other meals | Not usually | Sometimes | Yes |
| Has a check-in desk | No | Sometimes | Yes |
| Must be licensed by state | Not always | Usually | Always |
| Conforms to restaurant code | Not usually | Sometimes | Always |

For those who have the country inn fantasy but don't want the full-time occupation of owning a country inn, becoming a private-home Bed and Breakfast host may be the answer. Although it is comforting to hear that the average guest will be a middle- to upper-middle-class tourist or business person, hosts often experience some trepidation before their first guest actually walks through the door. But being a B&B host is a far cry from being a hotelier, an altogether different mentality. Remember that it is the private-home ambiance that appeals to the B&B guest. It is the quality of the private home that sets this form of accommodation apart from all others and makes each B&B a unique experience. From a strictly business point of view, operating privately allows hosts to run their business as they wish—picking and choosing guests according to their own standards, selecting dates to take or not take guests, setting house rules, and ultimately deciding how well they wish to get to know their guests.

❖❖❖❖❖❖❖

**Question:** If I offer B&B in my home, how do I respond to criticism that I am weakening the position of area hotels and motels or competing unfairly with them because I don't have to follow the same rules (such as a restaurant health code)? I wouldn't want to start something that could lead to a decline in local business.

**Answer:** *Although you and the public establishments in your area both provide accommodations for paying guests, lumping together what you do and what they do is neither accurate nor fair. You provide personal hospitality on a prearranged basis. You do not serve the general public. In most states your operation usually does not fall within the purview of the hotel-motel-restaurant code for the simple reason that you are not in that business. With the possible exception of the most popular cities and tourist attractions (where B&B can approach a full-time commitment for a host), you provide accommodations on a limited schedule when it is convenient for you.*

*Jean Brown, founder of Bed and Breakfast International, San Francisco, America's first reservation service for private homes, stresses to hosts in her network that what they really offer is community service. The benefits to both host and guest extend to the community at large.*

> *The publicity B&B receives may encourage travel to an area because it describes friendly hospitality and offers a greater variety of options for people with special needs and interests. It also enables more people to attend events when local hotels are full.*
>
> *Beyond this, short-term accommodation in private homes is a needed innovation which many states and local governments encourage because of the economic benefit it brings. The State of Maine, for example, has made a videotape showing how to become a B&B host. Architectural preservationists support B&B as a way to achieve restoration and maintenance of existing dwellings which might otherwise become dilapidated due to the rising cost of keeping them in good condition. This is especially true of houses of past eras. There are millions of Americans interested in preserving our unique residential architectural heritage. Older*

*people who may not be physically capable of performing routine maintenance themselves and cannot afford to pay someone else to do it for them, and younger people who find the need for extra income, use B&B to pay for restoring an older house they'd love to own and live in. All of this activity adds up to keeping America's older neighborhoods in excellent shape and owner-occupied. B&Bs generate fewer occupants and cars than would be the case if a room were permanently rented to a boarder or if a large house were subdivided or turned into condos.*

*One example of how this works comes immediately to mind. We visited a 73-year-old prospective host, who owned a beautiful home. However, she was beginning to neglect it. Her yard was becoming an eyesore in the neighborhood, and she complained that she could no longer garden because of her arthritis. We sent her guests about eight nights a month. At $30 a night, she earned $240, enough to hire a gardener and do some household repairs. She had reason to keep her house clean as she looked forward to her guests. Her life took on new meaning. On our return visit, she showed us thank-you letters from people all around the world who had stayed with her.*

*We believe that the B&B movement is a useful and beneficial development in this country. It is an extension of traditional home hospitality and is a property right of the homeowner. City councils, planning boards, and the travel industry should encourage this use of private homes.*

Jean takes great pains to distinguish private-home B&B from the operation of a public guesthouse or inn operating illegally in a residential zone. Private-home B&B is self-limiting, she explains, because there are only a few people in each community who have both the interest and the space available to offer the service.

Another factor that keeps B&B a one-to-one business is the time-consuming nature of making custom reservations that match specific hosts with guests who have special needs.

Meeting the needs of people in transition at an affordable cost is a hallmark of B&B everywhere. Here are just a few of the situations in which Bed and Breakfast has eased a stressful time for people pulling up their roots.

- A single manager was transferred by her company to the Albany area. She stayed at a Bed and Breakfast for several months while she started her new position, got oriented to the area, hunted for a house, and waited to move into it.

- A European scientist came to America to work on a short-term project for a Rockland County chemical plant. We arranged a stay for him in an apartment in a two-family house owned by one of our hosts. This gave him the convenience of having his own place. His hostess lived in the other part of the house and was available to answer questions about how to get places. When his family came to visit, he used his network membership to stay with them at Bed and Breakfasts in other parts of America.

- An English banker came for a two-month stay in New York City. He called us from a $170-a-night hotel. We found him an unhosted garden apartment on the same street as his hotel for $75 a night. His bank saved almost $100 a day, and this guest was much more comfortable.

- The Japan Travel Bureau sent a new employee to one of our B&Bs so that he would be forced to speak more English. His hosts eased his learning of the language and even helped him get his driver's license.

- A sales representative who travels 75 percent of the time started using B&Bs. Here is her reaction to her first experience: "I felt so welcome and comfortable in this home. It was the first time I was away that I didn't spend the bulk of the evening on the phone to my family. I sat down to chat with my hosts, got involved in a game of Scrabble, and suddenly it was time for bed. I felt safe and wondered how I had spent so many years staying in cold, impersonal commercial places."

- A married lawyer started a new position and needed a place to stay while he worked four days a week and began to look for a house. He went home to his family on the weekends. This continued until the end of the school term, when his wife and child were able to join him.

- *A California contracting firm was able to submit a lower bid and consequently win a job in Westchester County, New York, because they housed their people at nearby B&Bs, saving close to $350 per week per person over housing them at a conventional $85-a-night hotel.*

For many women traveling alone or with children, B&Bs are a welcome alternative to hotel accommodations. Women appreciate the security, warmth, and friendliness. This may include a light snack before retiring, a friendly chat after a hectic day out, a list of baby-sitters the hosts have used, some special bath salts, an ironing board set up for touching up clothes, laundry facilities, a hall closet well stocked with extra personal grooming and hygiene items, or simply a needle and thread to sew on a stray button. I have often supplied a typewriter to a guest with last-minute changes to make in an important presentation. Although they generally seem more resigned to the inconvenience of traditional forms of travel, men, too, are reporting that B&B makes their time on the road less stressful.

Both men and women appreciate the unpressured environment of a private home. Some women, however, find it especially desirable. They may be worried that in a hotel they will be harassed or receive second-class service in bars or dining rooms. Rather than run that risk, they may wind up ordering meals from room service and watching television, not a pleasant prospect. Often, their families feel better knowing that they are safe and secure in a cozy family home. In my experience, businesswomen report that staying at B&Bs makes working away from home much easier. Communities where such accommodations are available are high on preferred assignment lists with executive and management women. As one suburban hostess commented, "B&B here is a women's network. A lot of valuable information is exchanged around my kitchen table over a late-night cup of tea." Looked at in this light, an area's Bed and Breakfast network is an important community asset, an enterprise that attracts people to the area who are likely to explore it while they are there, generating increased revenues for all sorts of businesses.

*In an area where there is considerable seasonal fluctuation (such as the skiing or hunting season), there may not be enough off-season business to make a commercial establishment feasible. During the busy season, the B&B network provides an attractive community service, but a host might see only an occasional guest the rest of the year. In other words, Bed and Breakfast complements the rest of the travel industry; it does not supplant it.*

## CONSULTANTS

A number of folks with considerable expertise are available for consultation and seminars. Some also offer "innternships" where you can apprentice at their inn, trying out your skills as innkeeper for a short time. Some of the best known follow. See also Chapter 2 for more on specific innternships.

## East

Carl Glassman, Wedgewood Inn, 111 W. Bridge St., New Hope, PA 18938, (215) 862-2570.

Carl offers seminars and consulting. For graduates of his or other recognized seminars, he offers an innternship of at least a week during which the inntern rotates through various inn functions, getting to understand the workings of the inn and the community in which it exists.

COST: A $300 fee for innternship plus approximately $75 a day for lodging.

Barbara Notarius, Alexander Hamilton House, 49 Van Wyck St., Croton-on-Hudson, NY 10520, (914) 271-6737.

I offer two-day seminars for aspiring innkeepers. The seminar covers a wide variety of innkeeping-related issues, from having realistic goals to finding or creating your inn, start-up, marketing, record keeping, operations, food and beverage management, financing, and personnel.

COST: $175 for a single person, $250 for a couple. Lodging is available for $75 single or $95 double a day.

For graduates of my seminar or other recognized courses, I offer an innternship program that takes one week and offers hands-on experience in all facets of inn operations. This experience is appropriate for aspiring innkeepers who plan to have less than ten rooms.

COST: $250 for a single; $350 for a couple plus lodging. Breakfast and lunch are included each day.

Kenneth I. Parker, 60 Union St., Nantucket, MA 02554, (508) 228-4886, fax: (508) 228-4890.

Ken is a developer and general manager of a number of small inns, including the Tuckernuck Inn, the Parker Guest House, Seven Sea Street, Nantucket Breeze Condominiums, and the State House Inn in Providence, RI. Although still involved in the operation of these inns, he now does consulting and offers seminars in the spring and fall at the Tuckernut Inn. The seminar covers complete inn development, including property selection, economic feasibility analysis, zoning, mortgage packaging, renovation/restoration, furnishing, marketing, staffing, and operations techniques.

COST: Three-day seminars are $475 for one person, $675 for two (in the same room). Consulting is $500 a day plus travel expenses. Lower weekly rates are negotiable.

Greg Brown and Bertie Koelewijn, New England B&B Consultants, RR1 Box 41A, Whitefield, NH 03598, (603) 837-9320, phone or fax.

Greg and Bertie are former innkeepers who now run seminars and do consulting for small and medium-size inns. Their monthly seminar, "How to Open and Run a B&B Inn," is offered at the Jefferson Inn in Jefferson, NH, as well as throughout the Northeast. Other services include start-up assistance, marketing support and planning, goal evaluation, innsitting, buying and self-sales assistance, and business plan development.

COST: Weekend seminars are $350 to $400 a couple and include lodging with breakfast. Consulting rates are $60 an hour or $400 a day with discounts for graduates of their seminars.

William Oates & Associates, PO Box 1162, Brattleboro, VT 02840, (802) 254-5931. Best for purchasers of large, commercial inns.

## Midwest

Norman Strasma, *Inn Review Newsletter*, PO Box 1789, Kankakee, IL 60901, (815) 939-3509.

Bob Fuehr, PO Box 79, Okemos, MI 38805, (800) 926-4667 fax and phone.

Bob has two companies: Inn Broker, Inc., and Innkeeping Consultants. He offers a free flyer and a video highlighting thirty-five inns and potential inns for sale in the Great Lakes region. He teaches aspiring innkeeper courses at Michigan State University each spring and at Oakton Community College each fall. He has innkeeping books and videos available. Bob has over seven years of seminar experience and hundreds of graduates.

COST: Seminars are $95 for one, $150 for a couple. He also sells a home-study kit that includes three books and a video for $75.

Lynn Mottaz, 10500 Noble Ave. North, Brooklyn Park, MN 55443, (612) 424-8238.

Lynn teaches a four-hour class on innsitting and innkeeping for Open University, a community college. Contact Lynn if you want more innsitting experience. She suggests that innterns volunteer at an inn or up-and-running B&B, become a professional innsitter, join the Minnesota B&B Guild or the Professional Innsitters Association, or get a day of training at a B&B.

Lynn recommends charging $35 a day plus $10 a day per booked room.

## South

David Caples, Lodging Resources, 98 S. Fletcher Ave., Amelia Island, FL 32034, (904) 277-4851, fax: (904) 277-6500.

David offers weekend seminars at Elizabeth Point Lodge that include eighteen hours of instruction on the B&B industry, feasibility of inns, creating an inn product, acquisition, financing, and start-up. Each participant receives pro formas on five-, ten-, or twenty-room inns and a 250-page resource manual.

COST: $595 for the seminar. A lodging package at the inn for two nights includes dinner Friday night, full breakfast and lunch on Saturday and Sunday, and local taxes for $202 to $303 for a single and $249 to $350 for a couple.

A hands-on apprenticeship at the inn is available to graduates of this seminar. Only one apprentice or couple is accepted for a Sunday-to-Tuesday program. Apprentice innkeepers rotate through the different departments of the inn from night audit, to kitchen, dining room, front desk, laundry, and maintenance.

COST: $50 a day plus lodging.

## Southwest

Sallie and Welling Clark, 1102 W. Pikes Peak Ave., Colorado
    Springs, CO 80904, (719) 471-3980.

Sallie and Welling Clark have owned and operated the well-known Holden House Bed & Breakfast Inn in Colorado Springs since its establishment in 1986. They have been instructing approved seminars and conducting B&B consultation since July 1989. The Clarks authored the book *Colorado's Bed & Breakfast Industry Survey and Marketing Analysis of a Small Inn* and have been involved in state and national B&B issues. In addition to being the founders of B&B Innkeepers of Colorado Association, the Clarks have served on the Professional Association of Innkeepers International (PAII) advisory Board, the Colorado Hotel/ Lodging Association, and the Colorado Tourism and Travel Authority. Seminars run September to April.

COST: One-day seminars are approximately $60 a person and include breakfast. A 10 percent discount is deducted from lodging for seminar attendees. Consultations cost $50 an hour.

Kit Riley, Sage Blossom Consulting, PO Box 17193, Boulder, CO
    80308-0193, (303) 440-4227, fax: (303) 786-7716.

Kit does consulting and runs a three-day seminar for aspiring/perspiring innkeepers. In addition, Kit works with innkeepers to sell their B&Bs as well as with clients to help them purchase the right B&B. Seminars cover regulations, business plans, building versus buying your inn, budgets, the Americans with Disabilities Act, promotion, and daily operations. Graduates of Kit's seminars are eligible for innternships at one of a number of participating B&B inns.

COST: Seminars are $375 and include breakfast. Consulting services are $75 an hour with a two-hour minimum.

## West

Sharon Layne and Bill Priest, Commercial Services, 28 North First St., Suite 100, San Jose, CA 95113, (408) 279-3833 or (800) 634-2567, fax: (408) 279-3358.

Sharon and her husband Bill, a real estate attorney who cofounded the California Association of Bed & Breakfast Inns, offer a variety of services to the aspiring innkeeper. They have a video available for sale featuring many California innkeepers revealing how they got into the business and sharing some of their secrets for success.

COST: Their two-day seminar costs $365 for an individual or $495 for a couple, plus lodging, and includes a comprehensive workshop to prepare participants for the purchase and operation of a B&B or country inn. Participants go home with a complete B&B operations manual. One dinner is included.

In addition, they offer an individual focusing session to help the aspiring innkeeper develop a successful acquisition plan ($300 for seminar graduates, $500 if not a seminar graduate). Four hours of consulting time are included. An apprenticeship at their inn, the Hensley House in San Jose, is available for serious hands-on training at a cost of $800 a week plus lodging. A commitment of two weeks is suggested. Sharon also acts as an inn broker. She and Bill offer broad consulting services on all aspects of acquisition, including valuation feasibility studies, business planning, and financing. Fees vary, with a $2,000 minimum.

❖❖❖❖❖❖❖

This book deals with the most commonly asked questions and situations. It is a compendium of fifteen years' experience in setting up B&Bs and reservation services nationally. But, of course, each situation is unique. You will probably want to talk things over with your prospective reservation service well before you take any concrete steps toward opening for business.

A directory of reservation services, all of which adhere to high standards in conducting business and represent only homes that have been personally inspected by them, is found at the end of this book in Appendix A.

# 2

❖❖❖❖❖❖❖❖❖❖❖❖❖❖❖❖❖❖❖❖  2  ❖❖❖❖❖❖❖❖❖❖❖❖❖❖❖❖❖❖❖❖❖

# Is Bed and Breakfast for You?

It is necessary to examine the question of whether Bed and Breakfast is for you from three perspectives: an inventory of your personality and attitudes; how your family reacts to the prospect of opening your home to paying guests; and what, and how realistic, your expectations are.

Complete the checklist on page 29 to find out if your personality and attitudes are similar to those of successful hosts.

Although there is no such thing as the perfect host, there are certain attributes or personal characteristics that make it more likely for someone to enjoy hosting. If your answer to most of the preceding characteristics was yes, you are probably good host material.

The B&B hosts I have met are between the ages of twenty-five and eighty-three; single, married, divorced, widowed; active at professional careers, at home with children, or retired. In other words, it is personality rather than any particular demographic characteristics that the hosts have in common. Successful hosts are interesting people, usually satisfied with their lives, proud of their homes, and convinced that they live in one of the best possible places. Because of their enthusiasm for home and community, they are able to share an insider's view with guests.

## BE THE REALTOR'S ALLY

This enthusiasm is one reason that realtors suggest B&Bs to out-of-town buyers as a base from which to see the community and select a home. The host, often unknowingly, becomes a representative for the community. The fact that the host has enjoyed raising a family there suggests to potential residents that they will also enjoy living there. Because he or she is not selling anything, the host is not seen as having a vested interest in any sale and is therefore sometimes taken more seriously than the realtor.

## YOUR FAMILY'S REACTION

How your family reacts to the prospect of opening your home is a very important part of your decision to proceed. Instant agreement and enthusiasm are not necessary. Often, because of ignorance or a difference in expectations about what a B&B will entail, family members are reluctant at first. It is essential to have discussions about what will really be expected of each person. Let your family read this book or sit in on a seminar on hosting.

Consider who will receive the money generated by the B&B and what this money will be used for. In England, my husband and I stayed at a B&B run by a banker, his wife, and three young children. It seemed to us that the wife, who had no outside job, did most of the work (cleaning and breakfast preparation). The husband worked in London and left for his office each day before we awoke. He was quite warm to us on the weekend, however, and made us feel very welcome. The three children shared one room during our stay so that two of their bedrooms were available for guests. Our hostess told us that this was a family project. They take guests only during six weeks of the summer travel season. The money they earn permits the family to enjoy a wonderful holiday on an island off the coast of Spain for the last two weeks of summer.

If you live alone, of course, the decision is all yours. Nevertheless, you should be prepared to deal with the reaction of your friends and relatives. Children long grown and on their own often expect that when they return home for a family Thanksgiving or Christmas holiday, the room of their childhood memories will wait for them. It is sometimes necessary to remind these grown children that they now have homes and children of their own and that what was once their room has been redone in the decor of your choice.

| Characteristics of a Successful Host | Yes | No | Willing to Change |
| --- | --- | --- | --- |
| Knows and appreciates community and region | ____ | ____ | ____ |
| Is enthusiastic about meeting new people | ____ | ____ | ____ |
| Enjoys preparing for entertaining | ____ | ____ | ____ |
| Can sense ordinary needs of others | ____ | ____ | ____ |
| Can take risks | ____ | ____ | ____ |
| Likes keeping home in good order | ____ | ____ | ____ |
| Has a wide range of interests | ____ | ____ | ____ |
| Sees others as generally trustworthy | ____ | ____ | ____ |
| Can get excited about the interests of others | ____ | ____ | ____ |
| Is accustomed to having company at home | ____ | ____ | ____ |
| Communicates directly and diplomatically | ____ | ____ | ____ |
| Organizes time and schedules realistically | ____ | ____ | ____ |
| Infuses home with personality and comfort | ____ | ____ | ____ |
| Allows others the privacy they desire | ____ | ____ | ____ |
| Pays attention to details but is not fussy | ____ | ____ | ____ |
| Maintains significant nonbusiness friendships | ____ | ____ | ____ |
| Is flexible, can roll with the punches | ____ | ____ | ____ |
| Has a good sense of humor | ____ | ____ | ____ |
| A family free of alcohol or drug problems | ____ | ____ | ____ |

If the last of your flock is away at school, it is appropriate to offer that room to B&B guests, but you will probably have to re-decorate it to welcome adults. It can't look as though a teenage son or daughter could take up residence at a moment's notice. If you have fixed up one room for B&B and guests are coming with children, a room complete with posters of rock stars on the walls could appropriately be offered at a reduced price for the young-sters in the party. I will address more of the home requirements in Chapter 3.

If you live alone, family and friends may also be concerned that it may not be safe for you to take in strangers. You can reassure them in a number of ways. Explain that you will be accepting guests only through a reservation service that has screened them. Some hostesses who live alone feel more comfortable accepting only women, couples, or families. Rest assured that many singles own Bed and Breakfasts and have only positive experiences.

## Awkward Situations

In most cases, one member of the host couple or family is more involved in the business than the others. This is fine as long as the others are not openly hostile to the idea or the guests or un-willing to help out in a pinch. Problems develop in situations where one person feels forced to participate despite a strong ob-jection to the venture. I know of only three cases where such a conflict has caused the hosts to close their B&B. One involved a young couple who had traveled widely and enjoyed meeting peo-ple the world over. Their home had two rooms and a bath on a separate floor. Conditions seemed ideal for a B&B. But the hus-band had grown up in a series of foster homes and soon found that having visitors in the house touched off too many painful memories of his past. Although all the guests were wonderful, he felt strongly that he could not continue. His wife, despite feeling that the experience was wonderfully enriching to their lives, agreed and they closed their business.

In the second case, a well-liked hostess had asked our reser-vation service to send as many guests as possible; she loved the whole experience and wanted to see if she could make a financial success of her venture. Indeed, she started having guests every weekend and during the week as well and was thriving on the stimulation and feeling of a job well done. Guests always gave her rave reviews, and I was totally surprised when she stopped by the office to say that she could no longer take guests. What was the problem? She explained that the more business she did, the more her husband resented the attention she paid the guests. He became increasingly withdrawn when guests were there and hostile when they were a few moments late to the breakfast table. Although he knew that his wife loved her business and wouldn't force her to stop, he couldn't disguise his feelings, and she stopped on her own.

The third case involved a lovely B&B that had been in business for three years. When the hosts began, their ten-year-old daughter was very helpful and enjoyed the attention of the guests. By thirteen, however, she was experiencing adolescent growing pains, and she viewed the guests as unwanted intruders. Her negative attitude toward them made her mother uncomfortable, and the family chose to stop taking guests. But they plan to resume when their daughter passes through this phase or goes off to college.

Luckily, the financial investment of using a home as a B&B is usually minimal, and hosts can continue for as long as it seems right and they enjoy it.

Often hosts are fearful until they have had their first guest. With each guest thereafter, they become more comfortable and confident. They realize that they can expect the majority of guests to be lovely people. You meet an occasional pill, but B&B guests are a pretty terrific breed.

## Family Members Help Each Other

My ex-husband, George, a technical author and editor, was often more comfortable with books and figures than with people. Although he was not normally outgoing, he really enjoyed the opportunity that B&B afforded him to get to know people on his own turf. Although he was helpful when asked, he often scheduled racquetball at 9:00 A.M. on Saturday, leaving me to take care of the guests. B&B worked for us because I didn't mind this. If I had to be away, he magically became the epitome of the gracious host and didn't mind doing so because it was not expected of him on a regular basis. My daughter, now sixteen, has met people from all over the world and flourished in her interaction with them. She is learning languages and plans to travel when she gets old enough to see the world. As she has grown up and become more capable, I have asked her to do some of the chores related to keeping the house neat, such as stripping the beds and setting the table. I always make sure that she knows that the money earned by having guests enables us to enjoy a more comfortable life and do more things. Now divorced, I have a live-in assistant who shares the hosting with me. She has a T-shirt that says, "I don't do mornings," but she doesn't mind waiting up for latecomers.

## YOUR EXPECTATIONS

If your personality fits that of other successful hosts, your family and friends are supportive, and your timing seems right, it is important to know what you expect to get from the B&B experience. For most hosts, although the extra income or tax benefits play a part, the joy of meeting the guests is always paramount.

## The Joys of Hosting

The influx of guests from all over the world can bring great cultural enrichment to your home and family. Here are a few examples from my own experience.

A group of Japanese men came to the Croton Clearwater Revival, an annual music and crafts event that celebrates the Hudson River and its cleanup. When they made their reservation, they learned that we had a four-year-old child. They came with gifts for each member of the family, but the most special were the presents for Cydney. On Monday, she went off to "show and tell" at nursery school with a brightly colored cloth that tied in the corners, the Japanese version of the paper bag. Inside it were all kinds of paper animals and balloons and other children's toys. She was able to tell her fascinated classmates the Japanese name of each item and a story to go with it. For that day at least, Cydney was the most cosmopolitan child in her class.

On another occasion, our guests were a concert pianist and a concert violinist. They had chosen our place because we have a piano. Each night, after they returned from supper, they would ask whether we minded if they played. We were treated to wonderful concerts in the comfort of our own living room. We heard fascinating tales of their travels to perform in Europe and got a firsthand account of a totally different lifestyle.

An appraiser and his wife who were very interested in Croton's rich artistic history stayed over a weekend. We took them on a little tour of the town, describing the various people who have lived here and some of the architecturally interesting buildings and sites. One of these was the Croton Dam. Months later, at Christmas time, we received a large envelope from them containing an 1889 *Scientific American* with a photograph of the Croton Dam on the front. In the enclosed note, this couple told us they had enjoyed their stay with us so much that they wanted to repay us in some way for the extras we had shared with them.

Clifford, an IBM employee, made reservations for a short stay. He had just started what proved to be a long-term assignment at the company's research center (ten minutes from our home) and needed a place four nights a week for about three months. He lived a little over two hours away and would go home each weekend. Our daily rate was more expensive than what he could pay, so we arranged a prorated weekly price in exchange for some yard work three hours a week. This proved to be mutually beneficial because he loved to work out the frustrations of his day pruning the hedges and weeding the garden. I really got a double benefit: often when George came home, he felt guilty seeing Clifford already hard at work and was inspired to help out. Clifford's assignment was extended twice, and his stay with us went on for nearly ten months. This guest became a trusted friend who even baby-sat for us on those evenings when we had scheduling conflicts.

## What Do Guests Expect of a Host?

Guests have expectations, too. At the very least, they expect a clean and pleasant room, access to the public areas of your home (television room, yard, and the like), and a hearty American breakfast. They will expect you to be available to answer questions about the area and to give them the benefit of your insider's expertise.

A good host sizes up guests and within a few moments after their arrival has a good idea what to offer to make them feel welcome and settled in. Remember, you are in the hospitality business and that means personal service. Do what you would do for a friend or relative who has come to stay. If the weather is warm, offer a cold drink; if it's cold, offer something hot. Some guests will bring their own wine or liquor so that they can have drinks in their room before heading out to dine. These guests need glasses and an ice-filled bucket. While showing guests their room, experienced hosts offer to send up ice. Keep tourist information and local maps (photocopies are okay) in the room. Hosts who provide these materials allow guests to learn preliminary things about the area for themselves. By the time the guests approach the host, they will be asking more specific questions, which are usually much easier to answer than a vague question such as, "What's there to do around here?" It helps to keep an up-to-date newspaper listing local movies and events so that you can let guests know what's happening in the area, what time things start, and whether reservations are necessary. If you know that something is coming to town that guests may want to attend, mention it on the phone when they call for directions so that you can get tickets or make reservations for them. Your guests rely on you to be informative. After all, they may be coming from a distance and not realize that unless they plan ahead, they may arrive to find the event or best seats sold out.

Collect menus from local restaurants to give guests a chance to see both selection and price before they make reservations. I often call the restaurant for them to ensure that the restaurant knows that they are coming as a result of my efforts. It is always good to have the support of other businesses in the community. They may even be a source of new guests.

The guest room must be clean, with fresh sheets on the bed and clean towels. Beds should be made, wastebaskets emptied, and towels replaced as needed. The guest must know that you are available to see that his or her needs are met. If a guest stays more than a week, he or she should be informed of your room-cleaning schedule so that personal items will be removed from dresser surfaces and the like to enable you to clean properly. Beds should be changed and the room thoroughly cleaned, just as you would for members of your own family.

Bathrooms need daily maintenance. If guests share a bath, hosts should glance in whenever they pass by and wipe down surfaces; check the sink, tub, and bowl; and make sure that there is adequate toilet tissue, soap, and facial tissue. Wastebaskets in the rooms and bath should be emptied daily.

The public areas of your home and the kitchen should be kept sparkling clean, neat, and company-ready. This may sound like a burden, but most B&B families find that having a clean home is one of the extra benefits of taking in guests. Too many of us allow routine chores to get away from us when our busy lives focus our attention outside the home. With this type of home-based business, the need to keep the house looking attractive stops you from allowing a mess to accumulate.

A hearty American breakfast usually includes bacon, eggs, bread, juice, and coffee, or equivalent. Only your imagination limits the variety that can be offered here. (See Chapter 13, "Best Breakfasts," for some suggestions.) Just remember that no one should leave your table hungry. In some states, hosts are prohibited from serving foods prepared at home and must resort to packaged foods. This is disappointing to many guests and should, therefore, be explained in advance. Whether you set a breakfast hour or arrange breakfast according to your guests' schedules is up to you, but it should be clearly stated in any material written and distributed in your home. It is an unhappy guest who sleeps past the breakfast hour, especially if he or she was not told about it beforehand.

Some of your guests will arrive wanting total privacy and will retreat to their room; others will want company or be interested in hearing about the particulars of your restoration or decorating efforts or lots of detail about what there is to do nearby. A successful host responds to these various needs, always realizing that the guests are not there to amuse the hosts. Good hosts also balance their own needs for privacy and free time with their interest in meeting new people.

It is important to have integrity and not permit people to make you do more than you feel comfortable doing. Making exceptions as special favors often causes problems. It is therefore necessary to think through beforehand what you will and won't be willing to do for guests. Here are some things that fall into this category:

1. Will you pick guests up at the train or airport? If you do this, how will they be able to get around on their own? Does this mean you will have to provide other meals if they can't walk to a restaurant?

2. Do you want to supply other meals? Routinely? Only for singles? Only on holidays? Only when asked to ahead of time?

3. Can guests smoke in your home? Do you smoke? (It's hard to tell others they can't if you do.) Would you be comfortable with smoking restricted to certain rooms? What about cigars or pipes?

4. How much notice do you need before a guest comes? Are you comfortable with last-minute calls? If not, let your reservation service know, and be firm. Running around trying to prepare for an arrival on short notice can cause some people to become so frazzled that they make a poor impression on the guests they have gone out of their way for.

5. What if someone asks to bring a pet? If you have a pet, how is it likely to react? What if the visiting pet brings fleas or ticks into your home?

6. If a guest is going to arrive late, how do you handle it? If you are in a ski area, late arrivals on Friday night are often part of doing business, especially if you have a two-night minimum stay on weekends. In other areas,

you may well examine your normal bedtime and be firm about guests arriving by a certain hour. Often, a guest can stop by during the day to get a key, and then it doesn't matter what time they come back at night. Some hosts have a combination lock on the door. The combination can be changed regularly to maintain a feeling of security, but guests can be told the combination if the hosts know that they are arriving after bedtime. Sometimes, it's best to tell people to stay one night at a motel and come up in the morning. You are the best judge of this. It can be very aggravating to wait up until 1:00 A.M. for a guest who promised to arrive at 11:00 and then calls at 11:30 to say he or she had been delayed. The main thing to remember is that you are a private-home B&B, not a hotel with twenty-four-hour staff and round-the-clock check-in.

7. What about children? If you have children and lots of baby equipment, swings, and childproof locks on your kitchen cabinets, you will probably welcome families with young children. It is my experience that people who go to B&Bs with children usually have well-behaved youngsters. If it has been a long time since children came to your home and the presence of your crystal collection on the coffee table makes you cringe at the thought of a toddler, you may want to restrict your guests to children above six. If your goal is to offer B&B only to romantic couples who might find it distracting to share the breakfast table with anyone in a high chair, you may want to limit your home to adults. You can do this because you are operating a private-home B&B. If you were running an inn or other public accommodations, you would have to abide by the law that prohibits discrimination by age.

8. Do you want to let a guest have a wedding on your property? What would this entail? Would it cause parking problems or trouble with neighbors? If you want to do this, what should you charge?

# THE SCOPE OF YOUR INVOLVEMENT

You must decide how large a role B&B will play in your life. You may open one room or many. You may take guests only a few days a month or as often as guests want to come. You may be available only for festivals or football games at the nearby college, graduation week, or other times when there is a shortage of accommodations in your area. You can accept the money for yourself or donate it to a favorite charity or religious group.

It is sometimes prudent to begin on a small scale, fixing up one or two rooms, and then expand the amount of your home available to guests as demand warrants. As your business grows, realize that it is necessary to plan personal vacations in advance. Whether you get someone to be host in your stead or just stop taking guests, don't be talked out of taking your time off because a houseful of guests wants you personally. Everyone needs occasional R&R from B&B.

❖❖❖❖❖❖❖

**Question:** My husband and I have traveled in Europe and enjoyed our stays in everything from Italian *pensiones* to French *châteaux* and Swiss village *Zimmer*. We'd like to become involved with Bed and Breakfast in our area, but we don't like the idea of putting up a sign or distributing leaflets to just anyone through the local tourist information center. Our privacy and personal security mean a lot to us—and to our neighborhood. Any solution?

**Answer:** *Your concerns are typical of most newcomers to hosting in this country. In fact, American-style Bed and Breakfast owes its particular form to them. By far the overwhelming majority of B&Bs in North America operate with no overt commercialism whatever. In most cases, there is no sign to set apart the B&B from any other residence on the street. Guests are prescreened either by the host or, more commonly, by a professional reservation service to which the host belongs.*

*You usually know weeks ahead of time who is coming, their employment, their home address, their telephone number, their bank or their credit card number, their reason for coming to your* area, whether they are past customers of the reservation service, how long they will stay, their dietary restrictions (if any), and whether they will require any special assistance.

You are in the hospitality service business, and your guests will generally be the kind of visitors any community would welcome. Indeed, a very large part of hosting involves providing guests with access to the community that is simply unavailable at a reasonable price (some would say at any price) from the commercial hotel and motel industry. In many instances, your guests will be already known in the area. They may be about to move there permanently because of a job change, may be coming to see a new grandchild, or may be back for a class reunion or in town for a professional meeting. Some are doing precollege interviews, are staying close to a relative in a hospital or nursing home, are members of a wedding party, or are representing a local business in a legal matter.

Most guests stay more than one night, and most have a specific agenda. Many will have a reason to return in the future or to recommend you to friends and associates heading your way. After you have been operating awhile, you will find that word of mouth means a great deal.

Balancing your need for privacy and security with your interest in meeting new people and supplementing your income is one of the basic issues I discuss in this book. Bed and Breakfast is consistent with other occupations traditional in residential neighborhoods (e.g., accountant, doctor, piano teacher, computer or typing service) and generates less traffic than most of these. For the most part, hosting is so unobtrusive that until you inform them, your neighbors might not even notice!

❖❖❖❖❖❖❖

**Question:** I work full-time, and we have an active household (three school-age children). It would be impossible for me to be at home all the time to take reservations and wait for guests to arrive. Should I stop thinking about becoming a host?

**Answer:** Most hosts lead full lives. Unlike an inn, motel, club, or resort, your home is private. You set the limits and house rules.

*You advise your reservation service of your booking preferences (spelled out to them when they first visit your home) so that only those guests meeting your specifications will be matched to you. This information includes dates when you want to have guests and whether you will accept smokers, young children, unmarried couples, members of the opposite sex, or pets. You are not obliged to accept any other categories of guests. This screening and matching is one of the major reasons to join a reservation service.*

*The reservation service also takes care of your reservations and cancellations. A guest who has made confirmed reservations through your service typically contacts you by telephone a few days ahead of time to arrange a mutually convenient arrival time. You are not expected to sit there waiting all day. You are extending your hospitality as you would for any other invited guest. Clearly, you are not signing up to become a servant at the beck and call of anyone who chooses to knock on your door. B&B is highly flexible; simply notify your reservation service when you do not wish to receive guests. This can apply to vacations, certain days of the week when you work or have other appointments, or any other time when you just want to relax. The advent of reservation services in most parts of America has considerably simplified the business end for hosts opening their homes for B&B.*

❖❖❖❖❖❖❖

**Question:** What made your reservation service reject a B&B?

**Answer:** *I always looked for a pleasant setting, a convenient location, and a warm and gracious host. I could not accept people who are interested only in the money, whose homes are shabby, or who appear to be so lonely that their guests will be expected to entertain them.*

*For example, here is the story of a home I rejected because the host lacked both trust and the ability to put herself in the guests' shoes.*

*A woman from Rockland County, New York, called to discuss opening a B&B. After a lengthy conversation, I sent her an*

application, and she sent back pictures of a beautiful estate that
is on the National Register of Historic Homes. She was very
excited about the prospect of becoming a host. We arranged a
date for the home visit, and I told her that I would be arriving at
noon. In response, she told me not to get out of the car if the
dogs were in the yard when I arrived. I informed her that I was
no longer coming. Anyone who allows vicious attack dogs to run
loose when she knows that guests are arriving is not ready to
welcome strangers. I am well acquainted with the area and
would certainly have arrived on time, but guests who are new
to the area may misjudge their time and arrive early or late.
My reservation service has a stake in assuring guests that they
can reasonably expect to arrive with all limbs intact.

❖❖❖❖❖❖❖

**Question:** My husband is away a great deal on business. One of
my good friends is widowed. Another is divorced and has a teenage daughter living with her. We all have nice homes that we are
proud of, not historically significant or anything, but comfortable. And we have spare time. Would we qualify as B&B hosts?

**Answer:** Most B&B hosts are women. If there are other family
members involved, they usually play supporting roles, pitching
in as needed. You and your friends might be ideal candidates,
assuming you enjoy making people comfortable and do not need
to rely on the money you will earn from B&B to maintain your
lifestyle. The greatest skill you will need is the ability to be a
gracious host who takes pride in her personal achievements.

Most hosts have invested a lot of themselves in their homes,
are accustomed to dealing with people who have professional
backgrounds, have a variety of interests, and are sure enough of
themselves not to allow others to take advantage of their good
nature and goodwill. They also become experts on their community or region, welcome spur-of-the-moment entertaining, might
consider inviting visitors to participate in some family activities,
and gain satisfaction and pleasure from meeting the needs of
others. The most successful B&Bs combine the attractions of
a comfortable home, a willing host, and a desirable location.

*Without a genial host, the most intriguing house in the most styl-
ish vacation spot will have a short career as a B&B. To decide
for yourselves if you want to take the next step, you and your
friends can start by reading this book and spending some weekends at B&Bs to experience what it is like to be a guest as well
as to learn firsthand from some experienced hosts.*

❖❖❖❖❖❖❖

**Question:** Before we relocate and risk our savings on an inn, is
there a way to try out innkeeping?

**Answer:** *Lots of aspiring innkeepers are looking for innternships. (See Chapter 1 for a list of professionals offering innternships and seminars.) They are entrepreneurs who are about to
spend hundreds of thousands of dollars to purchase a historic
home or an already operating inn. They will very likely pull up
roots to relocate with the specific goal of beginning a new chapter in their lives as innkeepers. Making mistakes can be very
costly, both financially and emotionally. Consequently, more and
more people are doing their homework: reading books, taking
seminars, working with consultants, staying at a variety of inns,
and looking for an innternship.*

*Although some established B&B inns and larger inns are
offering innternships or apprenticeships, there seem to be few
industry guidelines. I interviewed Norm Strasma of the Inn Yellow
Pages, Carl Glassman at the Wedgewood Inn in New Hope, PA,
David Caples at the Elizabeth Point Lodge in Amelia Island, FL,
and Sharon Layne of the Hensley House in San Jose, CA. All of
us have been running seminars and doing consulting for aspiring
innkeepers for many years.*

*We realize that going to other B&Bs as a guest is not a good
way to find out if innkeeping is for you. Carl likes to say that
being a doughnut connoisseur doesn't mean you could run a
Dunkin' Donuts franchise. A good apprenticeship or innternship
allows the prospective innkeeper to get hands-on experience and
more realistically test the waters. David related the case of an
actor who had taken his seminar and planned to buy an inn
that his girlfriend would run. They were very enthusiastic until*

she had to get up at 3:00 A.M. in order to be fully made up and in the kitchen baking at 5:00 A.M. She suddenly decided that innkeeping was not for her and saved the actor from making a colossal mistake.

Norm has noticed a lot of requests for information about innkeepers offering innternships. In the Midwest, I couldn't find anyone doing them. On the East Coast, there seems to be more opportunities but very few that have been thought through. An inntern who was here in the fall told me that she just called inns in different places and asked if she could volunteer to get some experience. Her experiences varied from real training to just plain unsupervised slavery.

It seems time to set some standards in the industry. What constitutes an innternship? What are reasonable expectations for the inntern and supervising innkeeper to have? What costs should the inntern be expected to pay? How much time is necessary for this experience to be worthwhile? Are there tips to choosing the right innternship?

Carl Glassman's inn has eighteen rooms. He takes apprentices for at least one week. They are required to have taken an approved seminar to be eligible. This means a seminar recognized by the PAII, a state association, or given by someone that Carl knows to be reputable in our field. They pay for their accommodations at the inn plus a $300 flat fee to cover a number of meals. During the course of the week, they rotate through various inn functions, including following the chamber maid and shopping for produce, as well as visiting the tourist commission, the Chamber of Commerce, and other inns in the area. Not until day five is there guest contact.

Unfortunately, Carl knows firsthand of an innkeeper who offers trial by fire. Carl feels very strongly that nothing an inntern does at the inn should be unsupervised and is appalled by innkeepers who think they can train a couple during the week and expect them to run the inn unsupervised on the weekend while the innkeeper takes the weekend off. In a case like this, if the innterns are not fully prepared, the guests will suffer as well as the innterns. Carl takes no more than six innterns a year and tracks their future progress.

*David Caples offers extensive weekend seminars at his twenty-room oceanfront inn. Graduates are eligible for a three-day apprenticeship. During this period, the apprentice checks in Sunday night, tours the inn, and reports to the night audit manager. Monday morning, he or she is in the kitchen at 6:00 A.M. with the food and beverage staff. By 11:00 A.M., the apprentice is working with the housekeeping staff and also rotating through laundry. From 3:00 to 7:00 P.M., there is some free time. At 7:00 P.M., the apprentice again joins the front desk staff to check in guests and complete the night audit. On Tuesday, from 8:00 A.M. until 2:00 P.M., the apprentice covers the front desk, answering phones, making reservations, and doing check-outs. After 2:00 P.M., David meets with the apprentice to review procedures and forms and answer questions. All apprentices leave with a resource book that includes operating forms and reports that can be used as a guide to setting up their own inn systems. The cost is $150 plus lodging. Like Carl, David is adamant about supervision. He does seminars once a month and takes twelve to fifteen apprentices a year.*

*On the West Coast, Sharon Layne and her husband, Bill Priest, have their B&B in San Jose. They do consulting, run a brokerage service for inns, and offer seminars and a two-week apprenticeship program at their inn, the Hensley House. Their program offers hands-on experience in day-to-day inn operations. The cost is $800 a week plus lodging.*

*I have a seven-room B&B inn. Because the inn is smaller than either Carl's or David's, I have fewer staff members and, like most smaller innkeepers, I do much of the work with one full-time assistant and a few part-time staffers. For the aspiring innkeeper who plans to have fewer than ten guest rooms, we offer just such an experience. I accept only a handful of innterns each year, never more than one couple at a time. Cost is $250 for one, $350 for a couple, plus lodging. The fee covers training, lunch each day, and Friday evening dinner.*

*The innternship lasts one week. Innterns arrive on Sunday evening and are given a tour of the inn and material to read about the inn, nearby restaurants, tourist attractions, and the area. Once settled in, they can read through the material and*

start to acquaint themselves with it. Knowing the material is
necessary for answering guests' questions and practicing phone
sales. During the course of the week, the innterns observe breakfast preparation and service, get acquainted with room layout,
housekeeping, and inventory control, get an overview of our reservation system and record keeping, practice telephone skills
and check-in procedures, discuss marketing and advertising, run
reports and evaluate the marketing plan, participate in preparing
and serving breakfast, supervise housekeeping staff and laundry, and examine our brochure and discuss brochure making,
setting rates, and different ways to increase sales. They get to
plan a week's breakfast menu and shopping, discuss purchasing in terms of what can be bought wholesale versus retail or by
catalog. They make a trip to the market, hone telephone skills,
and have a look at strategic planning, including capital improvements, expansion, staffing needs, and marketing changes.

By Thursday, we discuss guest relations and issues of dealing with groups, special guests, troublesome guests, and so on.
They work on the computer and learn about making reservations, financial records, and bill paying. They prepare a chart of
arrivals for the weekend, visit the florist to pick up room flowers
and make any special orders, arrange the flowers in each room,
and spend the rest of the afternoon learning about bookkeeping,
payroll, and record keeping for tax purposes.

By Friday, innterns are involved in preparing and serving
breakfast, observing check-out procedures, checking rooms for
arriving guests, and preparing for Saturday's breakfast. Friday
evening is spent checking on weekend arrivals, discussing community relations, and evaluating the week so far. Saturday,
there is a chance to participate in any area that the inntern
wants more work in and to have maximum guest contact.

It seems accurate to say that those of us who are serious
about innkeeping consider offering an innternship as our way
of giving something back to the industry. It is by no means a
money-making activity for any of the people interviewed, but it is
a way to enable serious candidates to become one of us. We are
cautious about whom we select so that the experience will have
value for both the inntern and the innkeeper.

Going back to the original question, let's try to answer it in light of the experience of these innkeepers.

What constitutes an innternship? *It seems clear that to be of value to the inntern, an innternship should be well thought out so that he or she gets hands-on experience in as many facets of running the business as possible. Just calling inns to volunteer to help out may not give an aspiring innkeeper the variety of participation needed.*

What are reasonable expectations for the innkeeper and the inntern to have? *Certainly the innkeeper should expect the inntern to be willing to participate in all tasks, from cleaning a toilet to evaluating the marketing plan. Innterns should arrive on time, bring appropriate clothes, and expect to eat most dinners out. A car, even if rented, is a good idea. Innterns can expect a good deal of individual attention but must give innkeepers enough space to breathe. Innterns should expect a well-thought-out plan for the time that they are at the inn that will allow them hands-on experience in many different aspects of innkeeping and sufficient time for questions and answers. Innterns should expect supervision and constructive criticism.*

*Innkeepers who offer innternships also usually do consulting. Although they are ready and willing to teach you about innkeeping in general, once you start asking questions specific only to your inn, understand that you should expect to pay for consulting time. It is unfair to expect someone to do your marketing plan for you for free.*

What costs should an inntern expect to pay? *The consensus seems to be approximately $50 a day plus lodging.*

How much time is necessary for the inntership to have value? *This seems to depend on how much past experience you have had. David's apprentices have all had first a three-day intensive course at the inn. Combined with the three days of apprenticeship, this seems to approximate the week that Carl and I find necessary.*

Are there tips in choosing the right innternship for you? *An inntern should probably select an inn of the size he or she intends to own. Be flexible about the time you can make yourself available. Know that an innkeeper will have more time for you off-season, but this will not give you an accurate picture of what innkeeping is like in season. Speak to the innkeeper. Ask for written material about the inn and the innternship. Expect to fill out an application that will ask for some serious thoughts and honest answers on your part. Remember that you get out of something what you put in.*

To find out more about the innternships described above, contact:

David Caples, Lodging Resources, 98 S. Fletcher Ave., Amelia Island, FL 32034, (904) 277-4851, fax: (904) 277-6500.

Carl Glassman, Wedgewood Inn, 111 W. Bridge St., New Hope, PA 18938, (215) 862-2570.

Sharon Layne and Bill Priest, Commercial Services, 28 N. First St., Suite 100, San Jose, CA 95113, (408) 279-3833 or (800) 634-2567, fax: (408) 279-3358.

Barbara Notarius, Alexander Hamilton House, 49 Van Wyck St., Croton-on-Hudson, NY 10520, (914) 271-6737

# 3

# Evaluating Your Home's Assets and Liabilities

O ne of the joys of B&B is the chance it offers to sample other lifestyles as well as other locales. My reservation service offered accommodations in diverse settings. For example, a fifty-two-foot yacht anchored in Long Island Sound, a dairy farm overlooking the Mohawk River, a mansion near Saratoga, a working farm with a cow named Ma, lakeside cottages in the Catskills, a loft with a waterbed in a solar-heated contemporary-style house near Albany, and an apartment, complete with doorman, in a Manhattan luxury high-rise.

It is very important for hosts to realize that when a commercial facility puts the words "Bed and Breakfast" or "Complimentary Breakfast" on its marquee, that doesn't make it a B&B. It is the noncommercial qualities that are most essential. A commercial place has staff that comes on and off in eight-hour shifts. The person who says "hello" is seldom the one who says "good-bye." Not so at your home. Your guests' enjoyment or dissatisfaction is your direct responsibility. It is therefore in everyone's best interest for you to take a good hard look at what you have to offer.

## RATING YOUR HOME

The B&B life is not only for those with property of extravagant beauty or opulence, though of course such B&Bs are perennially popular. For the business traveler, a suburban split-level with all the comforts of home and a location down the road from corporate headquarters may be just the thing. There is no set prescription for the perfect host, and there is no single type of home that meets all needs or suits all tastes. It takes only a short time to realize how much success depends on diversity, the incredible mix of people, occupations, interests, and locales that make up our society. Whereas the hotel and motel industry has adopted a cookie-cutter approach to most of its establishments, B&B thrives on offering only absolute originals, unique combinations of hosts and homes.

*Although B&B accommodations can be offered in many different home settings, it is imperative that prospective guests be accurately informed about what you have to offer. For a realistic estimate of how much business you might do and as an aid in pricing your room(s) sensibly, compare your accommodations with this checklist of typical features for standard, executive, and deluxe accommodations. (Your reservation service will also help you to do this.)*

| Feature | Is This Your Home? |
|---|---|
| **STANDARD** (minimum requirements for a B&B) | |
| Usually convenient to some desired location | _____ |
| Shared bath (sometimes with host family) | _____ |
| Sleeping room kept ready for use (clean, aired, neat) | _____ |
| Kitchen and other public areas kept company-ready | _____ |
| Guest room outfitted with the following basic comforts: | _____ |
| • Two pillows | _____ |
| • Firm mattress | _____ |
| • Mattress pad | _____ |
| • Two sets of sheets | _____ |
| • Extra blankets | _____ |
| • Soft, fluffy towels (two sets) | _____ |
| • Room-darkening curtains or shades | _____ |
| • Reading lamp by bed | _____ |

| Feature | Is This Your Home? |
|---|---|
| • Clock radio | _____ |
| • Towel rack | _____ |
| • At least two empty drawers in bureau | _____ |
| • At least half of a closet | _____ |

### EXECUTIVE (includes features of *standard*, plus)

| | |
|---|---|
| Generally a grander house with more rooms | _____ |
| May have historical or architectural interest | _____ |
| Usually has quality furniture | _____ |
| Guest room(s) share bath separate from hosts' | _____ |
| Some have private bath | _____ |
| Usually convenient to businesses or attractions | _____ |
| Has some special amenities for guests' use: | |
| • Library | _____ |
| • Sitting room | _____ |
| • Fireplace | _____ |
| • Pool | _____ |
| • Garden | _____ |
| • Hot tub | _____ |
| • Sauna | _____ |
| • Views | _____ |
| • Stable | _____ |
| • Access to clubs (tennis, swimming, golf, yacht) | _____ |
| • Host shares hobbies (weaving, bridge, restoring antique cars, outlet shopping) | _____ |
| • Phone in room | _____ |
| • Fax | _____ |

| Feature | Is This Your Home? |
|---------|--------------------|
| • Waterfront | _____ |
| • Piano | _____ |
| • Kitchenette | _____ |
| • Jacuzzi | _____ |
| • Exercise equipment | _____ |
| • Office equipment (computer, typewriter) | _____ |
| • Sports equipment (bicycles, croquet set, volleyball) | _____ |
| • Videocassette recorder | _____ |
| • Darkroom or art studio | _____ |
| • Collectibles | _____ |
| • Sewing room | _____ |
| • Music room or sound system | _____ |

**DELUXE** (includes many features of *executive,* plus)

| | |
|---|---|
| • Usually a historic or otherwise noteworthy property in top condition | _____ |
| • Only private baths | _____ |
| • Expensive furnishings (custom decor) | _____ |
| • Variety of amenities | _____ |
| • Gourmet breakfast (possibly in bed) | _____ |
| • May not be conveniently situated but is so interesting that people will want to visit | _____ |
| • Antique or luxury linens | _____ |
| • Fine china and crystal | _____ |
| • Separate quarters for guests (cottage, carriage house, pool house) | _____ |
| • May have staff in addition to host | _____ |

You may notice that none of these categories mentioned any particular number of rooms. In fact, B&Bs in each category may have only one room set aside for guests. Quantity is not the same as quality. Some guests prefer the charm of a very small place where they can really get to know the host family; others prefer a larger place where the mix of guests from all over the country or the world will add enjoyment to their stay.

## EVALUATING YOUR LOCATION

- How much demand is there in your area for overnight lodging?
- Is this demand constant?
- Is it seasonal?
- Is it related to events at a local college or other institution?
- Are there any tourist attractions nearby?
- Do they have special events?
- Are there any local festivals that occur every year?
- Are there any wineries?
- Are there any large businesses?
- What hotels and motels are within a ten-minute drive?
- Within twenty minutes?
- Within thirty minutes?
- What are their capacities and rates?
- How often do you notice "No Vacancy" signs?
- How far are you from a large city whose residents may be looking for weekend getaways?
- Is there skiing nearby?
- Will guests be able to arrive by public transportation and get around without a car?
- Are there other B&Bs in your area?
- How are they doing?
- How does your place compare with them?

In answering the preceding questions, you are getting a good idea about the desirability of your location. If you are near a large city or corporate area, your location will be more interesting to business guests, the Monday-through-Friday crowd. Tourist traffic is more seasonal; guests are typically getting away for a weekend or staying at a B&B en route to a long vacation. The vacation season depends on the part of the country you are in. North of the Mason-Dixon line, it is usually considered April through October. In the Sun Belt, the season may be the reverse. Maine offers a spectacular seacoast and lots of tourist attractions but a limited season. Most traffic to Maine is in July and August. The difference between the cost of a house in Maine and that of one in Massachusetts is enormous. The difference in seasonal demand will be similar. If you are under two hours' driving time from a major city, guests can get there for a two-day weekend and still have time to enjoy the area. A drive time of more than two hours is usually considered too long for anything less than a three-day trip.

In the travel industry, some places are considered final destinations, and others are stopping points along the way. Maine, for example, is considered a final destination; like Alaska, it is not usually considered as being on the way to anywhere else. Massachusetts, on the other hand, might be either a final destination or a stop on the way to Maine, Canada, Vermont, or New Hampshire.

Remember, your B&B is likely to have under five rooms for guests. If ten couples want to stay on any particular night, you will have to turn five of them away. If a festival is in town and 100 couples want to stay, you will still have only five rooms and will have to turn the rest away. Of course, you can bet that on weekends of high demand in your region, you will have a full house. But what you should be most interested in is how many times demand outstrips supply in your area, not how great occasional demand will be. You can be sure that if there were high demand in your area on a constant basis, more hotel and motel rooms would be built. Commercial facilities have to pay overhead year-round and can't survive on sporadic periods of high demand. But you can as long as your expectations are realistic.

Once you have answered the preceding two lists of questions, you should have a good idea about the desirability of both your location and your home. Demand for your accommodations can be judged on the basis of these two factors. Remember, a stand-ard B&B in a desirable location may do more business than a deluxe B&B in a remote location.

## TAKE A GOOD LOOK AT YOUR HOME

### First Impressions

Your guests' first impression of your home will be formed as they drive up to your home. What will they see? Is there any repair work, painting, or yard work that needs to be done? Would flower-filled window boxes or better-trimmed hedges make your home more inviting? Can your house number be seen from the street? The last thing you want is for a late-arriving guest to wake up your neighbors.

When I was a small child, my parents bought a waterfront home in Larchmont, New York. It was a big move for them, and much deliberation and numerous visits were necessary before they made up their mind. The odd thing about visiting this house was that sometimes the owner would only be available to show it in the morning, but at other times, she was only available in the afternoon. What we didn't realize was that she was available when the tide was high. At low tide, the house backed on a cove of mud twelve feet down, not the most appealing sight. This taught me that because first impressions mean so much, you should show off your house to its best advantage. If you are giv-ing directions and there are two ways to approach your home, send your guests by the most scenic route even if it is not the fastest or the most direct. Later you can tell them about short-cuts. If they are arriving after dark, have the house well lit. Make their welcome warm and inviting. In the winter, for example, a fire burning in the fireplace makes a house seem cozy.

### The Interior

Walk through the public rooms of your house, and look at them as a stranger would. What do you see? What feeling do you get? Are there repairs to be made? Is something frayed or broken?

Should it be fixed, replaced, or simply put away? What will it cost in time and money to make these changes? Look at each of the potential guest rooms. Are they large or small? What type of beds do they have? Will you need new furniture? Will you have to redecorate? Should you start by fixing up one room and see what comes of it? These are some of the questions you should be asking yourself. If any of the answers are yes, you will want to examine your rooms in more detail. If some changes need to be made, the questions that follow will help you determine how much work needs to be done, how long it will take, and what it will cost.

## The Guest Rooms

Before you offer a room to a guest, make sure to sleep in it first. You need to find out firsthand what else needs to be done.

### CHECKLIST

Do the shades block out the early morning sun? _____

Is the temperature comfortable? _____

Will you need to adjust the thermostat in this portion of the house? _____

Will a fan or air conditioner be necessary come summer? _____

Are there extra blankets in the closet? _____

Is the bed comfortable? Is it long enough for tall person? _____

Are the bedsprings too noisy? _____

Do the windows and screens work easily? _____

Are the pillows comfortable, not too hard or soft? _____

Is the air circulation good, no musty smells or stuffy closet? _____

Do the dresser drawers slide in and out easily? _____

Is the reading lamp good to read by, not too bright or too dim? _____

Are there enough hangers in the closet? _____

What sounds do you hear? _____

The last question is especially important because most people sleep on one side of a house for years and aren't aware that other bedrooms may not be as quiet as theirs. Rooms at the front of the house may be less desirable on days when the garbage men arrive at 6:00 A.M. to pick up the trash. For example, I visited a home near Cooperstown, New York, and was shown to a beautiful, well-appointed room where I slept soundly. Early the next morning, however, I was awakened by the sound of a rush of running water behind my head. It turned out that the shower pipes were in the wall at the head of the bed; when the host's son got up early to shower before school, the running water and clanging pipes were enough to rudely awaken any sleeping guest. It was quite a startling experience.

When I mentioned this to the hostess, she said, "Oh, I forgot to tell you. The room just doesn't look as good if the furniture is arranged differently. There are too many doors and windows to move the bed from that spot." My advice was to utilize this room last, to rearrange the furniture even if it isn't the nicest way artistically, and to ask the young man to shower before retiring. I also suggested that if all the other rooms were booked, she should warn guests that this room backs on the bathroom and that they may hear the sound of running water. In this way, guests will take the room knowing its drawback and won't be frightened by the noise.

You will find that guests who are told about your home's weaknesses as well as its assets won't complain if those shortcomings cause minor inconvenience. For example, a very old house may have a small hot water tank. Until you are able to get a larger one, share this problem with guests so that some will shower at night and others in the morning.

Here are other examples: Guests staying at homes along the Hudson River all want to enjoy the river view. They need to be told that the railroad line was built at the river's edge and that in any home from which they can see the river they can also hear the train. If you work outside your home and must leave early, don't accept guests who don't know this. A guest who awakens at 10:00 A.M. surprised to find a note from a host who has left for the office will be very dissatisfied. But a guest who has accepted the accommodation knowing that breakfast is served at 7:00 A.M. and that late risers must prepare their own meal will do it in good spirit.

# The Bathroom

Use the guest bathroom, too.

Is the bathroom clean and shiny?                                          _____

Is extra lighting or a flashlight necessary to get there after dark?       _____

Does the tub drain well?                                                   _____

Are the cleaning things and extra toilet paper handy?                      _____

Is the water temperature appropriate?                                      _____

Does the door lock work properly?                                          _____

Is there a nonslip surface or rubber mat in tub?                           _____

# Safety and Comfort

Here are more questions to ask yourself as you evaluate guest accommodations.

| Points to Check | Date | Professional to Call |
|---|---|---|
| Smoke detector installed in each guest room | _____ | _____ |
| Smoke detector in hallway(s) | _____ | _____ |
| Smoke detector in kitchen | _____ | _____ |
| Nonskid pads under throw rugs | _____ | _____ |
| Night-light for hallway(s) | _____ | _____ |
| Night-light for bathroom | _____ | _____ |
| Adequate outdoor lighting | _____ | _____ |
| House number visible at night | _____ | _____ |
| Secure pool fencing | _____ | _____ |

Bushes, vines, and other plants trimmed
back from walkways         _____     _____

Escape ladder (collapsible) for
second-floor bedrooms if needed     _____     _____

Fire escape rehearsal         _____     _____

Fire escape map         _____     _____

Nonskid treads on outdoor steps
(or textured paints to improve footings)     _____     _____

Secure pet restraints and fencing as
needed         _____     _____

Child/toddler stair gates as needed     _____     _____

Flashlights in sleeping rooms
(with working batteries)         _____     _____

Eight-hour supply of candles in case
of power failure         _____     _____

Air conditioner or fan in working order     _____     _____

Several run-throughs with any new
kitchen equipment (especially
microwave oven)         _____     _____

Fireplace(s) cleaned         _____     _____

Fireplace(s) inspected for flue problems     _____     _____

Ample supply of kindling and wood     _____     _____

Appropriately sized fireplace screen(s)     _____     _____

Fire extinguisher for each room     _____     _____

List of emergency telephone numbers
placed next to phones         _____     _____

Items needed by family members
removed from guest rooms     _____     _____

Hot water temperature checked     _____     _____

Hot water availability adequate for family
and full number of guests (check
number of showers possible before
water cools. Can you run washer or
dishwasher without affecting hot water
supply to showers?)         _____     _____

Water-saving devices installed     _____     _____

Bed slept in by you to check comfort    _____    _____

Extra bed space for children as needed
(high riser, trundle, inflatable mattress,
rollaways, cot, futon)    _____    _____

Privacy locks on bedroom and bathroom
doors above reach of small children    _____    _____

Grab bar installed on wall beside bathtub    _____    _____

Wastebaskets in bedroom and bath    _____    _____

**At poolside**

• Life jackets    _____    _____

• Water wings    _____    _____

• Pole    _____    _____

• Life preserver    _____    _____

• Garbage pail    _____    _____

• Scooper for pet droppings    _____    _____

**Guest closet extras**

• Bathrobes or pool cover-ups    _____    _____

• Hair dryer (or in bathroom)    _____    _____

• Curling iron (or in bathroom)    _____    _____

• Hot rollers (or in bathroom)    _____    _____

• Sewing kit    _____    _____

• Iron (may be in hall closet)    _____    _____

• Ironing board (may be in hall closet)    _____    _____

• Small refrigerator (optional)    _____    _____

• Electric hot water device (optional)    _____    _____

• Padded hangers (optional)    _____    _____

• Wooden hangers    _____    _____

• Sunscreen or sunblock cream
(may be in bathroom)    _____    _____

• Plastic glasses and dishes (optional)    _____    _____

• Paper napkins (optional)    _____    _____

• Vase    _____    _____

- Candles and matches         _____   _____
- Sachet or potpourri (optional)   _____   _____
- Neck pillow (optional)       _____   _____

**In the bathroom**

Tile and grouting scrubbed to remove
  and prevent mildew           _____   _____

Bathtub, sink, and toilet bowl scrubbed   _____   _____

Shower curtain scrubbed with vinyl cleaner   _____   _____

Shower stall and floor scrubbed   _____   _____

Drains unclogged and treated with a
  drain cleaner               _____   _____

Automatic toilet bowl cleaner installed   _____   _____

Decals (nonskid) installed in bottom of
  tub or shower               _____   _____

Bath mat with nonskid backing   _____   _____

Windows and mirrored surfaces cleaned   _____   _____

Metal fixtures shined          _____   _____

Towel rack and shower curtain rod tightly
  secured                    _____   _____

Full-length mirror installed on back of door   _____   _____

Bathroom cabinet or closet stocked with:       _____

- Paper cups                  _____   _____
- Tissues                     _____   _____
- Extra toilet paper           _____   _____
- Liquid soap (by sink)        _____   _____
- Bar soap (in shower or tub)   _____   _____
- Air freshener               _____   _____
- Hand lotion                 _____   _____
- Band-Aids                   _____   _____
- Cotton swabs                _____   _____
- Cotton balls                _____   _____
- Nail polish remover          _____   _____

- Emery boards                                    _____    _____
- Cleanser                                        _____    _____
- Glass cleaner                                   _____    _____
- Sponge(s)                                       _____    _____
- Paper towels                                    _____    _____
- Sample-size toothpaste, mouthwash,
  shampoo                                         _____    _____
- Replacement light bulbs                         _____    _____

Window shades or curtains for privacy            _____    _____

Functional exhaust fan in room or window         _____    _____

# WHAT IF YOU DON'T HAVE THE RIGHT HOUSE?

Use the material presented in this chapter to evaluate a possible new home. Many people who take my course in New York City live in small apartments and hope that B&B will be a way to help finance a larger apartment or a move to a house. Older couples considering a change in lifestyle after retirement may also anticipate moving. First, decide where you would be most happy living. Not everyone enjoys country life. Remember, your guests will visit for short stays, but you will be living there all the time. Examine the seasonal nature of the location, and ask yourself the other location questions that determine how often people will be seeking out your area. Evaluate the house in terms of amenities and number of rooms. Calculate how often you will have to have guests in order to bring in enough money to supplement your income. (Read Chapter 4, "Financial Considerations," before doing this.) How often will you be comfortable having guests in your home? Does this fit with how much business you need to do?

# SEPARATE QUARTERS

From my own experience, as well as from speaking to numerous B&B owners, I have found out that as the business becomes more successful, your own private space becomes more elusive and sought after. Time away from the inn helps, but it does not make up for a sense of not having a place to go to do personal things without being interrupted. Toward this end, innkeepers add private quarters, buy the house next door, or, as in my case, are planning to build a house next door. I have spent this winter getting the permits. Soon, construction will begin, but at least this time I won't have to live there until the construction is over.

## BUYING AN ESTABLISHED INN OR NOT?

Now that there are existing B&Bs for sale, prospective innkeepers wonder whether to buy an existing business or start from scratch. Most people choose an area first, one that will be compatible with their own future interests. If there are both an established inn for sale and a large home suitable for conversion in the area, it is often unclear which way to go. There is no simple answer. It partly depends on your finances and how soon you need to start making money. Certainly, a turnkey operation will allow you to begin taking guests right away. You will benefit from placement in guidebooks that may take you years to achieve on your own. You will also benefit or suffer from the reputation of the past innkeepers, so make sure they have a good one, and expect to pay for this. The savings in time and stress from renovating or building and the advantage of a good reputation are often worth the extra cost.

## DO A MARKET SURVEY

A market survey is necessary before you spend many hundreds of thousands of dollars and change your way of life. You can hire a consultant to do the market survey or try it yourself. Begin by speaking to the local or larger regional chambers of commerce. Get a good idea of how many travelers come into the area each year. See if there is a discernible trend, preferably upward, in these numbers. How often are the existing facilities at full occupancy? State agencies usually provide figures about methods of transportation used by travelers to your area. Determine the attractions that make your location a final destination. In addition, determine how many people will pass through your area on their way to another destination.

Know your competition. Determine which establishments are comparable to yours, and especially examine how well they are doing and what they charge. This will be important in pricing your rooms because the room price, multiplied by your estimated occupancy, will result in how much money you can expect to take in from your business.

## UNHOSTED BED AND BREAKFAST

Sometimes a B&B accommodation is referred to as *unhosted.* This is usually a city apartment or a freestanding cottage or carriage house on the host family's property. In many cities, the demand for reasonably priced apartments for the business traveler on short-term assignment is great, but supply is short. A person who owns or leases an apartment that he or she is not currently using may list it with a reservation service for guest use on a daily or weekly basis. For example, a host may be living with someone but may be reluctant to give up his or her apartment in case the relationship docs not last. He or she may be trying to hold on to a small apartment after moving to a larger one because apartment values are rising and selling it next year may mean more money. Using that small apartment for B&B pays the carrying cost and possibly more during the interim. A host may be on vacation or sabbatical for a few weeks or months and allow guests to use the apartment during that time. I know of two young women with small apartments, neither big enough to share with a guest, who take turns sharing with each other, freeing the second apartment for guest use. They split the proceeds.

These are a few of the many types of unhosted places made available for guest use. In many cases, there is a host who makes sure that the apartment is clean and stocked with breakfast food for the guest to prepare. When a host is not in town, he or she must arrange for a friend or concierge service (a company set up to stand in for you for a fee) to be at the apartment to greet guests and acquaint them with any particulars about the place or neighborhood as needed. One host I know makes his studio apartment available for guests in New York City and has put together a beautiful book of handy information for his guests. It includes information about restaurants, theater, shopping, as well as laundry facilities and garbage disposal. In all unhosted situations, it is essential that the guest have the phone number of the host or the person in charge in case of emergency. For more information about unhosted B&B, see Chapter 11, "Specialty Bed and Breakfasts."

## REAL ESTATE SPECULATION

Few are those who have an intuitive sense of the real estate market and of areas that they believe will rise in value. Such a person can purchase an undervalued home, make improvements to it, and use it as a B&B to offset some of the expenses and enjoy the tax benefits while building equity to reap at the time of sale. These people, however, realize that they are gambling. If this type of property is not the owner's primary home, he or she may pay a manager to run the B&B. Making a profit in this situation is unusual, but because the business is planned for a short term only, the losses sustained may be more than made up by the sale of the property.

❖❖❖❖❖❖❖

**Question:** I have one guest room on the ground floor with a private bath and private entrance. The upstairs guest room shares the family bath. There is a large closet in that room that could be made into a small bathroom. Would it be worthwhile for us to make this additional bathroom?

**Answer:** *My answer to this question is another question: How long have you wanted to do this? If adding this bath is something you have wanted to do for a long time, now is the ideal* *time. Understand that the difference in what you will be able to charge for this room may be only $10 a night because of the private bath, but you will probably have more call for the room. The cost of the new bath will be a tax deduction, and you will also be increasing your equity in your home. If you decide not to add the bath, you will attract guests who are willing to share the family bath in order to pay lower room cost. Make sure that you are also comfortable sharing your bath with guests. All personal items must be removed from the bath so that guests don't feel that they are invading your personal space.*

❖❖❖❖❖❖❖

**Question:** We bought our home a few years ago, and it needed lots of work. Now the public rooms are ready, but all the bedrooms still need to be decorated. Would it be premature to fix up one room and begin while we work on the other two?

**Answer:** *No, most people take it one room at a time. Select your largest room to prepare first. Ideally, a queen-size bed plus a daybed will give you maximum flexibility. You can work on your other bedrooms one by one and open them as they are ready and your business grows.*

❖❖❖❖❖❖❖

**Question:** Please describe a home that you rejected when you had your reservation service.

**Answer:** *A potential hostess in Yonkers, New York, arranged for me to visit her two-bedroom, two-bath apartment. The guest room was large, airy, and recently painted light lavender. The bed was covered with stuffed animals. I remarked that with the animals removed and a little decoration, the room would be quite suitable for a businessperson on short-term assignment or for anyone while looking to relocate in lower Westchester. She smiled and asked, "How many animals will have to go?" All of them, said I, assuming that they belonged to a daughter who was now married or at least away at school. She told me that her daughter was fourteen years old, went to high school, and* lived at home. Her clothes were in the closet and dresser drawers, and she would get very upset if her animals were dispossessed. She explained that the girl falls asleep on the living room couch watching TV every night and no longer sleeps in her own bed. What this woman didn't understand was that she really didn't have a room to rent. No B&B guest at any price wants to feel that he or she is invading anyone's private space.

❖❖❖❖❖❖❖

**Question:** In looking at my home, I think guests would enjoy my master bedroom most because it has its own bath and a fireplace. The current guest bedroom is next to my daughter's room and shares a bath with her. I think both the guest and my daughter might be uncomfortable with such an arrangement. My daughter is sixteen and will be going to college in two years. Should I give up my master bedroom?

**Answer:** *The answer to this question depends on a few conditions. First, are you married? If you are, discuss the idea with your spouse. You may decide that relocating is a poor idea after all. You might wait the two years until your daughter leaves for school and then have two guest rooms with a shared bath. However, if you are alone and don't mind changing bedrooms, you are right, this would be an ideal B&B situation. Starting now will certainly help you accumulate the funds you will need to keep your daughter in college. If she knows that this is your motivation for opening your home to paying guests, you may find her very helpful in keeping the house neat and clean and welcoming in the guests.*

❖❖❖❖❖❖❖

**Question:** Are there state or local regulations that pertain to using my home as a B&B?

**Answer:** *Chapter 5 goes into considerable depth about these. Please make sure to read it carefully before opening your home or purchasing a place for B&B.*

# 4

# Financial Considerations

**B**ed and Breakfast does not guarantee any homeowners any minimum amount of money per year. It is best to think of this income as money for extras, not money you must have in order to meet basic obligations. Many successful hosts combine their B&B activities with other compatible uses of their homes to generate the money they need if they do not work outside the home. The financial considerations discussed in this chapter include estimating your B&B income, pricing your accommodations, taxes, and record keeping. I also touch briefly on ways to offer additional services to bring in extra income.

## A PROFESSIONAL OPINION

Since the first edition of this book was published, I have been fortunate to have as an advisor Arthur D. Levy, a New York City CPA who gives financial advice to innkeepers around the nation. I asked him to read my existing financial chapter and add his expertise. Throughout the chapter, you will see quoted material that came from my interview with Arthur.

## BED AND BREAKFAST IS A SMALL BUSINESS

"Operating a Bed and Breakfast is similar to operating any other type of small business. The income you earn is variable. Small businesses fail constantly for a myriad of reasons. Among them is procrastination: 'Always put off till tomorrow what you can do today,' 'The check's in the mail,' 'Don't worry about it, it will take care of itself.' Avoiding decision making is one of the most common causes of business failures.

"Another reason businesses fail is as a result of the basic failure to establish goals. For you to properly determine where your business is going and how it should operate, a business plan is a *must*. A business plan will answer questions like, 'What are you selling?' 'To whom are you selling?' 'Why do they buy from *you*?' 'What else can you sell them?' 'What do you do to secure a market?' 'What are your advertising and promotion policies?' 'What are your pricing policies?' 'How big is your competition? Who are they? What are they doing (that you're not)?' You will be surprised at how many of these questions apply to you when you really start to think about it."

## ESTABLISH GOALS!

"Be sure your goals are reasonable and precise—not, for example, 'I want to rent a lot of rooms,' but instead, 'I have three available rooms that I would like to rent for five nights a week, forty weeks a year.' Obviously, it would be unrealistic to set a goal to rent all of your rooms, all of the time. We have seen situations where hosts have aggressively estimated income without consideration for the number of rooms available. This is not an example of good business planning."

## ESTIMATING INCOME

How much you might earn from doing Bed and Breakfast is highly variable. Much obviously depends on the types of rooms you offer, how many you have available, how often they are filled (which is sometimes a function of your location), the price you charge for each overnight stay, and your overhead. Often your reservation service can help you arrive at some good "guesstimates." Remember, there is tremendous variation from season to season and place to place. And be reassured that your second year's estimates will be much more accurate than those for your first.

In a major metropolitan area where room rates in hotels are in the $100-a-night category, a Bed and Breakfast with three or four executive-level guest rooms that are occupied 60 percent of the time, with no restrictions on who is an acceptable guest, and serving good but simple breakfasts might gross $60,000 to $75,000 a year.

A spare room used during only part of the year for guests, in a house in a small college town in the Midwest, where smokers and children are not welcome might have guests on half of the weekends March through October and bring in $1,600 a year.

Remember, the gross income is not the only consideration. Bed and Breakfast is usually most beneficial as a second income. Certainly no one could live in a six-bedroom Victorian home in Croton, NY, with a gross income of $25,000 a year. The fact that my ex-husband's income was highly taxed made the advantages of writing off many of our home expenses another good financial reason to offer Bed and Breakfast in our home.

It is best to make very conservative estimates: after all, it never hurts to find you've surpassed your expectations. Let's first try to estimate how many *roomnights* you can expect in the coming year. A roomnight is the number of rooms multiplied by the number of nights a party stays. If a party of four comes for a two-day stay, they represent two rooms times two nights, or four roomnights of business. You may be wondering, "How can I estimate my number of roomnights?" Talk to the reservation service in your area. Find out when the travel season is. Are there tourist attractions near you that will bring people during the travel season? If so, estimate that you will be three-quarters full on at least half the weekends in the travel season. If you are very selective about who comes (for instance, if you take only nonsmoking couples with no children and no pet allergies), reduce your estimate to two-thirds full.

Following are a few brief examples of how different B&B hosts figured out their likely rates of occupancy.

❖❖❖❖❖❖❖

**Becky's B&B** is executive quality, about an hour from a major East Coast city, has four rooms that share two baths, is near some tourist attractions, and takes only nonsmokers, but will accept singles and children. A chain hotel room of comparable quality in the area begins at $85. Becky's room rates are $35 for a single, $50 for a double on a daily basis, $200 for a single and $280 for a double on a weekly basis. The travel season in her area is April through October (seven months, twenty-eight weekends). If we estimate three-fourths full for half of those weekends, she will average three rooms of guests two nights per weekend, or six roomnights times fourteen weeks. This would come out to eighty-four roomnights for weekend guests in season. Estimating a 50 percent cutback off-season, three roomnights times ten weeks (half of the five-month off-season) would give her another thirty roomnights of weekend guests. This leaves four weeks of vacation or time that her house is used for personal friends and is not available for B&B guests regardless of demand. Since most weekend guests will be doubles, $50 times 114 roomnights would be $5,700. Becky's place is also near a few major corporations. She can expect either one long-term stay (a single executive relocating into the area) of two or three months ($200 a week times ten weeks yields $2,000) or perhaps a few two- or three-week guests on short-term business assignment (auditing a plant, supervising new construction) bringing in five weeks of business times $200, equaling $1,000. Her home is on the way north to a ski area, and some guests will want to stop over on their way to or from their vacation. So add ten roomnights at $50 ($500). In addition, there will be some weekday business from people coming into town to visit relatives who are ill, have a reunion, christen a new baby, attend graduation, or to do other personal activities; add twenty roomnights at $50, or $1,000. A conservative estimate for Becky's B&B would be a gross income of $10,200. Of course, this is not all profit. But Becky can certainly expect that as she becomes better known and gets repeat business and more referrals from satisfied guests, her business will grow and perhaps double in two to three years.

❖❖❖❖❖❖❖

**Susie** has a two-bedroom, two-bath New York City apartment in a good location. It is a deluxe accommodation in an area where hotel prices are high. Until now, she has had a roommate who paid $500 a month in rent but was always around and had kitchen privileges. There was never anyplace to accommodate Susie's friends or relatives when they came to town. Susie decided that her place would appeal to businesspeople and that she would like to try to have the apartment for personal use on weekends. It is available Monday through Friday. Rates are $60 single, $70 double. If she has paying guests ten days a month, she grosses $600 minimum, or $7,200 a year. If she does more business or has doubles instead of singles on a few of the nights, her income goes up considerably.

❖❖❖❖❖❖❖

**Marsha** lives in a rural area a good two hours from the nearest large city. There are no chain hotels nearby, but there is a mom-and-pop motel that charges $40 a night. Although there are no major businesses nearby, she is in a very scenic location with lots of acres for hunting and fishing, and pond for swimming and skating on her property. There is a college twenty minutes away, and the exit to the main highway connecting two major cities in the state is only five minutes away. She has three rooms available for guests; they share a guest bath. One daughter still lives at home, and there is an extra bed in the daughter's room for a visiting child. Marsha can expect to have guests on the four weekends that the college has home football games, parents' weekend, graduation and also to have an occasional parent coming up overnight with their son or daughter to visit the college for a personal interview. Estimate thirty-eight roomnights of college-related guests at $35 per night, or $1,330. If Marsha markets her B&B properly, city folk might make the trip to enjoy three-day weekends in this nature lover's paradise. Add another thirty-six roomnights, or $1,260. Residents of the town will also call on Marsha to accommodate guests for weddings, family reunions, and the like. Add twenty-five roomnights, or $875. Marsha can expect to gross $3,165.

❖❖❖❖❖❖❖

**Diana** has a fabulous place—a bedroom with fireplace, king-size bed, mountain views, private bath, and Jacuzzi. She likes to feature gourmet breakfasts or breakfast in bed. She and her husband love to entertain and have a VCR and a large collection of old movies on tape. The location is close to a number of colleges, tourist attractions, and businesses in southern California. The problem Diana faces is that the area is overbuilt, with hotels that offer rooms with breakfast for $29.95. Diana's house is worth over $500,000. It is not worth her time to try to compete with a cheap motel by offering a lower price. She realizes that what she offers is a fantasy, a romantic getaway. She charges $125 a night for a couple and for $175 will include a candlelight supper. She expects her guests to come only from a certain segment of the travel market, exactly the type she wants to entertain, people who will be much like her husband and herself, with similar interests. She limits her business to two weekends a month and expects to earn $6,900 (about $300 per weekend, twenty-three weekends a year).

❖❖❖❖❖❖❖

**Donald** is a mystery writer who has restored a six-bedroom home in the French Quarter of New Orleans. Each room now has a private bath. Two of the bedrooms open into a sitting room suite. Two ground-floor bedrooms open onto private gardens at the rear. Donald's rates are $150 a night for the two-bedroom suite, $95 each for his garden rooms, and $85 for a room with a queen-sized bed. Donald's decor is deluxe, and the location is very desirable for business travelers, conventioneers, and tourists. He is fully booked about five days a week, which brings in $445 per day, $2,225 per week. Donald enjoys traveling and finds that the summer is his off-season, so that's when he closes up and goes off on his own. Open forty weeks a year, Donald grosses $89,000 from his B&B.

❖❖❖❖❖❖❖

**Sue Ellen** and her husband and three youngsters (ages five, seven, and nine) live in a rural area in Wisconsin. They have a dairy farm and have fixed up the farmhand's cottage to sleep a family of four. Guests who come there are welcome to take all meals with the family because there are few restaurants within a twenty-mile radius. (Meals other than breakfast are extra.) Guests can relax or pitch in with farm chores. Children are welcome to learn to milk a cow, meet the newborn calf, gather eggs from the chickens, or play inside by the wood-burning stove on cold rainy days. Sue Ellen keeps lots of games handy for such days. Guests can go for a moonlit ride on the hay wagon in the summer and snowmobiling in the winter. The hunting season in the fall draws hunters from as far away as Chicago. Rates here are $30 for two people, $10 each for children over three years old or adults sharing the cottage. Her first year, Sue Ellen got a lot of hunters during the brief hunting season ($500). Winter (November through March) offered lots to do, but there was so much snow that a number of guests canceled their reservations because they couldn't get there. She grossed only $1,000. In summer, families of four came about four days a month ($400). In total, Sue Ellen earned about $2,000; she could probably have rented her cottage full time and earned about the same thing. Instead, she enjoyed the variety of guests and found that her children benefitted from the interactions with other children from less rural surroundings.

## PRICING

In the preceding examples, the information given included how much each room cost. Understand that location is one of the key ingredients: B&B rates vary across the country and around the world for some of the same reasons that the cost of housing varies (supply and demand). It is usually more expensive to stay in the city than in the country. The other factor in determining price is amenities. A deluxe accommodation will charge more than a standard or executive one in the same location.

In the beginning of B&B in this country, the media focused on the "sleep cheap" aspect. As more high-quality accommodations became available, guests who called to get reservations were stunned to find that prices were far more than $15 a night. It is important for guests to realize that whatever a B&B charges, it should be a real value compared with an equivalent commercial accommodation. For example, if a chain hotel's rooms in your area cost $85 and do not include breakfast, an executive-quality home should probably charge no more than $50 to $60 with breakfast. Bed and Breakfasts generally average half to two-thirds the cost of a comparable-class hotel or motel. Certainly, there are going to be cheaper places to stay in the area, but they won't be as nice as yours, and you should not try to compete with them on price. Guests looking only for a low price aren't usually going to be the ones B&B hosts seek, anyway.

Your reservation service will be the best place to turn to for help in pricing. The staff knows what comparable places go for and can sometimes give you pricing ideas that will make your place very attractive to potential guests. You can always adjust your rates in the future, but it is good to set a price that you can live with for at least a year because it would be awkward for any-one representing you to print prices, send them out to guests, and then have to say that the printed prices are wrong.

When thinking of pricing, decide if you want to give a dis-count for children, weekly stays, or senior citizens.

There is customarily no charge for children under two stay-ing in the same room with parents. For children over three and under twelve, the rate is generally $10. If the children stay in a separate room, you have the option of charging a child rate or an adult rate. Logically, if they take up another room, they should be charged for it. Unfortunately, many B&Bs don't have space or extra beds to accommodate children with their parents, and the charge for two rooms can be more than a family wants to pay. For this reason B&Bs don't get very many families as guests.

Weekly prices may be the equivalent of six nights' stay, five nights' stay, $10 off per night, or a reduction of 10 percent. The lower rate is charged because usually weekly stays are much eas-ier on the hostess (not a lot of bed changing), and guests staying for a long time don't usually expect a gourmet breakfast every day. Because so much of the business is on weekends, weekly rates encourage people who will be in town during the week to use a B&B. Increasing your number of roomnights increases your business. A $50-a-night room that is empty brings you in $0. But if you reduce your nightly rate to $40 to bring in a week's stay, you will make $280.

Guests sometimes think that they can book a room for Saturday night, arrive Saturday at 10:00 A.M. and hang around until late Sunday afternoon, really enjoying a full weekend at the cost of a one-night accommodation. This is why hosts in desirable locations have two-night minimum stays on weekends and even three nights on long weekends. This is particularly true in places with very short seasons, such as beach and ski areas. Decide if you want to set a minimum length of stay. If you have a two-night minimum and are free on a Saturday night, you can always accept a last-minute one-night guest. Some hosts offer one-night stays as long as a surcharge of $10 to $15 is paid.

## BEFORE YOU OPEN

Arthur Levy recommends that before you open, "Some consideration should be given to the type of legal entity you will operate your B&B out of. Recent changes in the tax law and the increased surveillance by the Internal Revenue Service (IRS) requires that you do proper tax planning so that you are able to take advantage of the available rules to minimize your potential income tax exposure. You should review your personal tax situation by examining your non-B&B income expenses as well. Portions of your mortgage payment, house maintenance expenses, utilities, insurance, and other items are deductible from your non-B&B as well as from your B&B income. For many hosts, tax savings are a far more important reason for getting into the business than the actual dollars they are going to receive."

## RECORD KEEPING

Arthur reminds us that "It is necessary (very early on) to establish basic books and records. Your accountant can help you with this, but at a minimum you will be required to keep records of cash receipts, cash disbursements, payroll, and personal expenses that may be deductible by the B&B. It is also important to determine what, if any, local, sales, occupancy, and/or room taxes are applicable in your location; to be sure to register with the authorized agencies to collect them; and to arrange to pay promptly to the appropriate authorities. Failure to deal with taxes on time can subject you to penalties. Your local accountant should be able to assist you in complying."

## EXPENSES

There are definitely expenses related to operating a Bed and Breakfast. At the very least, you will be sprucing up; freshening paint, investing in new sheets, towels, and table linens; and purchasing a guest book. You may want to invest in new furniture or antiques, landscaping, a pool, and who knows what else. You may have structural repairs to make or restoration to do. The important thing to understand is that because these expenses are now related to business use, not just personal use, you must keep receipts and understand how they will be reflected in your tax obligations.

## INCOME TAX

"The IRS has raised numerous questions concerning Bed and Breakfasts. Among the current issues are the following:

1. Are Bed and Breakfasts a business or a hobby?
2. Are Bed and Breakfasts tax shelters or businesses?
3. Are proper business records being maintained, since with the absence of records there can be no proof of any losses?"

Several issues have been raised by the IRS in the last few years. The IRS National Office has issued a technical advice memorandum on B&Bs. This release provides the basic ground rules as to how and when a B&B may qualify to be treated as a business. It is imperative that B&B owners and their tax advisors be familiar with this memorandum to be sure they establish the strongest possible case to protect their deductions.

"Generally, expenses that are required exclusively for the maintenance of your B&B will be deductible. Examples of these are furniture for guest rooms, newspapers, magazines, repairs, sheets, towels, linens, breakfast-related costs, as well as other items that are required."

## Tax Strategies

To help some B&B owners avoid some of the issues that the IRS has raised in the past, Arthur Levy established a new operating strategy for them. His basic ground rules are as follows:

1. Incorporate the B&B.
2. Because the real estate (the home) is generally owned by them, the owners should enter into a lease agreement with this corporation.
3. The corporation that is formed solely to operate the B&B files a Sub-Chapter S with the IRS and state tax department. This election enables the stockholders of the B&B to include in their individual tax return the income or loss of the Sub S Corporation. The Sub S designation is merely for tax purposes and has no effect on the legal status of the corporation.
4. The B&B pays rent to the individual owners of the real estate, who in turn make the necessary mortgage, interest, and amortization payments, real estate tax payments, and other expenses directly related to the real estate. In addition to these expenses, the owners may deduct depreciation attributable to the portion they own that is used exclusively for B&B.
5. This strategy enables the owner to show the B&B operation on the individual income tax return as a distributive share of profits from a Sub S Corporation rather than showing each line item on the individual tax return.

"To date, B&B owners have been successful in reporting losses in this manner and have thereby avoided being targeted for IRS audits. This is an extremely sophisticated and complex tax planning method and should be done after consultation with your tax advisor, accountant, and/or attorney."

## Itemizing Expenses

You will be able to claim expenses only if you itemize your deductions, so you will want to keep accurate records of them. Most will fall into one of five categories: guest capital expenses, guest maintenance expenses, house capital expenses, house maintenance expenses, and business expenses.

*Guest Capital Expenses.* These are expenses for things that you purchase exclusively for guest use that will last longer than a year—for example, an antique bedroom set with bed, marble-topped dresser, and armoire: $1,000. Other guest capital expenses might include:

- TV for guest room

- Blankets or quilts

- Breakfast trays

- Plants for guest room

- Furniture for guest room

- Draperies or window shades for guest room

- Guest room carpeting

- Artwork for guest room

- Towel rack

- Smoke detectors and fire extinguishers

*Guest Maintenance Expenses.* There are expenses for things bought exclusively for the guests' use that will last less than a year—for example, flowers for the guest room: $2.50. Other guest maintenance expenses might include:

- Fruit placed in guest room
- Newspapers in guest room
- Magazines for guest bathroom
- Repairs to guest furniture
- Sheets, towels, and table linens
- Breakfast-related costs

*House Capital Expenses.* These are expenses for things for the house that will be used in common by your family and the guests and that will last more than a year—for example, a new room: $4,000. Other house capital expenditures may include:

- Furniture for public rooms
- A new kitchen or appliances
- TV in the family room
- Hot tub, Jacuzzi, pool, tennis courts
- Carpeting
- Outdoor landscaping

*House Maintenance Expenses.* These are expenses for things for the house that will be used in common by your family and the guests but that will last less than a year—for example, the gardener's services. Other house maintenance expenses may include:

- Heat
- Electricity and gas
- Telephone
- Rent

- Housekeeper or laundress

- Painter

- Handyman

- Plumber

- Heavy cleaning service

- Pool service

- Interior designer

*Business Expenses.* These are expenses incurred in order to do business—for example, your accountant's fees. Other business expenses may include:

- Your attorney's fees

- Your ledger

- Business cards or stationery

- Liability insurance

- Membership in a reservation service, chamber of commerce, or other professional group

- Telephone answering machine

- Reservation service commissions

- Advertising

- Baby-sitter's fees while you take guests on tours of your area

- Office supplies: postage, fax, telex, phone

What will not fit into these five categories are items bought for the exclusive personal use of you and your family, and these are not deductible. It is wise to sit down with your accountant and discuss the tax implications and benefits. I am not an accountant, but it is my understanding that you can deduct your total guest maintenance expenses, your business expenses, and a portion of your home maintenance costs in the tax year in which these expenses are incurred. Your guest capital expenses will be fully deductible but depreciated over time according to the IRS ruling on the life of each type of expense. For example, furniture is depreciated over ten years; so the $1,000 antique bedroom set would be depreciated at $100 a year over ten years.

House capital expenses are also depreciated. But because you use the house in common with the guests, only a portion of these expenses will be allowed. It is necessary to determine the amount of your home used for business and the proportion of the year during which it is used for business.

For example, in Donna's four-bedroom home, two bedrooms are used exclusively for B&B. The first floor of the home includes the kitchen, where breakfast is prepared; the living room, where guests sit in front of the fire and relax; the dining room, where breakfast is served; and the family room, where guests watch television. Half of the second floor (where the bedrooms are) is used exclusively by guests. The first floor is used in common by the family and guests. Thus, half of the home is used for business.

If the family has guests in any week, the house must be heated or cooled, cleaned, have electricity, telephone, service, and so on. These things are not turned on and off daily, so it seems appropriate to count weeks that a B&B does business. If there were guests overnight during ten or more weeks, it is fair to say that the B&B did business one-quarter of the year. If guests came in more than twenty weeks, the B&B did business half of the year. More than forty weeks represents full-time use because every business is entitled to some vacation and time when the business is open but makes no sales.

Since Donna uses half of her house, if she is in business one-quarter of the year, it would be fair for her to use one-eighth (one-half times one-fourth) of all house maintenance and house capital expenditures as deductions. If her business grows and she builds it into a full-time business (half of the house times one year), it would be appropriate for her to deduct half of all house expenses. This same figure applies to the amount of house maintenance expenses in the year incurred and the portion of house capital expenditures written off over time.

To keep track of my expenses and to make it easier for my accountant, I have always kept five large envelopes to which I have attached ledger paper. On each envelope, I write the type of expense (e.g., guest capital expenses) and the tax year. I look at each receipt, ask myself which category the expense falls under, write the amount and what was bought on the ledger paper, and drop the receipt into the envelope. This way, I have made a record of the expense while it is still fresh in my mind, and the backup is in the envelope in case of an audit.

## BREAKFAST COSTS

Because most hosts don't want to have to group the food they buy for guests separately when they are in line at the supermarket, they find it easier to just keep an accurate count of how many breakfasts are served (the number of guests times the nights they stayed). This cost is then arrived at by multiplying the number of breakfasts served by $5.00 for a continental breakfast or by $7.50 for a full breakfast. If you serve a very elaborate breakfast—for example, with caviar or fresh maple syrup—the cost may go up to $10.00. Breakfast costs should include more than just the price paid for food. It also includes the cost of gas used driving to and from the market, refrigerating the food until it is used, waste and spoilage, gas or electricity to cook the food, washing the dishes in your dishwasher, and washing table linens in the washing machine. If you purchase fancy centerpieces, fine china, or silver, these costs are included as maintenance or capital expenses.

## STAFF

### Independent Contractors and Salaried Employees

As long as people who work for you file a self-employment tax return and send you a bill for services rendered or work for you under terms of an independent contractor agreement, you are not responsible for any payroll expenses such as Social Security or federal or state withholding tax. But if you pay them more than $600 a year you will be required to file Form 1099 with the IRS.

If you hire a full-time housekeeper, for example, you will need to speak to your accountant about setting up a payroll ledger and withholding Social Security, unemployment insurance, and disability. This procedure is a nuisance, but absolutely essential if you are to claim these expenses.

## Hiring and Supervising Staff

If you are already established in an area, you may have an accountant and an attorney. If you are new to an area, you will be selecting these professionals as well as a realtor, insurance agent, gardener, plumber, electrician, and so on. The best way to choose from the vast array of vendors offering these services is to speak first to your neighbors and your reservation service. Your neighbors will certainly have had experience with local people and can steer you toward some and away from others. If you have a number of good recommendations, interview them, and make your selection based on whether or not you will feel comfortable working with them, they have appropriate credentials, are liked in the community, and have time to give to your business. When I decided that I needed a bookkeeper, I first interviewed the three women who answered my newspaper ad and then had my accountant talk to them. He felt that two were equally qualified, so I hired the one who offered me flexible hours and a reasonable wage.

If you are unhappy with the work that someone is doing for you, speak to them immediately. Make clear exactly what the problem is. This will put them on alert. For example, my gardener didn't seem to show up for work on any particular schedule and sometimes appeared early Saturday morning with two helpers, all making a huge racket with their power mowers, and waking my guests. We discussed it, and he promised to come on weekdays only, when I have very few guests who expect to sleep late in the morning.

If you hire household help, it is necessary to make a schedule for them so that they will know what your priorities are. The same holds true for workers such as painters and carpenters. You are the client, and those who work for you are the employees. You need to monitor the work done and give people feedback. If you have been satisfied, tell them or write a letter of thanks for a job well done. You will be remembered as appreciative; and if you need another job done in the future, you will have established a positive bond. If you are not satisfied and talking to the person responsible doesn't help, you may need to find someone new to do the work. It is often hard to fire someone, but it is necessary if you don't want your warm nature to be taken advantage of.

## Tipping

Most guests are confused about whether they are expected to tip. The general rule is that if there is a housekeeper or other staff, tipping is appropriate. If the B&B is owner-occupied only, tipping is not expected.

Since the guests don't know this and it is a lot easier to keep good help if they are earning good tips, it is a good idea, if you have staff, to find a nice way to explain this to guests. I usually do this when guests pay the bill. I say something like "Thank you. You're now paid in full unless, of course, you'd like to leave something for Brenda when you go."

I have stayed at B&Bs where there is a little envelope in the room with "For the maid" printed on it. I have resented this, especially if I've never seen the maid.

## Hiring Your Children

Don't forget that under the 1987 tax law, children over fourteen can earn money that will be taxed at their own rate, not yours. If you use them to help care for the house, yard, and guests, and pay them for these chores, this part of your profits will be taxed at a low rate and can help to build their college fund. Also, many host families find that running a B&B unites the family in a common purpose, and it is an excellent way to introduce children to the world of work and responsibility. Separate tax returns must be filed for your employed children.

## EXPENSES OFFSET YOUR TAXABLE PROFIT

You will pay taxes only on that part of your B&B income that exceeds your expenses. As in any new business, start-up costs in the first few years, in combination with low initial volume, may result in losses, which of course are paid for from your other income. In certain respects, this does shelter other income. However, you cannot continue to show a loss year after year. In five years, two years must show a profit. After that, if you make a major investment in your home (e.g., to remodel, restore, or add a pool) to increase its desirability as a B&B, you will again be able to justify a period of loss.

The important thing is that you must be able to prove that your B&B is a serious business, not a hobby. The IRS considers hobby income to be very different from that of a small business. Although all the income from a hobby is taxable, expenses related to carrying it out are not. For example, if you decided to keep bees for a hobby and incidentally sold a few jars of the honey to your friends and neighbors, the money paid to you would be taxable, but the cost of the jars and lids would not be deductible.

## DEPRECIATING YOUR HOME

One of the most complicated issues most hosts face is whether or not to depreciate that portion of the home used as a business. Although it may be wise for an older person in a very high tax bracket who has lived only a short time in a very expensive house to depreciate as much of it as is allowed, it may be unwise for someone who is younger, intends to move in a few years, or bought the house a long time ago to depreciate it. Only you and your accountant can figure out what is best for your particular circumstances. The important thing to remember is that if you depreciate a portion of your house now, when you sell it, only the portion that has not been depreciated will count as the expense subtracted from your selling price when computing capital gains. What this means to you varies according to tax bracket as well as age. Some people qualify for a one-time credit on the sale of their primary residence that exempts some of the profit from tax. Others intend to spend the rest of their lives in their home and don't care if their children inherit a house that has been partially depreciated.

❖❖❖❖❖❖❖

**Question:** Is it permissible to include information about other services I can provide for an extra fee to interested guests? I have a small crafts business and can also arrange special interest tours to wineries and the studios of other artists in my area.

**Answer:** *By all means, list these interests and capabilities with your reservation service, and make it clear than an additional fee is charged. Ask your service to place a feature on what you do in your network newsletter so that other hosts can tell their guests, too. Include a descriptive flier or brochure among the materials on tourist attractions in your guest rooms. Here are some examples of supplemental services some hosts offer.*

- *Real estate sales or brokering*

- *Breakfast in bed (with the works, popular for honeymooners)*

- *Shopping tours (especially to outlets and fashion discounters)*

- *Picnic lunches or fireside suppers for two*

- *Running local errands at an hourly rate*

- *Interpreting and translating*

- *Crafts and collectibles (for sale in the B&B to guests only)*

- *Antiques for sale*

- *Lessons (sports, needlework, languages, typing)*

- *Office services*

- *Child care*

- *Horse boarding and grooming*

- *Cosmetics or wardrobe consultation*

- *Walking tour of the area*

*If you offer a tour that must use a car, please go in the guests' car. If you use your car, you will need a chauffeur's license and livery insurance. Remember that it is fine to have literature in the guest room that will let the interested guest know how to avail themselves of your extra services, but don't push. You don't want guests to feel uncomfortable if they aren't interested.*

# 5

## Starting Up

**M**ost newcomers to Bed and Breakfast needn't reinvent the wheel when starting up. With the experience of 20,000 host families behind them, most reservation services are well versed in assisting new hosts in complying with regulations in their area. Using your reservation service as a resource during your start-up phase will be a great time-saver.

### REGULATIONS VARY FROM STATE TO STATE

Because the status of Bed and Breakfast varies from state to state and community to community, based both on written laws and on local custom, it is impossible to provide a specific set of steps to follow to ensure that your B&B will open without a hitch. It is possible, however, to outline the areas of concern every new host must deal with before greeting the first guest.

This chapter presumes that you have established a working relationship with a knowledgeable and responsible reservation service or state association. If there is no service in your immediate area, find the closest by checking the Reservation Service Directory in Appendix A, and call them before you call anyone else. Follow their suggestions for dealing with any agencies or officials. They've been through this many times before, and they want you to open as much as you do. If there is no reservation service covering your area, consider starting one to extend the benefits of B&B to many more people. In fairly short order, you can become the expert advising newcomers.

## DETERMINING YOUR NEED FOR A PERMIT

Whereas most commercial places are required to have a license or permit to operate, a private-home B&B may or may not, depending on its location and size. Here are two examples.

New York State looks at it this way: If the occupancy of your home (including your family) averages, on a daily basis, fewer than ten persons, no license or permit is required, and your business is categorized as a private-home B&B. New York also exempts B&Bs from the state restaurant code, but does require that all meat served be bought in a store to ensure that it has been inspected by the U.S. Department of Agriculture. It also requires that your water and septic systems be adequate for the needs of your business and that hosts collect sales tax on all stays.

In Wyoming, the Department of Health and Social Services sees the matter very differently. It regulates B&Bs and what it terms *ranch recreation facilities* stringently by requiring that any person operating such a facility shall possess a current, valid permit from the Division of Health and Medical Services. A Bed and Breakfast is defined as any private home that is used to provide accommodation for a charge to the public and that has not more than four lodging units or is occupied by no more than a daily average of eight people during any thirty-day period and in which no more than two family-style meals are provided in any twenty-four-hour period. Clearly, this rule could include B&B inns as well as older-style tourist homes. No distinction is made between walk-in clientele and screened guests. Wyoming reserves the right for the state health officer to make an inspection of any B&B during normal operating hours to ascertain compliance with health and safety conditions. Furthermore, the Wyoming rules specify in detail the types of food one may serve to B&B guests and where food must be prepared (on the premises). The guest may not be offered a choice from a menu. The code also specifies the minimum allowable size of escape windows, the location of mandated smoke detectors, a written record of monthly checks of the smoke detectors, and the type of fire extinguishers to be available in good working order.

Your state may lean toward the New York approach or to the Wyoming approach. Because B&B is evolving very rapidly in North America, it is important for you to stay informed, through your reservation service and area networks, of new developments that may affect the conduct of your business.

## KEEPING UP-TO-DATE

The need to provide legislators with background on B&B was one of the main reasons for the formation of Bed & Breakfast Reservation Services Worldwide—A Trade Association, in 1985. Ultimately, though, the responsibility for being in compliance with whatever your state requires falls to you because you are the individual actually providing the service. Attend get-togethers sponsored by your reservation service and state association, and read your business newsletters to stay up-to-date.

By the way, if your business is larger than your state's definition of a B&B, you will probably have to comply with all the provisions of the state's commercial code, just like any inn, hotel, or motel, even if you accept only screened guests through your reservation service. It is important to know from the very start what scale of business you want to get into. The regulations and the cost of conforming to them may help you decide.

Make it a point to attend seminars and workshops for small-business operators that may be offered by your community college or local bank. (Many are organized specifically for women starting new businesses.)

## FIRE AND SAFETY CODES

In January 1984, New York State passed the most stringent fire and safety code in the country in response to a terrible hotel fire the year before. When an investigation found that the hotel had not been in violation of the existing code, the legislature decided that something was wrong with the code. The new code applies to any place that opens after January 1984 and takes more than four guests on a routine basis. The implications are that private-home B&Bs with more than three guest rooms have to conform to the new code. This is very expensive, involving sprinkler systems, self-closing fire doors on each guest room, extra stairs or full fire escapes, and more. The imposition of these commercial fire codes has hindered the growth of the industry in New York. Both the Bed & Breakfast Association of New York State (BBANYS) and the Bed & Breakfast Council of the State Hospitality and Tourism Association have fought them. In the summer of 1995, Governor Pataki signed a bill that permits B&Bs with up to five rooms to adhere to a modified fire plan that includes hardwired smoke detectors, sprinklers in the stairwells, and a rope ladder as an alternative to a fire escape in lieu of a second staircase for escape. I include this information because often one state will follow another in developing statutes, and New York has often been such a leader. Before you open your door to guests, check your state's fire and safety code provisions. If your house is on a historic register, you can sometimes secure an exemption from various requirements, but you can't ignore requirements just because you have a historic home.

## SALES TAX

In most states, you will be required to charge guests sales tax. Your reservation service may or may not handle this for you. It will always inform a guest that this tax is due and to whom it is to be paid. But remember, your reservation service does not maintain your business records; you do. The easiest way for you to keep track of all your B&B business matters is by entering expenses and income into a common ledger. Some hosts now use a computer spreadsheet designed for the small-business operator, but this level of record keeping is probably not necessary or helpful unless you have several rooms and do a considerable amount of business.

You will need to inform your state sales tax department of your business to obtain authorization to collect sales tax. Your certificate of authorization should be framed and hung in plain sight.

The reservation service typically receives the required deposit on a reservation and forwards the entire sum, minus its commission (usually 20 to 30 percent) to you. You should enter the entire sum to be paid by the guests under income and the reservation service commission as an expense of doing business.

Sales tax is payable on the total nightly cost for your room(s). You compute the tax applicable in your area based on tables supplied by your state and collect it in addition to any balance due from your guests. The sales tax is not entered as income to you because you are merely acting as an agent in collecting it. Because it is not income, it is not deductible on your tax return. It is a good idea to talk to your accountant about your tax responsibilities and how to take care of them with the least amount of effort.

Generally, sales tax is reported and remitted to the state every quarter. Failure to collect or remit sales tax may be punishable by a fine in many states. In New York State, a law was passed in 1985 requiring that sales tax forms be filed even for a quarter in which you had no income and collected no tax. Failure to file costs you a $50 fine. Filing late can cost you interest on tax money due the state, so take the few minutes that are necessary each quarter to fill out and send in your tax forms and money on time. Keep current at the end of each month and quarterly filing will be a breeze.

## OCCUPANCY TAX

Local authorities often require the collection of an occupancy tax for hotels, motels, and often B&Bs. Whether this applies to your operation usually depends on the number of rooms. In Westchester County, places with more than four guest rooms are required to collect a 3 percent occupancy tax on the room cost. This tax is payable quarterly. It is important to find out if your region has such a tax, how many rooms trigger this requirement, and how often the tax is to be paid. You must contact the department that is in charge of this particular tax, so that you will receive the certificate authorizing you to collect the tax. Once your certificate is received, it should be hung in a visible place. I have framed mine in a small Victorian frame and hung it next to my sales tax authorization certificate in the pantry.

# RECORD KEEPING

Most hosts will not need a bookkeeper. The records you maintain to monitor your business and pay sales, occupancy, and income tax should be perfectly adequate. For sales tax, use the remittance schedule and forms supplied by the state and county. If your B&B is not incorporated, federal income tax requires that you file a Schedule C with your annual return, itemizing your business expenses and deductions. State and city income taxes are usually based on your adjusted federal income. Corporations file a separate return by March 15.

## Your Guest Book

You will need to keep a guest book for your guests to sign when they arrive. It can be simple, perhaps nothing more than a composition notebook, or fancy. There should be space for the guest's name, home address, telephone number, and comments. Some hosts place photographs of guests in the book, cover the book with decorative fabric, and send copies of the photos in holiday cards. This serves to increase repeat and word-of-mouth business. Moreover, this type of register can help you keep names and faces together long after guests have departed. You may even want to jot down something next to the guest's name (for instance, "came for son's graduation") so that you will be reminded when you communicate with this guest in the future. In addition, it provides a legal account of your guests in the rare event that there should be an audit of your business or an inquiry by local planning, zoning, or other officials.

I also keep a lined piece of paper for each month with the following entries:

| Name | Nights | Dates | Number in Party | Total Paid | Commission | Sales Tax | Occupancy Tax |
|------|--------|-------|-----------------|------------|------------|-----------|---------------|
| Mary Smith | 2 | 9/15–9/17 | 2 | $80 | $16 | $4.60 | $2.40 |

At the end of each month, I total up the columns and compute the number of breakfasts served. I then know gross sales, commissions paid out, breakfast costs, and sales tax owed. I always keep the sales tax money separate from money that belongs to me, so that when it comes time to pay, it won't feel like my money. Your ledger and guest book are generally all you need to manage your sales and occupancy tax records. They are all you would ever be asked to produce to document that the sales tax you have paid for any given period of time is correct.

## Income Tax

For federal income taxes, a much more detailed and comprehensive set of records and receipts needs to be kept. Your accountant can help you set up a system for storing and organizing all documents for tax time, or you may wish to utilize my large-envelope method (see Chapter 4).

A number of firms now offer a *one-write system:* Each time you write a check, it is spread into columns for the various types of expenditures you have. At the end of each month, simply add up the columns to keep a current account of expenses. The same type of system can be used to record incoming funds and their sources. Keeping good records helps your accountant a great deal at tax time. It also gives you a very good idea of how your business is doing. You still need to keep actual receipts for expenditures (to produce in case of a tax audit to document that the checks you wrote did, indeed, go for payment of bills you claim), but this form of business checkbook tells you exactly where you stand whenever you want to know.

## Computerized Record Keeping

A variety of computer programs to keep track of your expenses and even write your checks are available. They are basically automated one-write systems that spread your checks and deposits as they are entered. Before you buy software, it is important to figure out what your needs are, as it is very easy to be talked into purchasing a program that does more than you need and is subsequently harder to understand and more time-consuming to use. Most innkeepers are not accountants and don't need a full-blown accounting program, but they certainly need one that does more than just balance their checkbook.

I am currently using People's Choice, a product of Safeguard Business Systems. For under $300, you get the software plus installation and some training. For a Safeguard representative near you, contact Safeguard, 455 Maryland Dr., Fort Washington, PA 19034, (800) 523-6660. This system is especially helpful for payroll. Payroll checks are tracked as written, and the information necessary for monthly, quarterly, and annual tax reporting is easy to access. It makes it possible for a small inn to operate without a bookkeeper and to need only an accountant at year-end for taxes and an occasional consult during the tax year. When I bring my beautifully printed-out summary of income and expenses to my accountant in February, his face lights up and my bill goes down.

## ZONING

Zoning is always a local issue. My experience with zoning will give you an idea of the worst-possible scenario, one that resulted in part because I was the first B&B in my area. It is unlikely that you will experience something similar, but what I learned should help you anticipate any obstacles with local zoning that might affect you.

Before starting my business, I checked with state agencies controlling licenses and permits and with the health department and got the okay to proceed as long as we had fewer than ten persons staying in our home on an average night. (New York State considers ten people on a daily basis the definition of a temporary residence, the smallest commercial entity of this type.) I thought I had covered all bases. It never dawned on me that sleeping and eating were not consistent with residential use. One of my neighbors, however, had other ideas. She could not have been more upset if we had opened a brothel. She went about the neighborhood gathering support to stamp out "the B&B menace."

Once we appeared on the front page of the local paper in a story about the reservation service; she complained to the zoning officials that we were operating a commercial business in a residential neighborhood and demanded that something be done immediately. The zoning official rang my bell and proceeded to let me know that, in Croton, only one boarder is permitted in residential neighborhoods. Therefore, if we had one couple or one family as guests, we were in violation of the zoning code. I replied that these were not boarders, but guests, about whom the code said nothing. He suggested that we go before the zoning board to get their opinion. Having never been to a zoning meeting, but being a rational person (however politically inexperienced), I agreed. I was in for a rude awakening. To start, the board sends out letters to every neighbor within 400 feet of a home to be discussed to let them know about the meeting.

Meanwhile, my adversary continued to gather support for her cause. Her fears were as follows: If Bed and Breakfasts were allowed in residential neighborhoods, soon there would be B&Bs all over town. Strangers would be riding around town looking for them. Large tractor trucks would be parked in the streets. Couples would be dropping by, by the hour. Property values would surely plummet. She convinced one gentleman down the road to write a letter to the local paper saying, "People will be ringing our doorbell at 3:00 A.M. looking for the mini-motel."

The night of the zoning meeting arrived. Clusters of people were seated all around the room. In one corner was the opposition to the local day-care project. In another were the neighbors who didn't want a family to increase the size of its driveway. Prominently seated were my neighbor and her supporters. In support of Bed and Breakfast were myself and my husband, one set of our immediate neighbors, and another couple from down the block.

I spoke. My view was that a boarder is, by definition, a resident of the community. When asked his or her address, a boarder gives your address. A boarder can get a library card, can send his or her child to the local school, and in general enjoys all rights and privileges of any other resident, including voting. Bed and Breakfast guests, by contrast, are under no delusion that my home is theirs. They have a home somewhere else, where they vote, pay taxes, and use the city services. Bed and Breakfast guests are merely visitors who come with travel dollars in their pockets to shop in our shops and eat in our restaurants, stimulating the local economy and taking home with them a pleasant memory about our town.

After I spoke, a number of other people stood up to have their say. They went on as though I had said that a B&B guest *was* really a boarder and should be allowed as such. The other citizens present clearly believed that a B&B guest was not a boarder. Indeed, the zoning board reached the conclusion that, although they didn't know what a B&B guest was, it certainly wasn't a boarder. I was amazed that in this public forum most of the speakers were content to give opinions based on emotion rather than fact. Many of those who spoke had not come for this issue in the first place and were totally uninformed about how our B&B worked. They didn't know that the reservation service did all the promotion and that we were not open to the public, only to those with reservations.

The zoning board seemed to be measuring the climate of the room. Was this group warm or cold to the issue at hand? They acted as though this small group of people truly represented the sentiments of the village at large, which couldn't have been further from the truth. Once the issue was getting front-page coverage in the local papers, strangers would come up to me in the supermarket to say what a lovely idea it was to have a B&B in town. But these people were not at the zoning hearing meeting. No doubt it never occurred to them that something so sensible would have any trouble being approved. The upshot of our appearance before the board was that because they had said B&B guests were not boarders, we felt it was perfectly legal to continue our business.

The board, however, thought that the ruling meant B&Bs were not allowed, although they had not said this as such. In New York State and most other states, anything that is not expressly prohibited in local zoning is permitted, so we continued to take guests. Again our doorbell rang. This time the zoning official said it was his duty to tell us to cease and desist this activity, or the village would issue a subpoena to take us to court. I knew it was time to talk to a lawyer.

I called a local attorney who had been instrumental in writing the zoning code. In his opinion, our B&B was a "customary home occupation." This is a category included in most zoning codes, but one that varies slightly in definition from locale to locale. Our code restricted a customary home occupation to one-third of the square footage of the house, forbade any sign outside, and permitted no employees. We agreed that we met those criteria, and our lawyer assured us that this would probably be the end of our problems because the village doesn't generally take residents to court. Famous last words! A few days later, a summons arrived charging me with flagrantly and knowingly violating the zoning code and ordering me to appear in criminal court. Panic! I envisioned myself in jail. Vertical stripes do nothing for my appearance. After some serious discussion with my husband, we agreed to spend up to our entire earnings to date ($1,500) for defense. I called the lawyer and told him to start his meter running.

I also decided that to justify the expense of the trial, I would do everything I could to make sure that publicity about it would appear on major television stations and in the *New York Times*. This was definitely the riskiest thing I had ever done. I knew that if we lost in court, we would have to fold our tent. But if we won, what a wonderful way to let the world know about B&B in America!

The day of our court appearance drew near. A large story about the controversy appeared in the real estate section of the Sunday *New York Times*. A national network did a five-minute spot on the 6:00 P.M. news. The day of the trial, a local television reporter sat in the courtroom with her camera crew, ready to interview the judge on the courtroom steps.

Our witnesses were ready. An author of a best-selling B&B book and officer of the American Bed & Breakfast Association testified that Bed and Breakfast was going on in 5,000 homes across America, 98 percent of which were in residentially zoned homes. A representative of the New York State Department of Commerce, Tourism Division, testified that the state encouraged the development of B&B because it would be especially helpful to small communities where demand for accommodations was too small or too seasonal to support commercial facilities. I testified as to how our reservation service worked to screen guests and send them by advance reservation to the homes listed with our group.

The best part of going to court was that the issue was truly whether we were violating a law. The neighbors were not in court. Witnesses were asked to state facts, not give opinions; and the judge looked at the law and the evidence, weighed both, and acquitted us. This case, although at the village level, has been a precedent-setting one in the state.

Today, more than fourteen years later, none of our neighbors' fears have been realized. There are only two B&Bs in Croton, and there have been no negative incidents related to them. In fact, property values around our homes have never been higher. The village has referred a number of guests to me. The judge even asked us if we would host a wedding at which there would be no guests and we would have to stand up for the bride and groom. The wedding took place on a beautiful spring day, the one weekend of the year when my weeping Chinese cherry was in full bloom, with pink blossoms from top to bottom. My daughter got to be the flower girl—in all, a very good omen for things to come.

## YOU BENEFIT FROM MY ORDEAL

Most hosts won't have to fight such a battle themselves. It is important to read your town's zoning code manual. It is best not to walk into your town hall and say, "I want to open a B&B." If you're the first one, you will most likely be told that it's not permitted even if they don't really know. They can confuse what you plan to do with a tourist home, which needs to be in the commercially zoned area. If you take guests only by reservation and have no sign outside, you can probably fit under the customary home occupation category and be legal in a residential zone. So just go into the town hall, purchase a copy of the zoning code, and read it carefully at your own pace. Look under "Bed and Breakfast," which you probably won't find. Then look under "Customary Home Occupation" and see if the requirements are compatible with what you plan to do. Realize that if you plan to have more than three or four guest rooms, your business may be too large to be considered a noncommercial use of your home. If you have any uncertainty, speak to a local zoning lawyer.

If it becomes necessary to get a variance from your zoning board, have your attorney represent you, and make sure to have as many local people as possible present to support you. If the codes seem compatible with what you plan, don't go before the zoning board unnecessarily. If your town passes a law pertaining to Bed and Breakfast after you are in operation, it cannot legislate you out of business. Your business would be considered a nonconforming but preexisting use. My town, after losing in court, developed a special permit required for any new B&Bs. But it does not apply to me, since I am covered by a grandfather clause. New B&Bs in Croton must now be inspected by the village inspector, must comply with current fire and safety requirements, must have adequate off-street parking, and must pay an annual fee to the village to renew the permit.

As Bed and Breakfast has become more common, it is less difficult for homeowners to work with local government. It is certainly an asset, especially in a small community, to have this type of accommodation readily available.

Where there have been serious problems for hosts (Carmel, California, and Santa Fe, New Mexico), the outcry has come from hotels and motels that are overbuilt and fear that every empty room represents a guest stolen from them by a B&B. The mayor of Santa Fe once made a speech saying how proud he was to have stopped the spread of B&B in his city. The industry has been forced to go underground there. America has always been a place that afforded freedom to all citizens, and I believe people should have the right to choose a cozy B&B environment over a cold, impersonal hotel room. Legislators must be made to see this point of view and to realize that those travelers who want to sample a bit of regional life will go to other towns that do have B&Bs. Surely it is in the best interest of towns all over America to offer this choice to travelers.

# Zoning Update

In July 1990, I testified as an expert witness for Sharon and Victor Keen of Stroudsberg, Pennsylvania. The Keens bought a 6,600-square-foot home in the Academy Hill section, the historic hub of the city. At one time their home was the academy after which the neighborhood is named. The Keens wanted to restore the home as a B&B. Pennsylvania, unlike many other states, requires that anything not addressed by local zoning be prohibited. If the zoning code doesn't address something, residents can propose a curative amendment to correct this oversight. The Keens made a proposal for a curative amendment that would permit Bed and Breakfast in historic homes over 5,000 square feet, with adequate parking and some other details. The Town Council gave them a very rough time, but the Keens finally won. Their home is perfect for this use, and they have decorated it with wonderful Mission Oak furniture and Arts and Crafts Movement pottery. The location, the decor, and their friendly, outgoing manner enchant guests.

Two important zoning cases occurred in Washington, DC (1990), and in New Orleans (1990). Both battles were heated, drawn-out, and costly, but the B&B movement prevailed. Jackie Reed of Bed 'n' Breakfast Ltd. and Millie Groobey of The Bed & Breakfast League/Sweet Dreams and Toast, both in DC, attribute their victory to keeping cool heads, being persistent, educating their government officials, getting a lot of neighborhood support from areas where B&Bs were operating with no problem, and producing guidebooks showing that B&Bs were flourishing all over America and that this was not just a Washington phenomenon. In addition, they received significant support from the National Trust, stressing that B&B is the best way to preserve our architectural heritage, and from the Washington, DC, Chamber of Commerce.

In Washington, B&B was accepted as a customary home occupation requiring a permit in a single-family residential home provided that (1) breakfast is the only meal served and only to the overnight guests; (2) the maximum number of sleeping rooms is two by right, and four with special exception, and, for historic buildings or those in a historic district certified by the historic preservation officer, up to six rooms may be offered to guests; (3) one parking space is allowed for each two rooms; (4) no cooking facilities are in the rooms; and (5) the building is owner-occupied, and the facility complies with all other parts of the general home occupation requirements.

In New Orleans, Hazel Boyce of Bed & Breakfast Inc. reports that B&B requires a license. Most B&Bs can apply for a conditional use license, which costs between $500 and $1,200 after two hearings—one before the City Planning Board and one before the City Council. They expect the city to streamline the process in the future. Any B&B taking four or more guests must meet the commercial fire code, but because of the historic nature of many of the homes, owners may sometimes obtain variances to get around requirements for enclosed stairwells and sprinkler systems. Bed and Breakfasts must be owner-occupied and comply with local zoning parking specifications. The biggest mistake made by naive hosts is to do extensive and costly restoration before getting approval from the life/safety (fire code) department.

## Other Battles

Muffy and David Vhay of Washoe Valley, Nevada, were planning to open their B&B in early 1991. They called me in July 1990 with a problem having to do with a fee from the State Department of Regional Transportation. After some research, they found that this fee is levied in some portions of California and Nevada on new construction or change of use for new businesses for infrastructure maintenance. Although the Vhays don't object to paying a one-time fee, they felt that they were being levied at a considerably higher rate than was fair for a small B&B that would generate very little extra traffic. I suggested that they pool together with other B&Bs in the state and form a citizens' group to help them approach the government. They were successful, and a new rate more appropriate to their level of business was assessed.

# SLEEPING ARRANGEMENTS

It's always necessary to ask your guests what sleeping arrangements are needed. Problems develop when hosts make assumptions. Often a married couple may require twin beds because this is the only way that they are comfortable sleeping. In today's culture, we also see a lot of unmarried couples traveling together. If you have a problem with unmarried couples sleeping together in your home, you should include this in your literature and inform the reservation service about it. Because your home is your castle, you are free to have only those guests with whom you are comfortable.

The following story illustrates an awkward situation that occurred before I routinely began asking about sleeping arrangements. As you will see, the story also demonstrates the need for checking on your insurance coverage.

In our second year of business, two women booked a room for the weekend. They came by train from New York City, and I put them in the twin-bedded room, which is what I assumed they would prefer. It became apparent to me as they gazed across the hall at the double-bedded room that they were gay. I had made a mistake, but was too embarrassed to offer them the other room. Since this occurrence, I routinely ask about bed preference when booking reservations.

Still, the day progressed nicely. We all swam and played volleyball in the pool and chatted. The women had wonderful senses of humor, and we really got to know and like these bright, articulate, and fun-loving people. Because they had no car and cabs in the country are expensive, we decided to invite them to join us for a barbecue dinner. Gloria (not her real name), a tall movie actress who reminded us of Katharine Hepburn in her youth, went off to the market with George to pick up a steak, while Suzie, a lead singer from a European rock band, came down to the garden with me to pick salad vegetables. She paused by my berry patch and asked me to identify a bright purple berry on a bush with large green leaves. It resembled nothing that I had ever seen in a store, and I told her so. She agreed, but before I could warn her about eating unknown berries, she popped one in her mouth, made a face, and said, "I don't think they are for eating."

We had a wonderful dinner and played some word games; and after a full day of sunshine, swimming, and fresh air, everyone retired early.

At 2:00 A.M. George and I were awakened by a knock on our bedroom door. There was Gloria, who said, "Suzie is lying on the floor of the bathroom, white as a ghost, having just thrown up everything she has eaten in days. It must be *the berry!*" In my mind, I saw large headlines: "Evil Bed and Breakfast Queen Poisons Gay Guest!" Quickly, I pushed George out of bed, ran to the phone to call Poison Control, and told George to take Suzie to the hospital. Poison Control was very helpful; they agreed that the best course of action was indeed to rush her to the hospital and to bring the berry bush with us. So in my nightgown, barefoot, flashlight and ax in hand, I rushed into the garden to cut it down. George and Gloria carried Suzie to the car, and they sped away. I remained at home with my sleeping toddler and my mother-in-law, who was visiting from California.

At 4:00 A.M., George and Gloria returned, but without Suzie. I was sure she was dead. She was not. The hospital had given her some fluid to counteract the dehydration and an injection to stop the vomiting, and she had fallen asleep. George and Gloria had watched her sleep peacefully for two hours before someone told them that they could go home and that when she wakened in the morning, we would be called.

Do you want to know what kind of berry it was? A pokeberry, which is indeed poisonous. The important point is that even though we survived this incident without any permanent damage or expense, it made us realize the need to have emergency numbers close at hand. Ever since, when we take a reservation, we ask the guest for the number of a person to call in case of emergency. It also emphasized the need to have adequate insurance coverage.

## LIABILITY INSURANCE

Most people who own homes have homeowner's insurance. These policies are difficult for most people to read and should be gone over carefully with the insurance agent. In some cases, homeowner's insurance will cover up to two paying guests; in others, it will not. If you are planning to open only one room for guests or rent your apartment unhosted, check to see if your current insurance is sufficient. If not, you should either change carriers or consider additional liability insurance. Liability insurance covers any losses to a guest that occur from injury because of your negligence. For instance, a guest might suffer an adverse reaction to something you serve for breakfast that had gone bad, trip on a loose scatter rug, or slip on some ice that you forgot to salt. If the guest sues and wins, your homeowner's insurance may not cover this. Settlements in liability cases have gotten out of hand; and in many cases, claimants have won even without proving fault.

For a number of years, reservation services were able to provide very low-cost liability riders to their host homes. In the three years that we participated in such a plan, we knew of only one paid claim: to two women who slipped on a patch of ice on someone's doorstep in Alaska. But the insurance company stopped offering the policy. Currently, if your B&B meets your state's requirements for noncommercial accommodations, you can qualify for liability coverage through many reservation services, state associations, and other professional groups.

The deductible is a way that the insurance company says, "We're in this together. Please keep your house safe." By taking all necessary precautions for the safety, security, and comfort of your guests, you will greatly reduce your chances of becoming involved in a claims action. Examine your home for potential problem spots. If there are any, make sure to remedy them before you accept your first guest.

## Inform Your Agent

It is important that your homeowner's insurance agent know that you are opening your home as a B&B and that you have or don't have additional coverage. Make sure that additional insurance does not jeopardize your current coverage. Many policies have a fine-print clause that says something like, "If you increase your hazards without notifying this insurance company, your policy is null and void." For example, if you store dynamite in your garage without telling your agent and the garage blows up, and with it your house, your homeowner's insurance probably won't pay for it even if you have been paying for fire insurance for twenty years.

Trying to anticipate any wrinkle of being involved in B&B, we asked an agent if this might be considered increasing our hazards. His response was that it would be a good idea to get approval beforehand. We did this and found that as long as we were up-front and could show our liability certificate, our insurance company was willing to continue our homeowner's policy without any stipulations or increase in price. The same thing may or may not happen to you; some insurance carriers are very conservative. If your carrier drops you, don't worry. There are many fine companies with good reputations willing to write your policy. Some are now offering B&B insurance, a low-cost commercial policy that includes liability.

## Bed and Breakfast Insurance

Many large insurance companies finally have come to recognize B&Bs and are offering commercial coverage for the B&B that includes not only liability coverage but also household personal property and loss of business income should you be forced to close during repairs. Again, you will get a better rate through a group. See Appendix D for a list of some agents specializing in B&B commercial coverage.

## SETTING HOUSE RULES

If you have definite house rules, share them with your guests, as you run the risk of being not only misunderstood but sometimes taken advantage of by guests who think they are renting your personal services as well as your room. Dissatisfaction on the part of both guest and host most commonly arises when the type of accommodation is not clearly spelled out, when there is failure to state mutually accepted house limits, or when guests confuse a B&B with a hotel or motel.

Here follows the rules for my B&B, the Alexander Hamilton House:

## Alexander Hamilton House Rules

1. No smoking inside. Smokers are welcome to go out to the back porch to smoke.

2. You are asked to use the guest refrigerator (located in the second floor hall) rather than put things in the kitchen fridge.

3. You are welcome to make coffee or tea in winter months or to pour from the pitcher of iced tea or lemonade that we keep chilled for you in summer. You can heat up something in the microwave, but you do not have general kitchen privileges. Please use plastic or metal glasses at poolside. They are in the pantry along with ice buckets. If you are traveling with small children, please speak to me about special exceptions.

4. Our outdoor lights are triggered by the movement of cars or people in the backyard. Don't try to turn them off from inside the house, or they won't go on for the next person. Cars should be parked nose to the curb, leaving room for others to park alongside.

5. Please do not write down the combination to our lock on anything that has our name or address on it.

6. Breakfast time is to be agreed on the night before. Please be prompt, or breakfast will be cold and your hostess disappointed. If you must change your breakfast time, please leave a note for us in the kitchen.

7. If you come in late, please remember that everyone else is already asleep.

8. If you have laundry that you would like included with ours, speak to Brenda the night before. If there is any ironing involved, please expect to pay Brenda for her time.

9. We have menus from most local restaurants. They are kept in the kitchen; just ask me or Brenda. We will be happy to call for reservations for you.

10. Guests are welcome to relax in the public rooms. The sun porch has a large color TV with cable and VCR.

There are three video stores nearby where you can rent movies. We also have many board games. Just ask.

11. In nice weather, you are welcome to use the tables and chairs around the pool to enjoy a light lunch or supper. We do not, however, provide the meals. No children are allowed at the pool without a parent. Nonswimmers must wear life jackets, which are stored in the garage.

12. Speak to Cydney about baby-sitting. If she is available she charges $2.50 an hour for one child, $1.00 an hour extra for each additional child.

13. We have bicycles in the garage for guests to borrow. Please ask us which are available. Cydney, Brenda, and I are very possessive about our own bicycles. If you ride it is at your own risk, and you will be responsible for the bikes.

14. If you need anything else, please just ask.

## SECURITY

If you feel uncomfortable about giving out the only key to your home, there are two simple solutions: (1) Add additional locks for use when you have no guests. When you have guests, use only the lock to which you have given guests the key. (2) Install a combination lock that can be reprogrammed. Give guests the current combination, and show them how to operate it. When these guests leave, enter a new combination.

In addition to door locks, you will want to advise your guests of any other security measures you normally employ, such as a burglar alarm system, direct-dial arrangements to local police departments, with or without an audible signal from an alarm, and window locks (especially important for fire safety). If you do not wish to provide details of your home security system to guests, you may choose to stay up and admit guests personally. Be aware, however, that this works only for overnight guests. One of my hosts had two women stay for a week. One was attending an art workshop; the other had come just for vacation and to keep her friend company. By the second day, the vacationer called to see if there were other accommodations available because she felt that the host was shooing her out in the morning and waiting up for them at night, all because he didn't feel that they could understand the alarm system. By no means should guests be made to feel that they must be out of the house all day or plan their schedule according to that of the host. Arrival times must always be mutually decided on, but after that, guests should be able to come and go at will.

Here are other steps hosts may take to ensure safety:

- Refrain from placing promotional brochures or business cards in public locations unless you put only your reservation service's phone number and no street address on this literature so that guests will be screened.
- Record the license plate number and make and model description of cars driven by guests. (This may be entered in a register separate from your guest book.)
- Telephone your reservation service at once if you notice anything out of line about the guests.
- Report any unacceptable behavior of a guest to the reservation service to prevent this guest from being referred to you or any other hosts in the network again.
- Discuss guest policies with all family members, including children, so that everyone knows what the guest is welcome to do in your home and which areas are the family's private domain.

To date, the screening policies of professional reservation services have resulted in fifteen years of B&B hosting in the United States with no known incidents involving jeopardy to anyone's personal security. Breakage or damage to a host's home or other property has been less than what one anticipates from family members. Thefts are virtually unheard of. (More frequently, a guest leaves something behind.) These facts translate into a very low cost of insurance for hosts.

There is one consequence of operating a B&B that may strike you as negative. Once neighbors have been informed that you are opening your home to paying guests, there may be a drop in their ordinary protectiveness toward your home. They may become nonchalant about reporting strangers seen about your premises, for instance, because they presume that any such visitors are anticipated and welcome. This may be less of a problem if you host infrequently and can let your neighbors know when you have plans to do it.

If a neighbor complains, keep in mind that hosting results in fewer visitors overall and fewer cars competing for parking than most other customary home occupations. Because visitors have been screened for compatibility with you and your family, they are probably just the type of people that your neighborhood wants to welcome.

## THE AMERICANS WITH DISABILITIES ACT

My editor, PJ Dempsey, was injured last year and forced to work at home for months because there was no ladies room at work that could accommodate her wheelchair. During the course of your normal day, count the number of activities that would be difficult, if not impossible, were you to need a wheelchair. You will quickly understand the need for the Americans with Disabilities Act (ADA). It was not created just to complicate unnecessarily an innkeeper's life.

As of January 26, 1992, the ADA became law. It was intended to make it possible for people with disabilities to live more normally and enjoy many of the pastimes that the able-bodied take for granted.

### Who Must Comply?

Innkeepers in owner-occupied Bed and Breakfasts with six or more guest rooms and innkeepers of unhosted Bed and Breakfasts with any number of guest rooms must comply. Compliance means that "All physical barriers in existing public accommodations must be removed, if readily achievable." If this is too costly or difficult, you must offer other ways of providing access. If installing a permanent ramp system is not possible without major architectural changes to your inn, a portable ramp might do the trick. Elevators are not required in new or old buildings that have fewer than four levels.

Understand that providing access for the physically challenged means making sure that doorways and parking spaces are wide enough, that pathways are smooth and flat, and that bathrooms, public rooms, gardens, swimming pools, and other areas are safe and accessible. Other types of disabilities include hearing, vision, and dozens of others.

## What Should I Do?

Inspect your property. Think about what you can do to make your place more accessible to those with disabilities. Start by making changes that are easily achievable, for example, by planning to purchase equipment that will make a room suitable for the hearing impaired. Realize that if you are renovating or constructing a new inn, your building will be expected to meet the needs of the physically challenged. One handicapped-accessible room is required for each twenty-five guests or for inns that have twenty-five or more employees.

## What Is Necessary to Make a Room Ready for the Visually Impaired?

Understand that such guests are not necessarily blind.

OUTSIDE:  Well-lit paths.
IN THE INN

1. Have printed information available in large type or Braille.

2. Your library can supply you with books on tape if you have a portable tape recorder to loan the guest.

3. Free the guest room of precariously placed decorations, and give good verbal instructions when checking in your guest to warn him or her about steps, protruding furniture, or unexpected things.

4. Color-contrasting strips on the top and bottom step or odd step from one room to another are very helpful and not expensive.

# What Is Necessary to Accommodate the Hearing Impaired?

More than 10 percent of the population is hearing impaired. A number of different pieces of equipment are available to aid the hearing impaired:

1.  TDD stands for telecommunication display device. A TDD costs under $300 and will enable you to make phone reservations and give your guest access to a phone. There is a not-for-profit service that also can act as an interpreter between you and a person with a TDD machine. You can expect to get calls identified as "relay" calls. The person using the TDD machine sends the message to this intermediary who calls you to relay the message. Waiting for the delayed responses is a bit difficult, but this system is a very good way to communicate with the hearing-impaired caller if you don't own a TDD machine.

2.  Telephone ring signalers and amplifiers.

3.  A vibrating alarm clock.

4.  Closed-caption TV. More and more TVs have this as an additional feature at no additional cost. If you've bought a TV recently, check to see if you can access this feature. It only requires reading the manual and pushing the right button on the remote control.

5.  A door-knock light.

6.  Smoke alarm with flashing light and horn.

Other than the TV, the TDD machine, and the smoke alarm, most items can be purchased for under $50. A portable piece of equipment that includes the smoke detector, door knocker, telephone-amplified handset, and alarm clock with strobe and bed shaker is available. The set can be used in any room. It is unlikely that you will need it in more than one room at a time. The total cost is under $350. Shop around.

# What Do I Have to Do to Meet the Requirements for Physically Handicapped Guests?

Access for physically handicapped people is the most complicated and costly type of change to implement.

ENTRANCES

1. You will need appropriate signs for accessible parking, entrance, and bathrooms. Your handicapped parking spot, 14 feet wide by 18 feet deep, should be as close as possible to your entrance.

2. At the least a portable ramp must be available. The cost will vary according to how many steps there are.

3. Doorways must be at least 32 inches wide. Doorway thresholds must be altered to permit wheelchairs to roll over them. The guest must be able to get from his or her room to the common rooms and dining area. Some rugs can make this impossible and must be changed.

4. New lever-type door handles may be necessary. It may also be necessary to lower door handles.

BATHROOM

1. The special toilet is higher than normal (48 inches in front and 32 inches beside or 32 inches in front with grab bars). Grab bars or portable arms must be mounted to the back of the toilet.

2. A bath seat needs to be placed in the shower and any impediment to shower access needs to be altered. Hardware that does not require grasping should be placed no higher than 44 inches. Again, grab bars are essential.

3. The sink needs lever-type faucets and should be 30 inches wide with a 48-inch turnaround in front, 27-inch height, and 19-inch knee space.

4. Outlets need to be lowered so they can be reached, or extension cords should be used.

5. The door to the bathroom needs to be 30 to 32 inches wide.

BEDROOM

1. A 48-inch turnaround space is needed for a wheelchair. Place your furniture with this in mind. Tables have to be 27 to 29 inches from the floor with a 19-inch knee space.

2. Closet bars or towel hooks probably need to be placed lower.

3. The doorway to the room must be at least 32 inches wide and have lever-type hardware.

4. Beds should be no higher than 24 inches, and 32 inches of space is needed beside the bed for wheelchair access.

5. Thermostats need to be approximately 35 to 44 inches from the floor.

6. Fire extinguishers must be accessible from a wheelchair.

## Don't Be Intimidated by These Changes

Certainly, if you are renovating or doing new construction, your architect can help you implement many of the structural requirements into your plan.

### FINANCIAL HELP

There is a disabled access tax credit available for businesses that covers 50 percent of expenditures between $250 and $10,250 up to $5,000 a year. The tax credit applies to barrier removal and equipment for the hearing or vision impaired. Any business grossing under $1,000,000 and that has fewer than 30 full-time employees is eligible, but expenses related to new construction are not. Barrier removal expenses up to $15,000 can be expensed in the year spent rather than considered a capital expenditure. This does not apply to new construction, either.

### DO WHAT YOU CAN!

The law states that a good-faith effort be made to remove any barriers without imposing an "undue hardship" on the innkeeper.

Make those changes that are "readily achievable" depending on your size and financial situation. For most places, this means physical access that can be achieved without extensive restructuring or burdensome expense.

Changes for the visually and hearing impaired are the least expensive and should certainly be done first. Make a plan that shows that you have thought through what changes are possible for your inn over the next few years, and rethink this plan if any renovation or new construction is on the drawing board.

## What If My Building Is Historic?

If barrier removal threatens to destroy the historic significance of a structure, it would not be considered "readily achievable."

## Will the Government Inspect My Inn for Compliance?

No. At this time there is no enforcement provision to the ADA. Private individuals can file complaints with the attorney general or file a lawsuit against you. This is unlikely to happen to a small inn if the owner takes steps to make access to the inn as easy as possible for those with disabilities. Do what you can within your financial means.

## Accessibility Is a Great Marketing Tool

Communicate to guests your accessibility. Use the international symbols on your brochure. Don't indicate compliance if you are only partially compliant. Be specific as to what parts of the inn are accessible and to whom. If you are compliant, you can promote your inn in a number of specialty newsletters, magazines, and guides.

## Where Can I Get More Information?

For more information on the ADA, contact:

PAII, PO Box 90710, Santa Barbara, CA 93190, (805) 569-1853. Send for their Americans with Disabilities Act Kit for the

Small Inn. The cost is $15 for PAII members and $30 for nonmembers.

TDD Hotline for information on free relay service between TDD and voice phones, (800) 332-1124.

Peter Robinson, a barrier-free environment specialist and consultant, (800) 963-0221.

The National Trust for Historic Preservation, 1785 Massachusetts Ave., NW, Washington, DC 20036, (202) 673-4296. Ask for Information Series No. 55, 1991, *The Impact of the Americans with Disabilities Act on Historic Structures.*

Every area has local and regional associations for the disabled. They will be more than happy to help you with information, sources for purchasing special equipment, and access to Braille printers or any other services you are having trouble finding.

## Hiring the Disabled

If you are considering hiring the disabled, read *Complying with the ADA—A Small Business Guide to Hiring and Employing the Disabled* by Jeffrey G. Allen, J.D., C.P.C. (New York: Wiley, 1993).

❖❖❖❖❖❖❖

**Question:** Although I enjoy entertaining at home and have done a good deal of it, I'd like some tips on handling the first few minutes after a guest arrives, particularly for the first time, in my home. Should any business be transacted then, or should it wait until the guest is ready to depart?

**Answer:** *I recommend that all business be transacted within the first twenty minutes of a guest's arrival. Some people feel awkward about money matters after they have spent some time with guests and gotten to like them. Guests expect to pay upon arrival, so it won't come as a surprise.*

*A reprint compiled for hosts with the help of Kate Peterson, formerly of B&B Rocky Mountains, points out what experienced hosts may do to make the arriving guest feel at home and welcome.*

## THE GIFT OF HOSPITALITY

1. Show room and house and give guests an opportunity to unload their belongings.
2. Offer a drink/beverage and ask if anything else is needed.
3. Take care of business (collecting money, signing guest register, giving receipt) within twenty minutes of guest's arrival.
4. Answer questions and mention local attractions.
5. Supply an information sheet containing questions and answers about the area.
6. Collect brochures about area attractions and have them available.
7. Offer breakfast in bed, if desired (some B&Bs charge extra for this).
8. Collect menus from a variety of popular area restaurants and clippings of restaurant reviews from local newspapers. Place in a folder available to guests.
9. Show guests where books, magazines, and newspapers are kept for their use.
10. Have good maps available: your region, your city, and your neighborhood (the latter with your house circled or highlighted for the guest's convenience in finding the way back at the end of the day).
11. Copy your local map with restaurants, movies, and attractions circled. Make enough copies so each guest can take one to keep. A simple promotional touch: use your business stationery with your B&B address, telephone, and illustration/logo at the top.
12. Put umbrellas you are willing to lend in a stand near the front door and tell guests about it.
13. Collect articles from newspaper tourism and events sections. Copy them and keep in folder easily available for guests. Copies hold up better than newsprint originals.
14. Collect discount and promotional coupons from nearby attractions and restaurants (evenings when there are specials on the menu, etc.) and leave them out for guests to use.
15. If it's all right with you for guests to use your deck or patio for eating, leave a list of places where take-out food is available in town or those that deliver to the home. Remind guests that payment in cash is always necessary for food delivered to them.
16. Make copies of your breakfast specialty recipes in case guests would like to try them again, when they arrive home. Again, using your business stationery will remind them of their visit whenever the recipe is used.
17. Set up a game corner or game shelf (garage sales can be treasure troves for these).
18. Tell your guests where they can find extra towels, more pillows or blankets, and the like. Let them know they should ask if they can't find something they need.
19. Invite guests to use the kitchen to boil hot water for tea or coffee or to place foods needing refrigeration or freezing away. Kitchen privileges for meal preparation are not part of your B&B responsibility to your guests; but if someone is staying more than a few days, you may opt to permit the use of your appliances and kitchenware as you see fit.
20. Place a welcoming tray in the guest room: fruit bowl, iced water or tea, drinking glass, mints, liqueur for after-dinner relaxation, a pretty napkin, one or two cut flowers from your garden, a deck of cards.

21. When guests arrive, find out what they like to drink in the morning and make coffee or tea early for those who drink it. A thermos outside the door so the first cup of the day can be drunk in bed is a real treat.
22. Place sample sizes of toilet articles in drawers of guest room.
23. If you have a historic home, guests may like to learn about it. You may want to take a course about tracing its history and keep the results of your work available for guests to read if interested.
24. Check with your library, historical society, or neighborhood association about the availability of walking tours in published form, so people can take them on their own.
25. If your setting is conducive to romance, offer your guests some private time in front of the fireplace with a complimentary decanter of cognac or wine and the use of your music system.
26. In cold climates, flannel sheets are a nice winter's touch.
27. If you have a special interest or hobby that others might enjoy sharing as participants or observers, invite them to join you. Let guests know you as an individual, your way of life, your part of the country, but don't convey the impression that the guest is there to amuse you. Be available at breakfast or in the early evening for those who want to talk, but recognize when a guest wants privacy.
28. Keep an up-to-date list of servicepeople in town (for example, in the event of broken eyeglasses, lost keys, spills on evening clothes, late-night pharmacy needs, copying of a business report, typing services, baby-sitting, pet services).
29. Take out a membership in the local video rental shop if you allow guests to use your VCR equipment or if you occasionally invite guests to join your family for a movie at home.
30. Provide a bedtime snack: cookies and milk, biscuits and hot chocolate, fortune cookies and wine, herb tea and scones, and so on. This is particularly thoughtful for people who have had very late days at a hospital, nursing home, or funeral home and may have missed meals along the way.

**Question:** Will I need to be able to accept credit cards from my guests?

**Answer:** *After being in business close to a year, I lost a large booking because the guest wanted to pay by credit card and we couldn't accept it. Since plastic of any type has always been repugnant to me and certainly one of the reasons B&B was so attractive was the lack of plastic associated with it, I had never tried to become a credit card merchant. But once this $1,000 booking slipped away, I knew the day had come to concede and apply for this privilege. I say "privilege" because that is the bank's attitude toward allowing you to help them make money. I naturally called my own bank first and was politely told by the* manager that the bank had a policy that home-based businesses could not qualify to be credit card merchants. I then called every bank in Westchester County and New York City, only to be told the same thing. Having wasted close to a full day on this fool's errand, I became depressed and gave up temporarily.

Shortly afterward I saw a story on a cable TV show about a business that allowed people to use their credit cards to pay for over-the-phone sexually explicit talk. I was outraged that this business was qualified to be a credit card merchant but my reservation service was not. I called the local chapter of the Association for Home-Based Businesses and was told by the chapter president that she is a credit card merchant because an exception was made by her bank after her husband threatened to move his million-dollar account to another bank if his wife's company was not made eligible to accept credit cards. Well, even if my husband had had a million-dollar account at a bank, I didn't think that this type of blackmail should be necessary. My rage mounted, and I started calling state legislators and the small-business administration. I threatened that if someone didn't take action, I would take my story to television. Within the week, the Union National Bank in Albany agreed to take my company on as a credit card merchant. They came to Croton and installed our credit card acceptance device in my kitchen.

We ask each guest for a credit card number to guarantee their stay. This helps ensure that they are serious about using their reservations. After many years of experience, we have found that no matter how nice people sound over the telephone, if they don't pay in advance, they are not likely to show up. Big hotels overbook because they know exactly what percentage will be no-shows. But a host with one to four guest rooms can't afford one no-show and can't overbook under any circumstance.

## BECOMING A MERCHANT

It is no longer difficult for a small inn or B&B to achieve merchant status with a bank. There will be some start-up costs if you want to have a "data capture" terminal that allows you to have the transactions directly deposited into your bank account once authorized by your credit card–approving bank system. This machinery can be leased or bought. Many associations have arrangements with specific banks that will process your credit card transactions. They do charge some fees. When figuring out which bank to work with, ask yourself how much the fees will amount to and how quickly you will be able to draw on the money. There are fees per transaction and also a commission based on the amount of sale. These commissions range from under 2 percent to almost 5 percent. American Express must be arranged separately from Visa, Mastercard, and Discover. American Express also has a fairly high discount rate (the commission charged), but they are often the easiest to deal with. If you belong to a trade association, you will probably benefit from its arrangement with a credit card banker. Small B&Bs who work strictly through a reservation service do not need to take credit cards themselves. The service will do it for them.

Understand that although you are able to have guests guarantee a reservation with their credit card, which may protect you from cancellations and make the callers aware that they must be serious about their reservation, consumers can still stiff you. They can "charge back" a stay, claiming that they never went, weren't informed of the cancellation penalty, or didn't receive what they ordered. This is rare, but it does happen. Protect yourself as best you can by clearly stating your cancellation policy and putting it in writing on the confirmation that is sent to the guest. In situations where the guest refuses to pay, it is difficult for the merchant to win without lots of documentation. Some inns tape-record the transaction on the phone with the permission of the would-be guest, making sure to verbalize the cancellation policy while the guest is on tape.

Some of the bank programs worth contacting include:

Retriever Payment Systems, (800) 877-2265.

NABANCO, (800) 622-2626.

NOVA, (800) 725-1243.

❖❖❖❖❖❖❖

**Question:** I have chosen a wonderful, very large house in a community that seems very receptive to my opening it to guests. I am terrified about decorating it. Can you give me any tips?

**Answer:** *For those who have lived in a home for a long time, have raised a family there, and now plan to start a B&B, there may be little more to do than touching up the paint, buying some new sheets, and selecting a few plants. With a new home (even if it's an older building), you will have to evaluate its needs, assess your budget, and proceed from there.*

*My own story should provide a helpful example. We weren't in the million-dollar house market, and decorating the house on a limited budget was a challenge to be tackled without decorator assistance. My decorating talents were a good eye for color and texture and knowledge gleaned from many magazine articles about how to make a small room appear larger. Moving into a house with high ceilings and rooms twenty-seven to thirty-five feet long forced some new insights on us. I owe one of the best to my Aunt Francine, who was one of the people who looked at the house when we first bought it and saw, as we did, how wonderful it would look when we finally finished decorating. She immediately offered me her dining room table and chairs, which had been in storage for seventeen years. I asked her how she could justify paying to store something for so long. She said, "My dear, husbands come and go, but furniture is forever!" She should know; she's had three husbands.*

*I traveled down to southern Jersey, where the storage company loaded the table and chairs on the truck, and happily rode back with my new treasures. When my husband arrived home from work that evening, we carried them in, only to find that a fifty-four-inch-long oval cherry table looked ridiculously small in the middle of a twenty-seven-foot-long dining room. This table now sits in the bay window, where I use it as a dessert buffet. So, decorating lesson 1: Large houses dwarf furniture. Although you now need to buy large pieces, this is not necessarily bad news. Very few homes can accommodate pieces of the size you need, so they are often available at garage and estate sales or auctions for a reasonable price.*

I found that my home has rooms that look into each other through many open doorways. Therefore, my choice of colors had to be fairly similar so they wouldn't clash. Wallpaper is a fast way to achieve spectacular looks yet provide continuity. I selected three different patterns (one for each room) from the same color family. Originally, my front hall had white and gold flocking and was quite reminiscent of a Victorian brothel. The living room and dining room were in the same drab gray textured paper, which added to the look of being a large empty barn. Victorian houses have carved woodwork, leaded windows, turrets, and other features that require some formality in the main rooms. Country Americana looked out of place except perhaps on our sun porch. To fit in with the formality, I used vinyl moiré wallpapers in the living and dining rooms and a floral print in the front entry hall.

To make these large rooms look cozy, it was necessary to group the furniture into smaller subgroups. I removed the wall-to-wall carpeting, had the hardwood floors sanded and sealed, and bought oriental area rugs that helped define the smaller areas. A decorator told me that this technique is now referred to as "having a series of episodes."

We did the upstairs guest rooms one at a time. The largest we furnished with large Victorian pieces, with marble-topped dressers and a settee. The other B&B rooms developed over time as demand for them grew. We put twin beds in one room. (Twin beds are in less demand generally; but when clients need them, double-bedded rooms just won't do.) To accommodate the beds, it was necessary to wall over one of the closets. When we grew from two to four rooms, we flew up to Maine, rented a truck, antiqued our way through country lanes, and came home with two rooms of country furniture at quite reasonable prices.

If you buy antique beds, they are almost always too short. Get a carpenter or handyman to extend the side boards six inches so you accommodate a normal mattress and box spring. Always purchase new, firm mattresses. Very few people like soft ones, and most bed complaints are because a bed isn't firm enough. Remember to ask people if they are over six feet tall;

most old beds have footboards that make for much discomfort if a person has no room to stretch out.

We have done each bedroom in a different color, varying the style to suit the size of the room. Your decor is a reflection of your unique personality and should remain so. One hostess I visited recently had bookshelves in each room. One room contained only mysteries, another romances, another classics, and so on. My rooms reflect Victorian romance, with candles, old-fashioned candies, and fresh flowers. Literature about the area and a train schedule in case they wish to visit New York City are also in each room.

Little extras are very memorable. Displayed collections are often focal points in a decorating scheme. Many hosts favor holiday and seasonal variations. Some hosts use fresh flowers or plants. At Christmastime, I decorate each room for the holidays, as well as the staircase and each of the tables downstairs. At breakfast, I try to feature seasonal foods, and I use butter molds to shape my butter pats into hearts, flowers, pumpkins, turkeys, and so on. It always surprises me that people rarely say anything about the Victorian antiques (I guess they expect them in a house like ours) but never fail to remark about the butters. Cloth napkins are also a nice touch. For guests who stay more than one night, I offer a choice of napkin rings shaped like little animals so that they will recognize their napkins the next day. This also saves on laundry, since most napkins will stay fresh for a number of days. The guests also get a kick out of choosing their rings. My little pig is the favorite; someone at the table always knows who is supposed to have him.

Decorating your B&B should be fun both for you to do and for your guests to enjoy. If you feel decorating is not one of your strong points, you might want to call in a friend whose decorating appeals to you. Remember, this is your home first and therefore it should be a place where you feel comfortable. If your taste is contemporary, don't feel that you have to change your house into country Americana for guests. As long as you do it with love and describe it accurately to prospective guests, those who come will not be disappointed.

❖❖❖❖❖❖❖

**Question:** We plan to have five guest rooms. Do we need a computer and special inn software? What do you recommend?

**Answer:** *In my life, a personal computer is as necessary as a car—both of them are time-savers I'd be hard-pressed to live without. Needless to say, there are plenty of people who live without cars and computers. The question you must ask yourself is, what would the advantages be? Would they be worth the cost?*

*There are advantages to having a personal computer over just a typewriter or word processor. With a special inn program, you can keep good financial records, as well as information about where your guests come from and how they heard about your place. This helps you plan your future marketing and evaluate your advertising and promotional effectiveness. The computer can simply be programmed to print mailing labels for past guests, making it easy for you to send out a newsletter, Christmas cards, or a special promotion notice. The cost will be high if you don't already have the computer. Decide on your software needs first, because the computer must have enough memory to run the program and a hard disk capable of storing your information. With five rooms, I think a computer is not essential but will be very helpful and save you a lot of time. Inn programs come for both IBM-compatible and Macintosh computers, so if you already have a computer, investigate whether the software is compatible with the one you have. A good list of inn software can be found in the* Inn Review Yellow Pages *(see Appendix B for address).*

*I am currently using Kozyware. As with all software, remember to ask yourself what you need it to do, and don't be talked into a program too complicated for your needs or skill level. Kozyware is not only very user-friendly but also a bargain. Kozyware is distributed by Forster & Associates, PO Box 551, Springville, NY 14141, (716) 592-2397.*

*Kozyware is available for $99 for two rooms, $10 for each additional room. If you use an IBM or IBM-compatible PC, this is a fabulous innkeeping software program at a phenomenally low* price. It offers a complete reservation system and calendar. Guest information is instantly available, including a photo display. It does invoices and confirmation letters with envelopes. Report writing makes it easy to track arriving and departing guests, referral patterns, and financial data, including tax obligations and travel agent commissions. Peter Figlioti and Jeffrey Forster have been very responsive to feedback and have upgraded Kozyware, so that it is easy to use for inns from two to ninety-nine rooms. A demonstration kit is available for $10 if you just want to try it out.

When selecting a software system, shop around. The price should not be the only factor. Ask for names of other inns currently using the product. Call them and ask how helpful the vendors are when questions or problems arise. Also check how satisfied they are with the product and follow-up assistance.

# 6

## Public Relations and Advertising

**A**ny business requires a combination of public relations (PR) and advertising to get off the ground, and both are necessary to keep an established business before the public eye and perpetuate a demand for it.

### PUBLIC RELATIONS

An article on Bed and Breakfast in a major magazine is often the result of PR efforts by a reservation service or a collective effort of a number of inns. In each article, certain B&Bs will be featured, usually those appropriate to the readership of that particular magazine. No one can pay to be included in the story. What goes into the story is an editorial decision made by the magazine. How, then, can a service's PR be responsible? The service may have sent in the story outline with pictures of sample B&Bs for an editor to look at or invited the editor to lunch or to a hosted get-together and suggested the article. They may have made a speech or given a radio interview that caught an editor's ear and then provided information when that editor inquired about B&B. The service may send press releases about an interesting event such as a gourmet or mystery weekend.

### The Seed-Planting Approach

I personally follow the *seed-planting approach* to public relations. This involves doing something every day that may result in letting the public know about my B&B or the joys of Bed and

Breakfast. It is called *seed planting* because as in gardening, some of the effort pays off this season, some in the future, and some not at all. Attending a Chamber of Commerce meeting to hand out business cards and brochures, speaking to a fraternal organization or a business group, or calling a corporation to set up an appointment with its travel or personnel department might be my PR activity for the day. Sending Christmas cards to my guests will remind them of an enjoyable stay and perhaps encourage them to visit my B&B again or recommend it to a friend headed this way.

## Professional Firms

There are companies that specialize in getting information about your business into the papers and magazines and on to TV and radio talk shows. They write your press releases, coach you for interviews, and so on. They are professionals who expect to be well paid for their efforts. Some contracts pay according to how often you are mentioned. This may or may not relate to how much business you do as a consequence.

Many PR professionals believe that it takes at least seven exposures for the average listener to understand a new concept. So public relations is not a one-shot deal. Rather, it is a continual effort to expose new clients to your product, create a demand for it, and make sure they come to you to buy it. If the publicity is positive, it may help you achieve all three. There are no guarantees, however. You may invite a travel writer to spend a night at your B&B gratis and then wait months to see the story. Perhaps the article will not even mention your B&B or will have something negative to say about your decor, your breakfast, or something else. Or the writer's editor may need space for a paid ad and cut the paragraph about your home. Should this risk discourage your efforts? No.

## Doing It Yourself

If you do not use a PR firm, you will have to act as your own publicist. The true cost of public relations efforts both in money and in personal time varies greatly. Some costs are direct, such as membership dues for a trade group, a reservation service, or a chamber of commerce. In these cases, you know what the cost is, but there may be a tremendous variation in what each group does for your business. Sometimes the results vary from year to year or season to season. Moreover, it may depend on whether you merely pay dues or also participate by attending meetings, volunteering for committees, and so on.

Many of your efforts may not produce business immediately, and it can be difficult to keep up your efforts in the absence of direct results. I have done many TV shows. My preparation for taping can take days, and the taping itself takes hours. But the final edited feature may be aired for less than five minutes. Although thousands of people may see the show, only two or three may follow through by calling to make a reservation. I justify the energy expended by assuring myself that such appearances are one of the seven exposures and that by promoting B&B in general, I am helping to build the demand for everyone in the industry. Successful entrepreneurs learn this early. The consistent and repeated mentions of the Alexander Hamilton House in stories about B&B are part of what has built our good reputation and why newcomers to this type of travel call us when they decide to make reservations.

## INCREASING LOCAL BUSINESS

Determining what kinds of guests will be attracted to your place is important in predicting how much business is likely to come your way. Certainly, asking yourself the questions in Chapter 3 about your location will be a good start, but these are focused on people who come for tourism, business, or just a romantic interlude. An important and lucrative type of business is guests coming to visit local residents who don't have room to put up visitors. This kind of business is not usually brought in by reservation services. It depends on your participation and reputation in the community. It is especially important because these are often your repeat customers, who, once they discover you, loyally return year after year.

## Make the Community Aware of Your Bed and Breakfast

If you are interested in local business, it is important that the community become aware of you. Keeping your home "company-ready" and always being happy to show folks around is only part of what it takes to create a positive image.

After the tremendous amount of publicity we had locally during our zoning trial, I thought there was no one in Croton who didn't know about our existence. I was shocked to find out years later that most people in town didn't know about us. I focused on doing some local marketing for the Alexander Hamilton House. First, I took out an inexpensive ad in the local paper. Then, the American Field Service was planning a historic-house tour in May. I volunteered my house and said I would be happy to host the reception at the close of the tour. I did this knowing that given the choice of ten houses on tour, most people wouldn't visit all of them. I certainly wanted them to visit this one, and food guaranteed that they would come. In addition, all the members of the committee came too. This was a wonderful activity to participate in because it enabled a favorite group to raise funds while giving us exposure to more than 150 people who came on the tour. I would be happy to host the reception at the conclusion of any historic tour in the future.

## HOUSE TOURS

House tours, in general, or an open house are good ways to spread the word about you. The first week in December is National Bed & Breakfast Open House Week. Band with the other B&Bs nearby. Write a press release to the local newspaper and let them know that you are participating by being open for tours during that week. Be specific about the days and hours so people don't show up when you are out marketing and so you don't feel like a prisoner in your own house.

## SUPPORT YOUR LOCAL
## CHAMBER OF COMMERCE

If you are part of your local chamber of commerce, participate actively in one or two projects a year, and attend monthly meetings so that you are in touch with what is going on and you get to know the other businesspeople in town as well. Our chamber was looking for a way to raise money for playground equipment in a new village park. I organized a silent auction. Chamber members were solicited for donations of goods or services. The auction was held at the winter blood drive at the high school. This is something that the village residents regularly attend. Most stopped in at the auction and placed a bid. At the end of the day we called the highest bidders and told them to pay their money to the playground fund and pick up their prize during the week at the Alexander Hamilton House. We raised $2,500 for the playground and had a chance to show off the B&B to the fifty-some people who stopped by. Most were delighted and wanted a full tour. We have since gotten considerable business and referrals from the folks who have had the opportunity to see our facility firsthand this year.

## OTHER IDEAS

- Host meetings of local groups in your parlor. The League of Women Voters, church or synagogue groups, charities, and so forth are usually looking for a centrally located place to hold meetings. The beverages and cake you provide give folks a chance to sample your hospitality and make a lasting impression.

- Donate a complimentary stay at your B&B to locally sponsored raffles or auctions. Understand that you will be solicited for donations to a myriad of fund-raisers. Many of these charities will be from other areas, even out of state. Donating to local groups is a far better use of your contribution. Local people are much more likely to refer guests.

- Invite the local realtors to tea. Give them a tour and let them know that you will be happy to accommodate folks looking for homes in the area or waiting for their closing. You may consider offering them a commission for these referrals.

- You will find that magazines pile up around the inn and need to be thrown out or recycled. Taking them down to the waiting room of the local hospital, doctor, dentist, or physical therapist recycles the magazines. Hospitals have cut down on subscriptions as a way to cut costs, and patients suffer from boredom. All are thrilled to see you coming with your old magazines. Glue on a mailing label or business card with the name, address, and phone number of your inn, so that readers will know where the magazines came from. It is a great way for locals to find out about you and have good feelings toward you, too.

- Invite the social workers at the local hospital for tea and a tour. They often are in a position to recommend accommodations to friends and family coming to visit patients. The same goes for local clergy. You will soon find your B&B called upon when local residents need extra space for guests coming to parties, bar mitzvahs, christenings, graduations, and even funerals.

- Invite the tour guides from the historic houses in your area for tea and a tour of your home. These are folks who know how hard it is to maintain a beautiful home and will really appreciate being on the receiving end for a change. They are in a position to tell many tourists about your gracious hospitality.

# SATISFIED CUSTOMERS HELP
# YOUR BUSINESS GROW

## Newsletters and Gift Certificates

Keeping your mailing list up-to-date is important. Many B&B and small-inn owners send newsletters to guests once to four times a year reminding them of upcoming attractions, events, and sales; offering special promotions; and sharing information about changes at the inn or with the family. The sample newsletter shown on the next page from the Silver Maple Lodge is a simple, one-color, single-page piece that semiannually updates guests on goings-on in the inn's area.

Notice the paragraph on gift certificates. This is an inexpensive promotional tool to encourage satisfied customers to send their family or friends on a trip. Make sure to print a lovely gift certificate and have a sample available at your B&B for guests to see. Gift certificates should be marketed before holidays. They bring in cash during the off-season. Sometimes they aren't even used. Make sure to put an expiration date on it (see sample on page 134). A year from the issue date is customary.

# ADVERTISING

Advertising is the buying of space in print media or air time on TV or radio to promote your name and product. Because you are the purchaser, you decide exactly what will be said about you. You pay for your own artwork and have the final say about copy. Depending on how much you pay, you can decide whether your message will be on a particular page or time slot. You also know precisely when and for how long your ad will run. But the public also knows that you have paid for this message and, therefore, may take what you have to say about yourself with a grain of salt.

Advertising agencies have graphic artists, layout people, copywriters and editors, and years of experience in knowing which vehicles have produced the best results. They are the professionals

# FAIRLEE
# GOOD
# NEWS

SILVER
MAPLE LODGE
and Cottages
RR1, Box 8, Fairlee, VT
05045

---

**(800) 666-1946**      **FALL/WINTER 1994-95**      **(802) 333-4326**

---

## FALL DAYS

We've survived a long hot, humid Summer here at the **Silver Maple Lodge** and are in the midst of a busy leaf-peeping season. The brilliant foliage colors are starting to fade and the leaves will soon be on the ground. We're looking forward to a snowy Winter season but hope it's not quite as cold as last winter.

## NEW COTTAGE - 2 MORE FIREPLACES

About this time last year we were about to break ground for an additional cottage on the rear of our property behind Leda's Restaurant. The foundation was poured by Thanksgiving and Scott worked most of the winter to have it completed in time for an early May occupancy. The cottage houses two units, both of which have king-size beds and working fireplaces. One of the units also has a sleep-sofa and kitchen area and one of the units is fully handicap accessible. The new units have been very busy all summer and we expect the fireplaces will be in demand all winter.

*Last Winter's Project*

## SPECIAL VALUE DAYS

From now until December 20, 1994, you can book any 2 nights for just $79 single or double occupancy! This rate will apply to any room except the fireplaced cottages. Call now to check availability.

## GIFT CERTIFICATES

As the holidays approach, don't forget that we offer gift certificates for lodging at the **Silver Maple Lodge** as well as for our hot air balloon package. A one or two night stay at the **Silver Maple Lodge** may be just the gift for someone you know. Call us for more information.

## WILD GAME SUPPER

The 38th annual Wild Game Supper in Bradford will be held on Saturday, November 19. Meats such as wild boar, moose, venison, bear, pheasant, rabbit, coon, buffalo and beaver are served buffet style. The menu also includes potatoes, squash, rolls, cabbage salad, beverages, and homemade gingerbread served with real whipped cream. There are six seatings between the hours of 2:30 and 8:00p.m., and tickets can be hard to come by. We have just a few rooms left for this weekend. If you are interested in attending this event give us a call as soon as possible. If we have space to accommodate you at the **Silver Maple** we'll also obtain tickets for you.

## HOLIDAY SHOPPING

For holiday fun and early Christmas shopping enjoy a weekend of Victorian-era nostalgia during the annual "DICKENS OF A CHRISTMAS" celebration in nearby Hanover, New Hampshire. From December 2-4, there will be street entertainment, window displays, "Santa" appearances, special menus in area restaurants, and lots more revelry. West Lebanon, NH and Woodstock, Vermont also have some great shopping!

# Alexander Hamilton House

## Gift Certificate

This certificate entitles bearer

*Brenda Barta*

to $ **100 —** credit toward a

Bed & Breakfast stay at our

Victorian Home or City Apartment.

Date and place to be arranged at the convenience

of bearer of certificate with Barbara Notarius

49 Van Wyck Street

Croton-on-Hudson, New York 10520

( 914) 271-6737

Certificate given by

*Barbara Notarius*

Expiration Date   *2 / 3 / 97*

*SAMPLE*

in this field, and they expect to be paid professional fees for services rendered. The price of advertising is often related to how many people can be expected to read or hear it. What may seem an outrageous cost for placing an ad in a magazine or newspaper with a large circulation can be justified by the very low per capita expenditure that exposure in such a publication guarantees.

The cost of an ad varies according to the circulation of the vehicle, the size of the ad, how many insertions you commit yourself to in advance, whether or not you supply camera-ready copy, and other factors. You will generally pay more to place your ad in a paper or magazine with a large circulation or exclusive clientele. The larger your ad, the more it will cost, but you will usually pay less per square inch. If you decide on a series of ads placed each week, month, or issue, your cost per ad will usually be less. *Camera-ready copy* is copy that can be run exactly as submitted, for which you have already silk-screened the photos, typeset the copy, and had your graphic artist do the sketch, layout, and border. If you are buying a two-by-three-inch space, your ad is submitted in that size. The term is usually applied only to *display ads*, that is, ads that are placed throughout a publication, usually interspersed with articles. *Classified ads* are found grouped together in a special section and are considerably less expensive. Like public relations, advertising is something you do not once, but repeatedly so that your clients will be able to locate you when they need to.

## PUBLICITY AND ADVERTISING FOR
## A BED AND BREAKFAST

Are you saying to yourself, "This sounds like a lot of money and a full-time job"? You're right. Hotels have people on staff whose total job is to plan and execute these tasks. A small B&B with fewer than six rooms would very seldom bring in enough money to justify such expenses. Still, without publicity and advertising, no one will come to your B&B. In many cases, this is where your reservation service really earns its commissions. Many big businesses spend up to 40 percent of gross sales on sales and promotion, and a business trying to increase sales will spend more than a business trying to maintain sales. A new business needs all the help it can get.

## Helping Your Reservation Service Promote You

When selecting a reservation service to represent you, one of the many things you will want to know about is what kind of advertising and promotion it has done in the past and plans to do in the future. (Before choosing a reservation service, please read Chapter 8, "Working with a Reservation Service," carefully.) If a reservation service is new, you may help it plan its strategies in this area. By volunteering to attend meetings, give speeches, or allow your home to be featured in an article, you can increase the demand for your B&B. Many reservation services ask their hosts for one free night if a travel writer wants to sample their B&Bs. If you are asked, accept and do your best to see that they get a good impression, but don't try to overwhelm. Travel writers are nobody's fools and will usually be quite able to see the advantages of a B&B by themselves.

Do local marketing for yourself. Distribute brochures to restaurants, friends, professional associates, local real estate salespeople, local corporations, women's centers, schools, catering services (who may refer guests to you when catering large events such as weddings with many out-of-town guests), funeral directors, maternity shops, nursery schools, senior citizen's centers, hospital auxiliaries, members of the clergy, and so on.

Let your reservation service know about events that will take place in your area as far in advance as possible. It sometimes takes three to six months to promote travel properly for an upcoming event. And be sure to keep your service informed about any changes in your household or B&B accommodations. If you get a cat, don't forget to share this news. A guest with allergies sent to you based on an earlier report of your having no pets will cause problems for the guest, may cause you to have to refund the money for the stay, and puts your service in the position of having misrepresented you to guests. If you get a canopy bed or antique bed linens, let your service know so that it can use these special features to entice couples looking for a romantic getaway.

## BEWARE OF SCAMS!

### Ad Scams

A company out of Chicago is targeting B&Bs and inns for advertising scams. Last year, they called my inn. The caller was very smooth, with a great phone voice and cheery come-on. The conversation went approximately like this:

> HE: "Are you familiar with the organization AARP?"
> ME: "Sure."
> HE: "Well, we represent the magazine *Modern Seniors,* the magazine for seniors. Some of our readers have recommended your inn to us. Because you were recommended by one of our members, we would like you to advertise with us and are going to offer you a low introductory rate of only $150 for our most popular spring issue. This is our travel issue, the one people save for months and refer to throughout the travel season. This rate is only for inns recommended by our readers."

*Modern Maturity* is the magazine of the AARP. If you aren't a member of the AARP, *Modern Seniors* sounds just close enough. These phone guys are con artists. They don't actually lie. They are flattering you and want you to think that your inn is getting something special. By the time the tearsheet arrives along with the invoice, it is very obvious that this magazine, if it even exists, is not what you were expecting. It is printed on newsprint. No calls follow from guests who have seen your ad. I asked the salesman to send me a copy of the magazine. It never came. I refused to pay for this bogus ad and was harassed by collection notices and then calls from a collection agency that threatened to get a judgment against me and ruin my credit. I finally stopped it all by going to the Better Business Bureau and calling the Chicago police.

This year, the call came again with a slight variation: "Have you heard of *Travel and Leisure Magazine*? We do a special issue every April called 'Escape Travel and Leisure,' and some of our readers have recommended your inn for this special issue."

Surprise! Surprise! For only $150, I could have an ad in this issue and I wouldn't have to pay until I got the tearsheet and the invoice. This time I knew enough to say, "Send me a copy of last year's issue and something in writing about your proposal." Never buy anything from phone solicitation alone. These guys don't want to risk charges of mail fraud.

Fool me once, shame on you. Fool me twice, shame on me. This time I was not fooled.

## Publicity Scams

A caller introduces himself or herself as a writer for a magazine that wants to do a story on you. Of course, he or she will need to stay at the inn, and it would be great if you could comp them for the stay because so much business will come as a result of the article. Often, this person is a free-lance writer who is doing the article on spec. This means that he or she has not sold the article yet and may never sell it to a magazine. If the article is never printed, this story will be worth nothing to you.

Make sure that you call the magazine to confirm the writer's story. Most reputable magazines will expect to pay for their accommodations. Don't call the number the "writer" gives you. Get the number of the magazine from information, and make sure that the features editor knows about the article and the writer. If the writer checks out, make sure to ask for copies of the article after publication.

## DEALING WITH "MAILPHOBIA"

Once you have been in business for a short time, you will be faced with the trauma of "mailphobia," a word I've coined for fear of the mail delivery. I can remember fondly when I was a child thinking how wonderful it would be when I was old enough to get mail. Now, of course, I long for vacations where there is no mail and no phone (I suffer from "phonephobia," too). What makes it so difficult to deal with the mail? At best, it is time-consuming. Much of it requires a personal response that can't be delegated to anyone else. With the growth of the industry, it seems as if every mail delivery comes with one more industry magazine or newsletter to subscribe to, a guidebook to be listed in, or a group or association to join. All these require decisions.

## General Recommendations

1. Deal with the mail daily if possible. Letting it pile up until the end of the week makes it look overwhelming. The idea is to handle each piece only once if possible. Moving it from pile to pile only makes this task more frustrating.

2. Sit in a comfortable, well-lit place, near the phone with a garbage can by your side. Do your best to resist being distracted until this task is done.

3. Open each piece and deal with it immediately if possible. Some people prefer to pay bills once or twice a month. If you do, bills go in a "To Pay" folder. Have another folder for letters needing a personal response. Try to keep this folder empty by responding immediately. Don't let these responses go more than a week. Anything left for the future when you have extra time is not important; you may as well toss it now.

4. Requests for brochures should be addressed and mailed immediately. Save the requests in a "For the Computer" file so that you can enter these people into your inn software or mailing list. Save time each week or month to enter this information.

5. When you receive checks by mail for reservations, make sure your confirmations go out the same day. People get very nervous if they don't hear back right away. Deposit your checks the day they come in, and make sure to enter them in your register.

# DECISION MAKING

With the growth of the B&B industry, one of the most noticeable changes has been the number of solicitations I receive in the mail. The following sections will give you some guidelines to help you make decisions when you too are faced with a mountain of mail before you.

## Guidebooks

When I first opened in 1981, there were no B&B guidebooks. Norman Simpson's *Back Roads and Country Inns* and Bob Christopher's travel guides were available, but only long-established commercial inns were included. At this time there are more than two dozen guidebooks that purport to be the definitive guide to American Bed and Breakfasts. If you are doing any of your own marketing, it is important to be in the right guidebooks. You cannot be in all of them. Please see Appendix B for a list of the most popular guidebooks. Some books charge you to be included. Cost may be factor in deciding which guidebooks you will be in and should be considered as part of your advertising budget. The AAA, Mobil Travel Guide, and the guidebook of the American Bed & Breakfast Association require on-site inspection. Many of these books have specific requirements that you may or may not meet. At one time AAA required that someone be on the premises at all times. For working hosts who didn't have live-in housekeepers, being included in the AAA guide was not possible. This is no longer the case.

Selecting which books you want to be in is important. Bernice Chesler, author of six B&B books, including *Bed & Breakfast in New England* and *Bed & Breakfast in the Mid-Atlantic States*, suggests that a large distribution is not necessarily indicative of your benefit. Make sure that you go to the library and a few bookstores to see these books. Call up a few of the B&Bs listed in the guides. Select ones similar to yours in size, style, and location and ask how well this guidebook has performed for them. Don't call the other B&B in town unless you're really close friends. Benefit from other innkeepers' experience. Most will be happy to share this information with you as long as it's not an inconvenient time for them. Make sure you ask first if it's a good time to talk, and if it's not, ask when to call back. Don't expect them to return the call. It benefits you, so you should pay for the call. Don't keep them on the line forever, or next time they won't be so willing to hear from you.

For a detailed list of guidebooks, including regional ones, contact the Professional Association of Innkeepers International (PAII).

## Timing

Remember that the nature of publishing is such that books come out once every one, two, or three years. Even though you send your information in and pay your fee, it may be six months to two years before your listing appears in print. If something at your inn changes, be it your rates, the ages of your children, or the number or type of your pets, it is necessary that your listing reflect these changes as soon as possible. People assume that any information they see in print is gospel, no matter how old it is. In sincerity, I happily gave all the information about my home to the late Betty Rundback in 1981 for her book *Bed & Breakfast USA*. At the time I started, we had one room with a private bath. The house had two baths on the second floor, so we designated one as our family bath and the other for the guests. A few years later, a guest called for the room with the private bath. By this time, we had decorated two other guest rooms and were describing our accommodations as having three guest rooms that shared two baths. We explained that there was no room with a private bath. In response, the guest in a sarcastic tone asked, "Where did you lose it?" He was annoyed, and we lost the booking.

## Evaluation

Just as with any other type of advertising, it is important to know what works for you and what doesn't, since you will be deciding each year whether to renew your listing or not. Ask every caller where they heard about you, and keep track of this information. If you are computerized and have inn software, this information will be part of your database. If you are not computerized, recording each booking, where the guest heard about you, and how much money you get from it on a page headed with the name of the guidebook or other advertising source will give you the information you need to plan for next year.

# ASSOCIATIONS

There are a number of local, regional, state, and national associations that want your membership. How important is it to join them? Must I belong to all of them? These are the questions everyone asks me. The major questions that need to be asked are "What will this association do for my B&B?" and "What will I be doing for it?" You cannot belong to everything, or you will pay a fortune in dues and be at meetings every night of the week.

## Local Organizations

Local organizations include groups such as the chamber of commerce, local charity groups, fraternal organizations, and even special short-term or religious groups organized to raise money for a local playground. Certainly, you will need to belong to the local chamber of commerce. It's important to be part of the business community, and often folks looking for accommodations will write to the local chamber for advice on where to stay. Your choice of charity work, fraternal group, or fund-raising project is up to you and may vary from year to year, but do try to participate in something local. You will get multiple rewards—gratification from helping others and also enhancement of your image in the community. (See Increasing Local Business at the beginning of this chapter.)

## Regional Associations

Regional associations usually organize because of a common purpose. They might do joint marketing on a regional basis as do the B&Bs of Cape May, New Jersey, who band together to promote off-season business by having special activities such as Victorian

Week in October and Christmas decorating contests in December. A regional group may be local or statewide but usually appeals for membership within the industry by doing such things as lobbying the legislature to ease the fire laws pertaining to B&Bs. Certainly, belonging to a trade organization, one that sets standards for membership, helps credential you.

When Bed & Breakfast U.S.A., Ltd., closed, many of the hosts who had been longtime members called me to ask whether I would start another reservation service. I was already focused on expanding my B&B and doing more writing and consulting. I did not want to go back to spending hours on the road inspecting B&Bs or days in the office on the phone. I suggested we start a Westchester County B&B Association. The B&B owners in the county met and decided to do some cooperative marketing, have monthly meetings, and encourage others to join. We got a phone number installed at the home of a woman in Croton who is retired and spends most weekdays at home. She answers the phone from 10:00 A.M. to 4:00 P.M. and refers guests to the B&B in the area they request. We pay her $50 a month from the association dues, and each member gives her $5 a night for reservations referred by her. This system works well because those with more rooms pay more because they benefit proportionally from how much business results.

The group is friendly. We meet each month at a different member's place. This allows us to know what the other B&Bs are like and feel comfortable referring to each other when we are full. Pooling resources to do cooperative marketing is also a good use of our advertising dollar.

In New York State at present, a B&B can join the Bed & Breakfast Association of New York State (BBANYS) or the New York State Hospitality and Tourism Association (HTA). The BBANYS was formed to act as a trade association for the B&B industry. It holds educational conferences, has standards for membership, presents information to the legislature, and produces a B&B brochure of member New York State B&Bs. The HTA was formerly the Hotel Motel Association but changed its name to reflect other facets of the tourism community, such as B&Bs and campgrounds, as a way to expand its membership base and to have more clout when dealing with the legislature. Within the HTA is a Bed & Breakfast Council that meets regularly and helps prepare informative sessions for the annual conferences. The HTA is very effective and has two full-time, highly paid lobbyists and many years' experience in working with state government. They have programs for low-cost property insurance, Visa/MasterCard merchant arrangements with low discount rates (commission to the bank), a widely distributed travel and tourism map of the state with all member properties indicated, as well as a host of other benefits formerly available only to commercial hotels.

In many ways the two groups duplicate services to their members. It would probably be better were there only one group that could say that it represents the industry in our state. Unfortunately, because there are two groups and membership is split between them, neither is as effective as it could be. Dues are $70 for BBANYS and $85 for the HTA; however, the BBANYS charges an additional fee of $150 for inclusion in its brochure. Presently, I belong to both but participate more actively with the HTA. The HTA meets closer to my home, and I feel that in the long run it has more power to shape legislative change, which is my actual need for a state association. I guess I have adopted somewhat of a wait-and-see attitude. As time goes by, I will evaluate the benefits of my membership in these two organizations and hope to decide on one.

## The IIBBEx

Elizabeth Shadwick runs the International Inn and Bed & Breakfast Exchange (IIBBEx) and produces a quarterly newsletter for innkeepers who are willing to make ten nights' lodging a year available to members of her group. Membership costs $63. As a member, you can avail yourself of the same ten free nights at other member B&Bs, one night at each, of course, and usually not on weekends. The idea behind this plan is that by welcoming other innkeepers, you are able to increase their referrals. Being in IIBBEx listings gives you international exposure at a very small cost.

"IIBBEx is not barter, as the exchange is not made on a one-to-one or even equal-value basis; it is not a gift, nor is it a reward. IIBBEx guests are not invited guests; therefore their stays are not taxable." IIBBEx has been operating since 1987, and Elizabeth has owned it since 1990. It has several hundred members. To get more information, contact her at IIBBEx, PO Box 615, Hayden, ID 83835, (208) 772-1994, fax: (208) 772-9287.

## Don't Lose Sight of the Personal Touch

I asked Bernice Chesler, the author of six books on Bed and Breakfasts, how she saw the B&B industry changing. She responded, "In some parts of the country, layers of rules and regulations and associations push for hosts to be more professional and make it difficult to be just a nice home away from home." It is a difficult balance to maintain both one's growing business skills and goals of increasing profitability without losing the human quality, the warmth of reaching out to strangers who you hope will enjoy the homeyness and comfort of your B&B.

This week, a potential guest called. My partner, Brenda, took the call and made the sale. Although this guest called two other places, she selected us because Brenda took the time to answer her questions and made her feel that we were offering exactly what she was looking for in a B&B experience. She selected us over a large nearby inn with much more luxurious facilities, including an indoor pool and tennis courts, because rather than answer her questions, they tried to rush her off the phone by promising to send her a brochure. She told us all about her experience during her one-night stay with us. She had such a good time in our home and felt so welcome that she will recommend to her women's group that they come for a full weekend this spring and take all the rooms in the house.

I'm sorry to have rambled a bit, but although I want you to take association membership seriously, I don't want you to fall into the trap of becoming so businesslike and "professional" that you defeat your own purposes.

Other regional associations that you may want to join include your state chapter of various sales groups, women's business groups, or larger-than-local business associations. Join only groups that you have the time and inclination to participate in actively. If you plan just to pay your dues and not attend the meetings or conferences, you will not get your money's worth. Consider joining a group that interests you, offers education about subjects you feel weak in, or has a member who will be good for you to get to know. You will want to belong only as long as you still feel that you get value from your membership. I belonged to Women in Sales and The Westchester Woman Business Owners for a number of years. After a while the meeting topics that had once been very stimulating seemed dull, and I found that I was missing meetings. I realized that when I first started my business, my need for basic business information was enormous. I was delighted to find people who willingly shared their skills with me, and I benefitted greatly. After many years in business, though, my needs from associations are different. I am happy when called on to share my skills with newcomers. If you are new to business, don't miss out on the wide variety of groups in your area that provide general business information. Know what your needs are, and participate for as long as you find these groups helpful. Don't sign up for every group you can find. Usually you can attend a meeting or two as a nonmember and then decide.

## The American Automobile Association (AAA)

If you have at least four guest rooms and are serious about your B&B business, then membership in the AAA is one of your best marketing tools. They have taken great care to make their inspection and rating system applicable to B&Bs and have produced a detailed booklet of requirements and guidelines. I will summarize them here, but I suggest that you write to AAA, 1000 AAA Dr., Heathrow, FL, 32746-5063, or call (407) 444-8370, and request their complete information on "Lodging Listing Requirements and Diamond Rating Guidelines."

The AAA defines a B&B as "usually a smaller establishment emphasizing personal attention. Guest rooms are individually decorated with an 'at home' feeling and may lack some modern amenities such as TVs, phones, etc. Decor may include antiques that reflect the ambiance of the facility. Usually owner-operated with a common room or parlor, separate from the innkeeper's living quarters, where guests and owners can interact during evening and breakfast hours. Many have shared bathrooms. A continental or hot breakfast is served and is included in the room rate. Parking may be on the street."

This is a major shift from the past. The AAA inspector comes unannounced once a year. Room rates are published in the tour book and must be kept up-to-date. They require that properties "honor reservations as confirmed. Cancellation and refund policies must be explained to the guest at the time reservations are made." Reservations must be made directly with the Bed and Breakfast, not through a reservation service.

### EXTERIOR AND GROUNDS

Properties must appear well maintained, safe, and easily accessible. The parking area and walkways must be illuminated and free from hazards.

### PUBLIC AREAS

Public areas should serve to provide a pleasant atmosphere.

### GUEST ROOM SECURITY

Each guest room must have a lock that permits a guest to lock the door when leaving the room. In addition there must be a dead bolt that cannot be opened from the outside when locked by the guest from the inside. The dead bolt must be bored into the door, and the bolt must be at least one inch from the edge of the door. "B&Bs, country inns and historic properties with original doors too thin to accept mortised hardware may be given special consideration on having surface mounted slide bolts. These properties are not required to have peepholes."

### FIRE PROTECTION

All guest rooms need smoke detectors and two distinct means of emergency exit. Guest rooms with only one exit are permitted at properties with interior sprinkler systems if the guest rooms are within fifty feet of an exit.

## HOUSEKEEPING AND MAINTENANCE

The property must be clean and well maintained at all times. Daily housekeeping service and fresh bath towels are required at all properties charging a daily rate. Linens need to be changed every third day of an extended stay.

## ROOM DECOR AND AMBIANCE

Guests must be able to move freely about the room. Windows must have adequate covering to provide privacy. Soundproofing should be adequate to muffle noise from public areas and other guest rooms. Furnishings must be coordinated in style and color to fit in with the rest of the property.

## FURNITURE

Each room must have a comfortable bed with two sheets, mattress pad, pillows with cases, blanket, and bedspread. A chair and bedside table must also be present. The bedroom and bath need to be well lit, clean, and safe and have adequate electrical outlets.

## THE BATHROOM

Bathrooms need the usual fixtures. The shower or tub should have a nonslip surface. Guests should be provided with a bath mat, toilet tissue, a waste basket, bath, hand and face towels for each guest, drinking glasses, and individually wrapped bars of soap. Liquid soap is permitted if a bar of soap is also available.

## THE RATING SYSTEM

The most important aspect of AAA membership is your rating. The AAA gives diamonds as a way to compare accommodations. The rating is determined by the conditions observed at the time of inspection.

- *One diamond:* Good but modest accommodations meeting the basic needs of comfort and cleanliness.

- *Two diamonds:* Accommodations that meet the needs of the budget travel, are clean and comfortable, and have nicer decor and furniture than one-diamond establishments.
- *Three diamonds:* More sophisticated establishments that offer finer decor, service, and luxuries.
- *Four diamonds:* Upscale lodgings with equally luxurious grounds and public areas.
- *Five diamonds:* Very well-known establishments where guests are pampered by a professional and attentive staff.

### OVERNIGHT STAYS FOR FOUR- AND FIVE-DIAMOND RATINGS

Inspectors must stay overnight at places being considered for four or five diamonds. They reserve rooms like any other guest and pay for their stay. In the morning, the inspectors identify themselves and share their evaluation with the owners. Few B&Bs will qualify for this level, although the AAA has adapted requirements for B&Bs and country inns to make this possible. For instance, instead of offering wake-up service, B&Bs can have alarm clocks in the room. They may have bathrooms with a shower only instead of a shower/tub combination. They can offer turndown service on request rather than routinely doing it. Writing tables are not required in guest rooms when guests have access to this type of furniture in public rooms.

### WHAT DOES THE RATING SYSTEM MEAN IN TERMS OF MARKETING?

The traveling public is familiar with the AAA and its rating system. They know that room prices are an important factor. The market for three-diamond places is considerably larger than the market for four- or five-diamond properties. Most business travelers seek out three-diamond properties, as well.

### WHAT DOES BEING A AAA PROPERTY COST?

The AAA does not charge to inspect, rate, and include your property in the *Tour Book*. You may buy advertising in the *Tour Book*, which enables you to hang a AAA logo on your sign (if you have one) or use their logo and diamond rating in your brochure or promotional materials.

You bet it is. Everyone I interviewed had only good things to say about the inspections and marketing results. I don't yet have a sense whether the additional advertising will be worth it, but I hope to hear from a variety of B&Bs who do advertise through the AAA. I hope to report these results in a future edition of this book.

# The American Bed & Breakfast Association (ABBA)

I have been a member of the ABBA since its inception in the early 1980s. Pat Wilson, who founded the ABBA, started her company as a way for reservation services to get together at a national conference and discuss the myriad of questions that arose as the fledgling B&B industry was born. Pat was immensely supportive of me when my B&B was under attack from the local zoning board. She knew that if there was to be a B&B industry in this country, it was important that positive zoning precedents be set. Toward this end she came to Croton at her own expense to testify for me at my trial, and for this I will always be immensely grateful. I have been loyal to the ABBA for more than a dozen years, even after Pat retired and turned over the organization to Sarah Sonke. Sarah has done some very positive things, including instituting a rated inspection system that has been very helpful for many innkeepers. It is especially useful for fledgling innkeepers who will benefit most from her expertise.

### MIXED REACTIONS

Unfortunately, there is dissension among longtime innkeepers I interviewed about the value of the ABBA inspection. Some expressed the feeling that there is inconsistency between inspectors and even from the same inspectors from year to year. Most people interviewed felt that Sarah Sonke gave the best feedback. She was straightforward and explained her opinions. The other inspectors were not as useful in their suggestions. A number of people I interviewed declined to be quoted. They had dropped out of the ABBA, which they referred to as "the taste police."

Joan Wells at the Queen Victorian in Cape May, New Jersey, feels that the inspection program is wonderful and worth the price of membership alone. Stephanie Melvin at Westchester House in Saratoga Springs, New York, left the ABBA because she felt that the rating system was unfair. Stephanie felt that her home was being compared to ones on the fanciest street in town, none of which could ever get the zoning permit to be a B&B in Saratoga Springs. Renate Kenaston at the Golden Gate Hotel in San Francisco liked the inspection but felt that she has little chance of ever being able to increase her rating from two crowns. Paul Welton at the Seven Gables Bed & Breakfast in Fairbanks, Alaska, resisted joining the ABBA for some years because he was afraid of the inspection. Once he had passed the AAA inspection, he bit the bullet and called the ABBA. He found their feedback very helpful. Marachal Goldstein at the Cain House in Bridgeport, California, described herself as "very pro ABBA." She said, "their rating system was fair and the criticism constructive." Frances Bochar at the Norton Brackenridge House in San Antonio, Texas, said, "ABBA inspections have been a nightmare. They seem to pick on such little unimportant things." Pat Wiley at the 1790 House in Georgetown, South Carolina, thinks inspections are a good thing, but, having only six rooms in her B&B, she felt that the cost of ABBA membership was too high. Donny Smith at the Maine Stay in Camden, Maine, likes the idea of inspections. Sometime she has differences of opinion with the inspector. "For instance," Donny said, "they want paper doilies under my drinking glasses and wrapped bars of soap rather than liquid soap in the bathroom. I'd rather give guests the choice. Just wrapped soaps seems so wasteful."

My own experience with the ABBA inspections has been mixed. I have received many useful suggestions. Some, though, seemed either impractical or financially unjustifiable for an inn of only seven rooms.

Bed and Breakfast is comprised of small homestays, B&B inns with under ten rooms, and small inns with ten or more rooms. I would like to see the ABBA create rating systems for each category rather than one category into which all must fit. That way, within what is reasonable to expect and afford, even the smallest B&B could be a five-crown establishment or know what has to be done to aspire to this status. The AAA has modified its expectations so that B&Bs would not have to meet hotel standards that are unrealistic for small establishments. Shouldn't our own organizations do the same?

### THE ABBA AS A MARKETING TOOL

It was clear from my interviews that all the innkeepers who track their referrals agreed that no more than three or four reservations a year were directly attributable to the ABBA guidebook. With so many guidebooks on the market, this one is not working at attracting guests. Innkeepers felt that being able to promote themselves as inspected by an objective outside agency was helpful. Those who participated in the ABBA's cooperative ad in *Country Inns Magazine* felt that they had some return on their investment, but not enough to do this again.

I discussed these issues with Sarah. She has addressed the marketing issues with a new plan to distribute 200,000 "handy, digest-sized, glossy publications" titled *Bed & Breakfast Travel's Companion.* They go out free of charge to auto clubs in the United States, Canada, and Europe; U.S. travel and tourism offices overseas; travel agents through *Travel Agent Magazine*; and through fellow ABBA members. Each ABBA member inn can advertise in this guide for $275, which entitles him or her to 100 words of copy, the rating, and a black-and-white photo of the inn. Six months of advertising in ABBA's new Internet service is included for advertisers (the ABBA's address on the Internet is http://www.abba.com). If you have access to the Internet, take a look.

### THE NEWSLETTER

*Shoptalk,* ABBA's newsletter, often tackles difficult topics and does it well. It is a very positive member benefit. Paul Welton found the issue about dealing with the IRS very helpful, a topic that other groups have traditionally shied away from.

COST: Basic ABBA membership is $300 annually. The cost of inspecting B&Bs necessitates such large dues. Unfortunately, although no B&B is too small to be part of the ABBA, membership is too expensive for many smaller B&Bs.

CONTACT: ABBA, PO Box 1387, Midlothian, VA 23113, (804) 379-2222, fax: (804) 379-3627.

## The Professional Association of Innkeepers International (PAII)

PAII, which is pronounced "pie," stands for Professional Association of Innkeepers International. It is run by Pat Hardy and Jo Ann Bell, former innkeepers with many years of experience in the industry.

### BENEFITS

The benefits of PAII membership are many and include the following:

- *Innkeeping,* their monthly newsletter
- Numerous money-saving discount programs for innkeepers, such as special phone rates and products needed for your inn
- Help finding staff or positions in innkeeping
- A travel exchange program
- Low MasterCard/Visa rates through a nationwide credit card processor
- Excellent research and discounts of 50 percent on their publications
- A fabulous national conference every two years (members get a discount on registration)

PAII conferences and newsletters are very valuable educational tools for anyone who takes his or her B&B business seriously. The conference serves up a menu of fascinating workshops, panels, and classes designed to inform, stimulate, and excite. In addition, it is a great opportunity to meet other innkeepers and share concerns and information.

NEW FOCUS ON SMALLER INNS

At the PAII conference in Reston, Virginia, in 1994, I was surprised and delighted to find that most of the people I met were truly small innkeepers with less than ten rooms, most with five or less. Although PAII originally targeted large inns for its membership base, it has been remarkably responsive to the growth of smaller places and their differing needs. PAII also offers an aspiring innkeeper's kit free of charge upon request.

COST: Membership is $150 annually.

CONTACT: PAII, PO Box 90710, Santa Barbara, CA 93190, (805) 569-1853.

## State Associations

State associations are now established in most states (see Appendix C). They offer their members many benefits. Most inspect their members, have meetings, produce a state brochure, and work with other state tourism bodies to promote B&Bs and small inns. Some have 800 numbers for guests to call for the brochure. Others pool resources to advertise cooperatively.

Certainly, membership in your state organization is a must. I have heard some mumblings about the political nature of state associations and some criticism of those who jockey for power. This can be a problem with any group. However, problems are better solved from within rather than by staying away.

## MAGAZINES AND NEWSLETTERS

***COUNTRY INNS—BED & BREAKFAST MAGAZINE.*** A bimonthly high-gloss magazine for travelers featuring B&Bs and country inns. Country Inns Publications, PO Box 182, South Orange, NJ 07079, (201) 762-4997. Subscriptions cost $19.95 for one year and $35.95 for two years.

***INN MARKETING.*** Publishes issues ten times a year at a subscription price of $47. You can get a trial copy for $5. Write to *Inn Marketing*, PO Box 1789, Kankakee, IL 60901, (815) 939-3509.

**INN TIMES.**  A bimonthly newspaper format, business and financial trade journal for innkeepers and guests. Subscription price is $14.95 a year. Write to Circulation Department, 2101 Crystal Plaza Arcade, Suite 246, Arlington, VA 22202-4600, (202) 363-9305.

**BED AND BREAKFAST: THE JOURNAL FOR INNKEEPERS.**  Begun in 1994 with its November/December issue, this beautiful, glossy magazine is published by Virgo Publishing, Inc. It is intended for the innkeeper, and a subscription is $24.95. Currently, they have a circulation of 15,000. In 1994, the magazine was bimonthly. By 1996, they hope to graduate to monthly issues. To subscribe, contact Virgo Publishing, PO Box 5400, Scottsdale, AZ 85261-9957, (602) 990-1101, or fax: (602) 990-0819.

**COUNTRY INNS YELLOW PAGES.**  An industry resource listing professional innkeepers and where to find information for products and services for the Bed and Breakfast industry. Cost is $20 (softcover, 120 pages). Contact Inn Marketing, PO Box 1789, Kankakee, IL 60901, (815) 939-3509.

**THE YELLOW BRICK ROAD.**  Call (800) 79-BANDB to order a subscription to this monthly consumer-oriented B&B newsletter. It includes inn reviews, consumer issues, and events at various inns. Send information about your inn to them at 2445 Northcreek Lane, Fullerton, CA 92631-1323. Subscriptions are about $40. Gregg Sallee, the associate editor, has written a report on what frequent guests are looking for at your inn. An additional national study of B&B guests includes hospitality issues, amenities, expenditures, demographics, and food preferences. Contact Gregg at (800) 79-BANDB if you'd like a complimentary copy of the newsletter, or if you'd like to buy a copy of the report or the study.

## PROMOTIONS

Each year you will be approached by a variety of people with promotional ideas. Some are one-time-only offers, such as the

Nabisco Company wanting you to offer two nights for the price of one for guests with their special coupon, or a coffee company giving you free coffee for a month in exchange for testimonials. This year, Q-tips did a similar promotion—buy one night, get one night free. You must evaluate the potential for increasing your business and the true cost of participation. Never promise specials during your busy times. If you are giving two days for the price of one, make sure it applies only during the off-season, Sunday through Thursday if your area draws primarily on weekends, or vice versa if you're in a business area. Although new innkeepers find promotions a good way to start out, most established places found them a nuisance.

Entertainment™, a discount club, charges you no fee. They produce a kit that offers their members 25 percent off at participating facilities. Contact Entertainment Bed & Breakfast™ Plus Division, Entertainment Publications, Inc., 2125 Butterfield Rd., Troy, MI 48084, (313) 637-8400.

## TARGET MARKETING

Target marketing is very focused marketing for a certain type of guest. It is often very useful to select a type of guest who will love your inn. My inn has obviously targeted the romantic couple. Our write-up in the *Best Places to Kiss in NY* targets just this market and works very well at filling our most romantic, and most expensive, rooms. Larry Miller at River Run Bed & Breakfast in New York's Catskill Mountains describes his technique as niche marketing. He opened his B&B in an area with many other B&Bs, but carved out a special niche for his. He found it difficult to find places that would accept his golden retriever, so he decided to market to dog lovers. Guests could bring their dog to his inn providing they conformed to his guidelines. He provided a large cage in the room. Guests could leave the dog in the cage during breakfast, but not in the room when they went away from the inn. He was able to advertise in dog-friendly publications and left brochures at veterinary offices in New York City. This strategy was immensely successful in filling his rooms. Despite numerous other B&Bs in his region, he has no competition for his targeted market.

Larry made the following suggestions:

1. Advertise in appropriate places. Target your message for best cost-effectiveness.

2. Bargain if you can with paid media; try to trade room-nights for advertising.

3. Promote interest and excitement through special offers.

4. Focus your effort on the most likely customers.

5. Leave brochures at places most frequented by your niche.

6. Attend niche-oriented events (i.e., for him, dog shows).

## SETTING UP YOUR PRESS KIT

Be careful when putting together any material, be it a business card, a brochure, or letterhead stationery. Think about who will receive it and whether you want to have your address available to unscreened travelers. Cautious hosts often include only a reservation service phone number on business cards and brochures. The reason the security record of reservation services has been so good is that they send hosts screened guests who have made and paid for reservations in advance. These are not the average hotel or motel guests who pull off the road when tired.

When guests call a reservation service to ask for a booking at a specific B&B, that is precisely where the service will try to book them. Your service may have affiliate's cards for your use, or you may have a designer do a drawing of your B&B for personalized cards. Logos are also a popular attention-getting device. Try to get some reliable advice about what looks good. Pen-and-ink sketches of your home usually reproduce well and are very effective eye-catchers. Printing can be quite an investment, so you don't want to have to reprint too often.

Here is a sample business card:

Alexander
Hamilton
House

Barbara Notarius
Innkeeper

(914) 271-6737
49 Van Wyck Street
Croton-on-Hudson, New York 10520

Your cards, however, are only one piece of a press kit. A press kit also contains:

- Your brochure or one-page summary of what B&B is and the specifics of yours. (See pages 159–161.)
- Photographs of the exterior of your house and at least one guest room. Black-and-white photos are preferable to color in case someone wants to reproduce them in a newspaper or magazine article. (As you can afford it, you will want to build a file of professional photos of your B&B.)
- A short (one-page) interview explaining your interests, what has attracted you to B&B, your community involvements, and the like.
- If you work only through a reservation service, an information sheet on your reservation service explaining how to make a reservation.

# Croton-on-Hudson's
# Alexander Hamilton House
### Bed and Breakfast Inn

Westchester's first bed and breakfast, the Alexander Hamilton House, circa 1889, is a stately Victorian home nestled on a cliff above the river, a short walk to the picturesque village of Croton-on-Hudson, gateway to New York's Hudson River Valley.

### Alexander Hamilton House
49 Van Wyck Street, Croton-on-Hudson, New York 10520

(914) 271-6737

Fax (914) 271-3927

### Alexander Hamilton House
49 Van Wyck Street, Croton-on-Hudson, New York 10520
(914) 271-6737    Fax (914) 271-3927

**Directions:**
**By Car:** From Route 9, exit at Route 129. Go east to light at Riverside Ave. Turn left onto Riverside for 1 block. Turn right on Grand St. Go 1 block. Turn left onto Hamilton which intersects Van Wyck right in front of #49. Go down the drive into the parking lot. Climb the porch steps and ring the bell.
**By Train:** Take the Metro North train from Grand Central Station. Hudson line to Croton Harmon Station. 41 minutes on the express train from NYC. If you call ahead, we will try to fetch you at the station.

Brochure for Alexander Hamilton House (*continued on pages 160–161*)

## Accommodations:

* **The Turret Room** — a large light, airy room with queen bed in a turret of five windows with a winter view of the Hudson. Private hall bath.
* **The Garden Room** - a spacious room with queen and day beds, and fireplace, overlooking the front gardens. Private attached bath.
* **The Victorian Suite** - a double bedded room with fireplace, sitting room. Mahogany headboard, marble topped dressers. Private attached bath.
* **The Library Suite** - queen bedded room with fireplace sitting room. Private attached bath. (First floor)
* **The Apartment** - a one bedroom, ground floor apartment with double bed in the bedroom, living room and a full kitchen on one wall, private bath and private entrance.
* **The Bridal Chamber** - our most wonderful third floor suite for special occasions. Please see insert.

## Amenities:

* Air conditioning.
* 35 foot in-ground pool, open Memorial Day through Labor Day.
* Telephones, color-cable TV, and clock radios in each room.
* Full breakfast including; fruit or juice, choice of hot entree of the day or cereal, hot beverages.

## Attractions:

* Historic houses open for touring: Van Cortlandt Manor, Phillipsburg Manor, Sunnyside, Lyndhurst, Boscobel.
* West Point (12 miles).
* Hiking: Teatown, Lake Reservation, the Appalachian Trail, Harriman State Park, Bear Mountain, the Croton Dam.
* Antiquing, apple picking and mountain biking.
* Sailing on the Hudson.
* The Storm King Art Center and Outdoor Sculpture Garden.
* 20 minutes to Westchester's corporate center along I-287.
* 15 minutes to Westchester Medical Center.
* Kykuit, the Rockefeller estate and art center, and the Rockefeller Archives.
* Easy access to New York City - 45 minutes by train.

## For Your Information

* Two night minimum stay on weekends.
* Smoking outside only.
* Well behaved children welcome.
* No pets, please.

Cancellation Policy: All stays must be pre-paid. Personal checks, cash, Visa, MasterCard, Discover and American Express accepted. Cancellations received less than seven days before a stay is to begin require forfeiture of one night's lodging cost per room reserved. Failure to cancel results in payment of entire stay.

# Alexander Hamilton House

**Rates:**

Turret Room and Apartment
  Single $75; Double $95
Garden Room
  Single $75; Double $105
Library Suite and Victorian Suite
  Single $100; Double $130
Bridal Chamber
  Single $175; Double $250 for 1 night,
  $200 for longer stays
Weekly stays - seven days for the price of six.
Monthly rates on request.
All rates subject to N.Y.S. Sales Tax.
10% gratuity will be added to bookings
involving more than two rooms.

  We are a member of:
    The Croton Chamber of Commerce
    American Bed & Breakfast Association
    AAA
    N.Y.S. Hospitality & Tourism Association
    Professional Innkeepers of America

# The Bridal Chamber
## at the
## Alexander Hamilton House

Westchester's most romantic getaway.

  5 Skylights
  King-size bed
  Private bath with Jacuzzi
  Fireplace
  Entertainment Center
  Elaborate Breakfast

Rates $250 for 1 night,
$200 a night for longer stays.

  Rated 4 Kisses in New York's
  Best Places to Kiss '92 & '94.

Alexander Hamilton House

- A copy of one article about B&B nationally.
- A folder to hold these inserts. Your business card should be attached to the front of the folder.

The press kit is what you give to businesspeople who ask for information or to members of the press before they come to interview you or before you appear as an invited expert on B&B. Bed and Breakfast is still a novelty in much of the country, so being a well-prepared spokesperson is a good reflection on the industry.

## Your Brochure

You may not feel that it is necessary to have a brochure describing your B&B. If you accept guests only through your reservation service, it will usually describe your offering in its catalog. But if you decide to create a brochure, include the specialties you offer. This is the place to let guests know all about your inn. Include your breakfast hours and whether you offer a full or continental breakfast. If there are house rules or restrictions, they belong here, too. Your brochure should be a reflection of your style and consistent with the atmosphere of your B&B. Indicate whether you are a member of a reservation service, and if your service is part of Bed & Breakfast Services Worldwide, use Worldwide's logo somewhere on your brochure, since the logo is used in public service pieces about high-quality B&B, and you will want to associate yourself with this group. The same is true for PAII, AAA, and ABBA.

### TIPS ON BROCHURES

1. Make sure your brochure will fit in a business envelope and brochure rack. Plan it to work as a self-mailer. This will save you time and money.

2. Select a color and type style that reflects your inn's image. Make sure the type is easy to read.

3. The location and name of your inn should be at the top front of your brochure, clearly visible to the potential guest scanning a brochure rack.

4. Have rate information on a separate insert so you won't have to reprint your whole brochure each time you change rates.

5. Indicate your cancellation policy.

6. Indicate any restrictions such as no smoking, adults only, and so forth. Don't forget to mention your best features—for instance, suite with fireplace, or full breakfasts include scrumptious hot entrees, homemade breads, and fresh juice. Make guests' mouths water. Include simple directions from the nearest major route. If you have room, a small map is very helpful. Mention nearby attractions.

7. A brochure with one-color ink on a different-colored paper is called a one-color brochure. Two-color brochures use two different-color inks, and four-color brochures are the glossy, full-color ones used by big hotels. One-color is usually more than effective and less costly for a small inn.

8. If you select a paper that isn't white, have your printer make up a sample of the color ink you plan to use on the color paper you have selected. Often, the color of the paper will change the color or the appearance of the ink. You want to catch any mistakes now, not after brochures have been printed.

9. See a proof of your brochure before you okay printing. Catch mistakes before they become costly.

❖❖❖❖❖❖❖

**Question:** There are many off-season periods when very few guests want to come to my area. I am intrigued by the idea of planning special events in association with other B&Bs. What should I expect to do to get this started?

**Answer:** *Talk with your reservation service, travel and tourism bureau, community affairs department of a local college, sports and hobby interests. Most reservation services need a minimum* *of three- to six-months' lead time to properly promote an event in directories or newsletters sent to guest members. Planning such events for your area's slowest season helps even out B&B business for hosts. Successful B&B promotions have included bicycle tours on weekdays, with guests biking between participating B&Bs to see fall foliage; a gourmet weekend, with each participating B&B responsible for preparing and serving a different meal or party; bridge blitzes scheduled for long February weekends (an interesting option for nonskiers bound for ski areas as companions to people who can't be kept off the slopes or for areas where there is no skiing); singles holiday celebrations; tennis tournaments; investors' seminars; and astrology sessions. One hostess I represented offered candlelight dinners for two in her guest rooms during January and February. The only limitations here are your imagination and energy. Reservation services are becoming increasingly skilled at aiding organizers in coordinating complex reservations involving several B&Bs and several events. On-line systems will make special events planning easier, which, in turn, will increase B&B business.*

❖❖❖❖❖❖❖

**Question:** All the B&Bs I read about have names. Is it necessary to name our house?

**Answer:** *It depends on how you plan to get your guests. If you have only a few rooms and plan to market strictly through your reservation service, you are considered a private homestay and no name is necessary. If you have four or more rooms and you will participate in the marketing, selecting a name for your home, and therefore your business, becomes a marketing decision. I created a two-room suite with private bath and sitting rooms with a fireplace that sells for $125 nightly. I asked myself, "What am I selling?" People don't need to pay $125 for a place to sleep. At this price they're looking for romance and are spending the money to provide the ambience. It's not romantic to stay at Barbara's house, so I decided to name the B&B. I couldn't think of a Victorian name that didn't seem overly pompous or*

*wasn't already taken. Since the B&B is at the end of Hamilton*
*Avenue, I thought about Hamilton House. I ran this by a friend*
*of mine who is a publicist. She said, "Hamilton House sounds*
*like a dorm at Harvard. If you're selling romance, the name*
*you pick has to sound romantic as it rolls off your tongue."*
*I responded with, "What about the Alexander Hamilton House?"*
*She said, "Now you've got it." Of course, everyone always asks*
*if Alexander Hamilton ever slept here, and I laugh and tell the*
*story of how we picked our name, since old Alex had been dead*
*for a hundred years by the time the house was built.*

## MURDER FOR MYSTERY LOVERS

Off season, many innkeepers fill the inn with murder mystery
weekends. The guests arrive in time for a buffet-style dinner and
begin to play. They may have been sent descriptions of their
characters in advance so they can come in costume. Play contin-
ues Saturday after dinner and is concluded Sunday after breakfast. Guests leave before lunch on Sunday. The weekend is sold
as a package. Contact Marguerite Swanson at (713) 868-4654 to
find out more about murder mystery weekends.

# 7

# New Marketing Strategies

**R**ecently, a number of existing companies have gone on-line with their databases. A number of new companies are vying to be your route to the Internet. A handful of CD-ROMs are being created to provide B&B guests with up-to-the-minute information, including photos of B&Bs that they can see right on their computer screens, and specialty books for inns appealing to certain market segments have come out. There is even an automated service that works through the telephone and fax machine to get your information out to the public.

## DEFINITIONS

Before I describe individual plans to market your inn, let me share with you some definitions that Dan McClure of Heron Street Publishing was kind enough to share with me.

## CD-ROM

Computer CD-ROMs allow home computer users to tap into large quantities of information from disks that look the same as CDs played on home stereos. Approximately seventeen million home computers were equipped for CD-ROM in early 1995, and the number of potential users is going up dramatically each month. CD-ROMs allow computer programs to include color pictures, large libraries of information, and even short movie clips. They have already been used extensively for educational and entertainment programs and are rapidly expanding into the travel market. CD-ROMs are typically purchased like books in retail stores or by mail order.

## On-Line Services

A number of companies have formed special services that are linked to home computers by telephone lines. Services such as CompuServe and America Online have millions of subscribers and provide a particularly easy-to-use environment for locating travel information. These services can display information about a wide variety of topics, including potential travel destinations. On-line services can include pictures, but it takes more time to display them than with a CD-ROM.

## The Internet

The Internet is similar to the on-line services, but much larger and less structured. Users from around the world can dial into an electronic network where almost anyone can create his or her own special data area. As a result, it is easy to place travel information on the Internet. However, the Internet is still fairly difficult to use, and there is no single directory of services, so many unsophisticated computer users have difficulty finding the information they are looking for.

## The Electronic Superhighway

Many of the big telephone companies are talking about installing fiber-optic cables in homes. The high-speed cables should allow many travel information services to be delivered quickly to the home without fancy computer equipment. It should combine the speed of CD-ROM with the variety of the Internet. The actual implementation of the electronic superhighway is still a number of years away for most parts of the country.

❖❖❖❖❖❖❖

I want to thank Dan for a very clear, concise view of the future. Not having hooked up my modem yet, I'm still a little behind getting familiar with the new technologies. I'm sure by the next edition of this book, we all will be more comfortable with them. Certainly, it is not important even to have a computer to know that many of our customers have them and will be using them to find us.

## AVAILABLE NOW!

The following section will inform you about a variety of marketing resources that are currently up and running but haven't been tested yet. I hope that by the next edition of this book, I will be able to evaluate how successfully they perform for the innkeeper. Please write to me if you want to share your good or bad experiences with the following systems.

*Altair's CD-ROM Guide to Inns and Bed & Breakfasts* retails at $19.95. They expected to sell 50,000 in 1995 in the United States, England, France, and Germany, and they have planned to distribute the CD-ROM in Spain and Japan by 1996. Your inn can be included with a page of copy and a picture for approximately $49.

CONTACT: Valerie Erde, Publisher, Altair Media, Inc., 511 Avenue of the Americas, Suite 391, New York, NY 10011, (212) 255-5506, fax: (212) 255-0027.

*Unique Accommodations*™ *Bed & Breakfast Inns* is a new CD-ROM. It is divided into geographic regions, making it easy to use. Your inn's ad is a full screen in color, complete with copy and a photograph. Ads cost $49, and an additional $30 gets you a twenty-five-word voice-over done by a professional voice-over artist. The CD-ROM sells at retail for $24.99.

CONTACT: Sheilia Thurman at InfoMedia, 4805 Lawrenceville Highway, Suite 116, Lilburn, GA 30247, (404) 923-3788.

*Heron Street Company* publishes particularly complete inn listings on CD-ROMs. Their first is a directory of B&Bs, country inns, and historic hotels on four CD-ROMs divided regionally that are sold individually and as a package. Your information can be listed free of charge. Inns are listed with up to five full-color pictures and can include several pages of copy. There is a small charge of $10 if you want to include pictures. They will be doing other CD-ROMs geared to specialty markets such as skiing, where accommodations are included to let the enthusiast know where to stay. They target both guests and travel agents here and overseas. They accept information year round, which they save for annual updated publications.

CONTACT: Heron Street Company, 31800 Northwestern Highway, Suite 380, Farmington Hills, MI 48334, (800) 474-3766, fax: (810) 626-1034.

***Inns & Outs*™ *International, The Bed & Breakfast Source*** is a complete B&B listing service that makes it easy for potential guests to participate in the B&B/inn experience. They supply detailed information on B&Bs and inns in North America via a cross-referenced on-line database. They currently have information on close to 25,000 properties. There is no charge to be listed with them. There are no deadlines because on-line information can be constantly added or updated. They plan to utilize multiple marketing channels, including the Microsoft network, to get your information to potential guests. A fairly significant marketing budget has been allotted to market their system in major travel magazines and Sunday travel sections of major newspapers and to fund a significant media campaign.

CONTACT: Eric Goldreyer at Inns & Outs International, 2310 West 9th St., Suite 1, Austin, TX 78703, (512) 708-9600, fax: (512) 708-9601. By April, 1996, (800) GO-BANDB, will make it possible for travelers throughout North America to access this database by phone, without a computer.

***The Bed & Breakfast Collection*™** has been producing a four-volume set of guide books covering B&Bs and inns throughout the United States, Canada, and the Caribbean. They now have added a CD-ROM and on-line database to their offerings, as well as a discount buying club for a large range of products particularly attractive to innkeepers. Joining the Bed & Breakfast Collection entitles you to the following member benefits:

1. Inclusion in the next edition of *Bed & Breakfast Guest Houses & Inns of America* (a four-volume national series sold at bookstores, now marketing 14,000 indexed properties)

2. Inclusion in national electronic editions published for travel agents, corporate travel offices, libraries, production companies, governmental agencies, auto clubs, and other interested subscribers available on a CD-ROM and on-line database

3. Quality assurance program that verifies your listing information

4. InnTravel™ Club frequent traveler club for innkeepers and guests that permits members to earn points for each stay that can be redeemed for free airline tickets, car rentals, gift premiums, or lodging at member properties

5. A discount club offering innkeepers 40 to 60 percent discounts off retail prices on national brand merchandise for furnishing, decorating, and operating their properties

6. Full market and media coverage with color photos in the electronic editions and black-and-white photos in printed books

7. Member properties featured in a regular newspaper column exclusively devoted to B&B accommodations. All innkeepers can apply for a complimentary two-line index listing.

The cost of membership begins at $100 for a 200-word description with additional charges for photos ($30 for the first photo, $25 for each additional photo).

CONTACT: Marie Baiunco Brindza, PO Box 38929, Memphis, TN 38183-0929, (800) 431-8258 or (901) 755-9613, fax: (901) 758-0816.

**U.S. Bed & Breakfast** offers an inexpensive way to market your B&B. Each member pays a $175 sign-up fee to U.S. Bed & Breakfast and makes the following commitments: (1) provide seven roomnights a year to a national advertising pool (you can select five months during which you honor the coupon); (2) permit U.S. Bed & Breakfast to offer a 10 percent discount for their referrals; and (3) offer one free night to Public Broadcasting Service (PBS) and National Public Radio (NPR) members after they have paid full-rate for three previous nights. In return, U.S. Bed & Breakfast provides an 800 number guest line. They act as a referral service to B&B properties throughout the United States and provide extensive publicity and promotion services for members in order to generate calls from prospective guests.

CONTACT: Tim Darby, U.S. Bed & Breakfast, 655 Fourth Ave., Suite 11, San Diego, CA 92101, (619) 238-6076, fax: (619) 287-6515.

*The Business Traveler's Guide to Inns and B&Bs* is a guide targeted at business travelers. It is available on a Windows-based computer disk. Their first disk came out in the fall of 1995, and it will be updated every two years. Cost to be included on the disk is $25, and the disk itself sells for $15.

CONTACT: Williams Hill Publishing, RR 1 Box 1234, Grafton, NH 03240, or Lisa Shaw, Publisher, (603) 523-7877, fax: (603) 523-7663.

*The Register* is an Internet guide to B&Bs, inns, and small hotels. Your B&B information and pictures can be available to ten million Internet users on the World Wide Web. Cost is $25 a year for a 150-word text listing, $45 a year for 300 words and one photo, and $65 for 300 words and two photos.

CONTACT: Bruce Murray, TravelASSIST, Assist Information Services, 11054 Ventura Blvd, Suite 109, Studio City, CA 91604, (818) 761-8796, fax: (818) 761-6804, e-mail: bcmurray@netcom.com or http://travelassist.com.

*Retreat & Reveille International* produces a directory advertised in military magazines. They also have had considerable publicity with military newsletters and news media. There is no cost to be in this directory, but you must give a discount to members of Retreat & Reveille. This can be only off-season, midweek, or however you structure your discount program. For $20, you may also join Retreat & Reveille International if you have ever been in the military or are a family member of someone in the military. You will then receive the directory and quarterly newsletter.

CONTACT: Captain and Mrs. Leonard A. Stoehr, U.S.N. (Ret.), 3106 Military Rd., Arlington, VA 22207-4136, (703) 525-3372.

*Inovatec, Inc.,* produces an electronic directory of B&Bs accessible on the Internet. Subscribers to any on-line service, including Prodigy, America Online, GEnie, and CompuServe, are able to access the information stored there by using key words such as *bed & breakfast* to view information and pictures of your inn. The cost of being included here is nominal, $25 for a 300-word description alone, $49 for the description plus a photo, and $99 for three photos and unlimited seasonal changes about area events, special offerings, or rate changes.

CONTACT: Inovatec, Inc., 3604 Galley Rd., Suite 130, Colorado Springs, CO 80909, (800) 473-1980.

*1st Traveler's Choice* is a directory of B&Bs and small hotels that is part of the Virtual Cities, an electronic mall on the Internet. Wanderers on the World Wide Web can access this directory by going to one of ten search engines and typing *Bed & Breakfast.* More sophisticated users can type http://www.virtualcities.com. Innkeepers' advertisements cost $50 a year and include up to 300 words and two pictures. This is the only directory that includes recipes from innkeepers, indexes the directory by language, and advertises inns that are for sale. *Country Inns Magazine* has chosen 1st Traveler's Choice as their Web site.

CONTACT: Lucinda Stone, 1st Traveler's Choice, 300 Montgomery St., Suite 500, San Francisco, CA 94101, (800) 809-7111.

*Bed and Breakfast Inns of North America* is another Internet directory. Your first three months in this guide are free, After that, you pay $15 a month for a page about your inn (usually three or four paragraphs of text and up to three photographs).

This guide can be accessed through any of the on-line directories, search engines, or news groups related to travel. It is one of the smaller guides, having only a few hundred listings, but it is growing rapidly. Their URL address on the Web is hhtp://cimatron.net.

CONTACT: Dan Blackburn, 4516 Lovers Lane, Suite 204, Dallas, TX 75225, (214) 368-6213, e-mail: danny@metronet.com.

*Innpoints,* a frequent-inn-visitor program, is new this year. David Brown, the company's founder, describes his program as similar to the frequent-flyer programs. For $25 a year, guests become members of Innpoints. They get a guidebook that will be updated three or four times the first year and routinely in subsequent years. Between guides, members will receive update sheets for each one hundred new inns that join the group. Each member also receives a quarterly newsletter that will feature special promotions from member inns. When a member stays at a participating inn, he or her receives four Innpoints for each dollar spent. These can be redeemed for TravelDollars that can be spent at participating inns, airlines, and car rentals. The Lacek Group, a specialty marketing company, is developing the awards program.

To participate, inns pay a membership fee of either $50 for PAII members or $139 for non-PAII members, plus an assessment fee of $10 for each room at the inn. Payments must be accompanied by a completed application form. Only inns that have passed a PAII-approved state or national inspection will be accepted. When an Innpoint memeber lodges with you, they earn Innpoints. You, in turn, must pay the company a 5 percent commission and report the stay. If an Innpoint member redeems his TravelDollars by staying with you, you will receive a voucher that will be redeemed by Innpoints at 95 percent of its face value. This program requires a little extra paperwork, because the stays must be reported, but the extra effort pays off since Innpoints should cost innkeepers less than traditional travel agents, and should encourage business travelers to stay at inns more often. In addition, innkeepers who sell memberships to their guests will receive a $5 commission for each sale.

CONTACT: David Brown, Innpoints, 757 East South Temple, Suite 290, Salt Lake City, UT 84102, (800) 466-6890, fax: (800) 364-3335.

**Internet Concepts** offers a free Internet site with a 200-word description of your inn if you are a member of PAII or one of its affiliated state associations.

CONTACT: Stephen Spenser, 1964 Barber Dr., Stouighton, WI 53590, (608) 873-7480, fax: (608) 241-5688, e-mail: http://www. insite.com.

**The Internet Guide To Bed & Breakfast Inns** should be thought of as an electronic guidebook freely accessible to users of the Internet. The *Guide* has already accepted several thousand basic listings of B&Bs across North America. It also has its own home page on the World Wide Web at http://www.traveldata.com/biz/inns. All listings are set up to be simple to use. The aspiring traveler need only enter any desired key words such as state, town, or amenity and all inns that match the chosen criteria quickly appear in a search list. The traveler need only click on each item in the list for more information or click a button to see a color picture of the inn, if available. Basic listings are short and without description. Advertising on the *Guide* gives your inn a considerably expanded listing with a full page of descriptive copy and a color photo of your inn for $16 a month. Your description can include amenities, ratings, and directions and be modified any time to promote seasonal specials or any other changes at the inn. This service is accessed through the various search engines and travel-related forums, cross linking to other travel sites.

CONTACT: TravelData, 172 Stearns Rd., Marlborough, MA 01752, (508) 229-2297, fax: (508) 229-2298, e-mail: jwilner @traveldata.com.

**1-800-BED N BREAKFAST** is a unique system whereby your inn information, complete with photo if you choose, is described or faxed free of charge to the caller interested in traveling to your area. The prospective guest can then call you directly to make reservations. Callers key in the state and area they wish to travel to and receive up-to-the-minute information. Although on-line services will undoubtedly be commonly used in the future, at present, there are many more people comfortable with phone and fax. Try the service by dialing 1-800-BED N BREAKFAST. I think you'll agree that the quality of the fax pictures is excellent.

Jeffrey Gross, the creator of 1-800-BED N BREAKFAST, has budgeted sufficient capital to get this number out in major newspapers and travel publications. Your information is accessible twenty-four hours a day, seven days a week. There is a small, one-time, setup charge for getting your information on the system, and then a monthly charge that depends on how large you want your ad to be. Pricing is reasonable, ranging from $4 to $16 a week.

CONTACT: Jeffrey Gross, PO Box 883, Chatham, NJ 07938, (800) 475-4859, fax: (201) 467-2676.

❖❖❖❖❖❖❖

**Question:** Do I need to have a computer to take advantage of the on-line directories?

**Answer:** *As an innkeeper, you can think of on-line directories as an alternative way to market your inn to those who are on-line. If you have a modem and become comfortable with the Internet, you will be able to converse with other users who are looking for B&Bs, but it is not necessary to be on-line yourself to get calls from people who have heard about your inn on-line.*

*The Alexander Hamilton House recently had a call from a cameraman for an early-morning ABC news program who found out about us on the Internet. He let us know that they like to broadcast the weather forecast from places where people get up early. Three days later, we were on TV about every ten minutes from 6:00 A.M. to 7:00 A.M. You would be amazed at how many people watch TV at that hour and how often they cut to the weather forecast. The weather forecaster showed a number of shots of our pool area, the exterior of the inn, our Hudson River view, interviewed our early bird guests, highlighted our breakfast, and even showed our Bridal Chamber. So far, we received fifty phone calls and booked eleven reservations as a result of that broadcast.*

# 8

# Working with a
# Reservation Service

The leaps-and-bounds growth of private-home Bed and Break-fast across North America is largely attributable to one unique aspect: the professional reservation services. Although it is possible to operate a B&B as an independent host, it is hard to come up with a reason why anyone would choose not to work with a quality reservation service.

## RECOGNIZING A NEED

The industry's pioneers saw the need for private-home B&Bs in America. They founded reservation services to encourage people to open their homes. Each service is an independent business, not a franchise. The founders come from diverse backgrounds. Most are well educated, have worked in service industries in the past, or have been educators.

The grass-roots B&B movement encouraged progress at different speeds in different parts of the country. For the most part, reservation services developed regionally, too. Being close to the homes they represented made it possible for the services to inspect each home and investigate any complaint. Thus, a service could represent high standards and ensure quality control. They knew the attractions of the area as well as the diverse accommodations nearby.

# PRESERVING HOST-HOME INDIVIDUALITY

Reservation services also saw the importance of ensuring high standards without interfering with how hosts managed their B&Bs. The appeal of B&B depends on the individuality of each host home and results from diversity of personality, architecture, and decorating style. At the same time, hosts could agree to provide clean, pleasant accommodations and a hearty American breakfast and to share their expertise about their region with guests. Reservation services thus came to stand for high quality while preserving the unique blends of style, personality, and menu that make B&Bs so attractive.

# SPECIALIZATION VERSUS
# A BROADER APPROACH

I have been to many national meetings of reservation service leaders. The first one I attended was an American Bed & Breakfast Association Meeting of East Coast Reservation Services in Washington, DC, early in 1983. Each of us talked about how to solve the same questions: how to screen travelers, develop host homes, and work with local and state governments to clarify rules and regulations that could affect the growth of this new industry.

As the meeting progressed, it became very clear to me that each reservation service had its own philosophy. One listed only historic homes. Another listed only homes that could accept guests who arrived by boat. Both were a far cry from my broader thinking that a B&B can be a simple room in a normal home convenient to something people want to attend. Others might want something unusual, historic, or deluxe, accommodations interesting in their own right. All, if clean, comfortable, and appropriately priced, would attract their own segments of the traveling public. Although there are still agencies that focus on very specialized travelers (for example, a reservation service that plans canoe trips in conjunction with overnight stays at B&Bs), most offer a wide variety of accommodations.

## REGIONAL LIMITATIONS

Despite the positive aspects of regionally defined reservation services, problems soon developed. Making reservations was complicated. A traveler on an extended trip needed to call a number of services in order to pull the whole trip together. Travelers who read a complimentary article about their local reservation service would call and ask to make reservations at B&Bs across the country. But because of the service's regional limitations, it was forced to refer these travelers to other services without knowing if the referral was acted on by the traveler. Statistics made it clear that most travelers who could not be helped by the reservation service they called did not call a second agency and went back to their traditional way of traveling.

## RESERVATION SERVICES EXPAND THEIR SCOPE

To keep from losing both types of travelers, services expanded their scope from bookings within their own networks to homes listed with affiliate services. Bed & Breakfast Reservation Services Worldwide was organized in April 1985 to set standards that services could agree on, so that each could feel comfortable about relying on others to inspect and follow through on homes that they all would now be sending clients to. To offset the added cost of doing long-distance business, many services became membership organizations, charging a reservation fee or annual membership to guests.

## MEMBERSHIP BENEFITS HOST AND GUEST

Such a membership works out well. Once guests have it, they are more likely to try Bed and Breakfast again rather than traditional accommodations. The more they use the membership, the better the value they receive. The more often guests use a service, the better it knows them and what pleases them, and this knowledge helps the service provide better matches of host and guests. Networking among services also increases the exposure of each host home because services across the country know about them. The reservation fees or membership dues help offset increased telephone costs, and the reservation services involved split the commission for each stay.

## BED AND BREAKFAST: THE NATIONAL NETWORK (TNN)

The National Network (TNN) is the oldest association of reservation services in America. It was established to help each member service market its hosts cooperatively. Members run very professional agencies. They have established cancellation and refund policies that are explained to guests during the reservation process. Members inspect any B&B they plan to represent and stand behind its quality. They take a very active approach to working with travel agents, paying commissions monthly, providing on-line access to information on World TravelFile, and 800 and fax numbers for most members. They even hold regional B&B workshops for travel agents. However, only one TNN member may exist per region. Consequently, there may be other quite reputable reservation services that are not TNN members because the area they represent overlaps an existing member's territory.

## RESERVATION SERVICES BENEFIT HOST HOMES

Reservation services have become a recognizable force in the travel industry through the formation of Bed & Breakfast Services Worldwide. They enable more people to stay at B&Bs and more hosts to do business. The services provide a myriad of benefits to their members, from being advocates of private-home B&B to legislatures, regulatory bodies, and the media, to screening both hosts and guests and relieving hosts of much time-consuming work so that they are better able to enjoy having guests.

## Advocacy

Your reservation service has probably been instrumental in clarifying state and local rules and regulations. Often, reservation services have helped point out inconsistencies between government agencies or conflicting state and local rules. The Alexander Hamilton House fought and won a zoning battle in Croton-on-Hudson that established a legal precedent in New York State for classifying B&B as a "customary home occupation" appropriate in residential neighborhoods. The findings of this trial have been shared with many other B&B hosts across the nation for use in similar zoning cases.

## Education

Services educate hosts by running seminars and holding meetings to keep them up-to-date on issues relevant to the growth of the industry and their individual businesses. In addition, as part of their publicity efforts, reservation services have educated the American public about the joys of B&B. This has created the demand that is helping the industry grow rapidly.

Education also includes sending guests tips for being a good guest that stress the differences between a B&B and a hotel. A sample of this type of educational piece  appears on the following page.

Public service messages written by Bed & Breakfast Reservation Services Worldwide are educating travelers about staying at a B&B for the first time. Guests unfamiliar with the more personal nature of B&B will understand and comply with respect and sensitivity toward hosts and fellow guests alike. This is very important as the industry's client base becomes broader.

Services also conduct regular seminars to encourage prospective hosts and to stimulate travelers to use B&Bs. These seminars answer questions about start-up and management and keep hosts up-to-date on new regulations that may affect them. Slides and photographs of host homes are prominently featured at such meetings.

## SAY YES TO BEING A GOOD GUEST

*Book Early:* You will have your choice of places to stay. Reservation services have business hours. Make sure you call during those times. Otherwise, you will probably have to call again or accept a collect call.

*Call Ahead:* Your host needs to know when to expect you. In private-home accommodations, hosts have many outside activities and no staff. It is very frustrating to have to stay at home all day waiting for a guest to arrive who hasn't had the courtesy to call ahead. Try to call at least forty-eight hours in advance. Your host will be ready to welcome you.

*In Case of Delay:* Call to let your host know your change in arrival time.

*Find out about Breakfast:* Let your host know if you have any special requirements, food preferences, or allergies. Different hosts have different rules about breakfast hours. It is a good policy to check at arrival with your host to determine when breakfast is served.

*Beds:* Always indicate your preference about type of bed, and let your reservation service know if anyone is over six feet tall. Most antique beds have footboards that can cause considerable discomfort for tall sleepers.

*Respect Other Guests:* If you are sharing a bath, tidy up after yourself so the next guest finds the bathroom as clean as you did. Make sure to bring a robe, since even B&Bs with private baths very seldom offer access to the bath without leaving your room.

If you come in late, remember that others are already asleep, and keep your voices down.

*Deposits:* Deposits are always necessary to reserve a B&B. Hosts often have only a few rooms, and holding a room for someone is taken seriously. Your deposit shows that you are taking the reservation seriously, too.

*Balance of Payment:* Expect to pay any balance due plus applicable sales tax upon arrival in cash or traveler's checks.

*Cancellations:* If circumstances force you to cancel a reservation, don't delay in informing your host and the reservation service. When booking, check to see how far in advance you can cancel without paying a penalty. Most places will charge at least a day's cost for cancellations made after designated dates. Certain places have no-refund policies at special times of the year.

*Get to Know Your Hosts:* They are an important reason you've chosen B&B travel. They know their locale well and are happy to share their expertise with you.

*Send Back Your Evaluation Form:* Reservation services use these for ongoing quality control and appreciate your reactions. By giving the service your feedback, you help it serve you better.

*In Return for Being a Good Guest:* Your hosts will extend a warm welcome, personal attention, and gracious hospitality at reasonable rates and help make your stay a memorable one and travel an enriching experience once again.

If you belong to a reservation service that belongs to the trade association, you will benefit from the power in numbers it represents. Whereas one person or family may have a difficult time getting the ear of someone in government, the media, or big business, a network that represents fifty, a hundred, or more citizens with similar interest can achieve its goals more easily. For example, by pooling our numbers nationally, we, as member B&Bs, have access to low-cost liability insurance. Legislators see us as a voting bloc. Suppliers of linens and other goods see us as a purchasing bloc. It is important to be united and well organized in good times. That way, when there are difficulties for the industry, they can be faced together by a group already clear about its goals and usefulness to the public.

It is only by having strong organizations supporting and representing their interests that individual B&Bs can have the power to fight other interests that seek to hamper their growth and success. For example, in 1986, the California Inn Association complained to the California Office of Tourism that private-home B&Bs should not be represented in state tourism literature compiled by the California Lodging Association. On behalf of the Bed & Breakfast Reservation Services of California and their member hosts homes, Susan Morris, Executive Director of Bed & Breakfast Reservation Services Worldwide, wrote a letter to the California Office of Tourism explaining both what reservation services do for the traveler and how B&Bs fill a need that brings more visitors and tourist dollars into the state. This was only the start of a unified drive to make the California Lodging Association understand that Bed and Breakfasts are also part of the lodging industry.

## Promotion

As any reservation service will tell you, promotion never stops. Each year, services conduct local campaigns that are responsible for numerous features about Bed and Breakfast on radio, on television, in the newspapers, and in magazines. Often, this involves encouraging travel writers to use B&Bs, so that they, in turn, can introduce new audiences to the concept. Reservation service representatives may attend travel industry conferences and seminars for the same reason. Press releases are sent regularly to hundreds of newspapers, magazines, and radio stations. Most reservation service directors have also become extremely skilled at presenting the B&B story to business groups, civic associations, and professional groups and at giving interviews and appearing on talk shows.

One reservation service spends over $1,000 annually on dues for membership in various chambers of commerce, convention and visitors' bureaus, B&B associations, business owner organizations, and other groups.

Cash outlays for direct advertising are also considerable. Each year, many thousands of dollars are spent to follow up on articles written about B&B and make sure prospective guests know how to find us. This involves distributing brochures and directories in response to inquiries and maintaining an up-to-date mailing list of people interested in B&B. Postage and printing alone (not to mention design, editorial, and layout) can cost more than $10,000 a year.

All this activity has put B&B in the public eye. Major stories have appeared in the following media (to name but a few):

- The *New York Times*

- *New York Daily News*

- *Chicago Tribune*

- *Woman's Day* magazine

- *Ms.* magazine

- Gannett Newspapers (*USA Today*)

- CBS TV

- NBC 6 and 11 O'Clock News in New York

- Cable News Network

- Independent News Network

- *Readers' Digest*

- WGY and WMCA radio

- The BBC

## A COURTEOUS AND CONSCIENTIOUS OFFICE STAFF

Your reservation service provides a courteous and conscientious office staff to answer inquiries and match guests to host homes during regular business hours. A new service may start as a very small operation with part-time hours in the home of the director. As it grows, a staff is hired and adjusted to meet the seasonally fluctuating demand for accommodations. These are the people who take a lot of the clerical drudgery off your hands. They are there to answer calls so that you can lead a normal life and not worry about missing business.

You should have an answering machine, so that the service can leave messages for you. You should answer these messages promptly because usually the service has only twenty-four hours to get back to a guest with a commitment about his or her reservation.

### Correspondence

The service staff is also responsible for dealing with mail, processing deposits, and getting confirmation letters and fees out to you and your guests. When an effective promotional piece is published, hundreds of letters can pour into an office. Many just want general information about B&B, but all have to be answered. Any time you want to volunteer at your reservation service, your help will be gratefully accepted.

### Credit Cards

Your reservation service can accept credit cards. This is important because when reservations are made at the last minute, the stay can be guaranteed by credit card payment, ensuring that your room will be paid for and the cancellation policy enforced if the guest does not show up.

## Screening

Reservation services take steps to ensure that guests are reliable. The vast majority of B&B travelers are lovely people, but the screening process occasionally discloses unacceptable guests. For example, one caller gave Bed & Breakfast U.S.A. a prestigious Park Avenue address but admitted, when questioned further by the staff, that this was his mother's address. He gave his mother as a reference, so before arranging the booking for him, the service called her. She said we would have to take him at our own risk. Needless to say, we did not accept him.

Similarly, the reservation service is sensitive to hosts' attitudes. This is a major reason home visits are mandatory before a reservation service accepts a new B&B. This procedure is costly and time-consuming, but it is essential in assuring the public of the quality that services represent. Although it doesn't happen very often, there are some prospective hosts who are so insensitive to the needs of the guests that they do not belong in B&B. One prospective host asked me if it was really necessary to have anything to do with the guests. His house was beautiful, but his attitude was inconsistent with the B&B philosophy of gracious personal hospitality.

## ONGOING QUALITY CONTROL

After a host is accepted by a reservation service, guests are sent rating sheets to be filled out and returned to the service at the conclusion of their stay. (See the following page for a sample.) This provides constant follow-up. Hosts often learn how to improve their service as a result of guests' comments. However, this information is not usually shared with hosts directly because most guests don't want to seem ungrateful. Also, this monitoring sometimes points out the need to make another home visit. If problems persist, a host is dropped.

## Sample Rating Sheet
### *(Courtesy of B&B Rocky Mountains)*

THANK YOU FOR STAYING WITH US! Your comments are valuable to us and help us provide the type of Bed and Breakfast accommodations you want. We hope to see you again. Please do tell your friends about us. Please return this form to our office after your trip.

Your name _____ Host _____ Dates _____

**Host Home** (1 is poor; 10 is excellent; please circle one)

| | | | | | | | | | | |
|---|---|---|---|---|---|---|---|---|---|---|
| Cleanliness | 1 | 2 | 3 | 4 | 5 | 6 | 7 | 8 | 9 | 10 |
| Comfort | 1 | 2 | 3 | 4 | 5 | 6 | 7 | 8 | 9 | 10 |
| Cost | 1 | 2 | 3 | 4 | 5 | 6 | 7 | 8 | 9 | 10 |
| Convenience of location | 1 | 2 | 3 | 4 | 5 | 6 | 7 | 8 | 9 | 10 |

**Host**

| | | | | | | | | | | |
|---|---|---|---|---|---|---|---|---|---|---|
| Courtesy | 1 | 2 | 3 | 4 | 5 | 6 | 7 | 8 | 9 | 10 |
| Friendliness | 1 | 2 | 3 | 4 | 5 | 6 | 7 | 8 | 9 | 10 |
| Helpfulness | 1 | 2 | 3 | 4 | 5 | 6 | 7 | 8 | 9 | 10 |
| Breakfast | 1 | 2 | 3 | 4 | 5 | 6 | 7 | 8 | 9 | 10 |

**Reservation Service**

| | | | | | | | | | | |
|---|---|---|---|---|---|---|---|---|---|---|
| Courtesy | 1 | 2 | 3 | 4 | 5 | 6 | 7 | 8 | 9 | 10 |
| Promptness | 1 | 2 | 3 | 4 | 5 | 6 | 7 | 8 | 9 | 10 |
| Accurate information | 1 | 2 | 3 | 4 | 5 | 6 | 7 | 8 | 9 | 10 |

Would you stay with these hosts again?   Yes/No

Would you tell your friends about us?   Yes/No

Additional comments _____

_____

_____

_____ Please send information about gift certificates

_____ Please send information to the travel planner at my business:

Name _____

Address _____

City/State/Zip _____

Telephone _____

Company _____

I learned about staying at B&Bs from a member host _____

_____ or another way (specify) _____

_____

## COSTS OF REPRESENTATION

Belonging to a reservation service is not costly once you realize how much work is being done for you. For example, at the American Country Collection, new hosts pay a $50 registration and membership fee the first year and $25 in subsequent years. The registration fee in the first year helps offset some of the cost of making the home visit. A 20 percent commission is paid on each booking made through the service or resulting from its advertising or public relations efforts.

Membership dues and the amount of the commission may vary slightly from service to service. Commissions usually range from 20 to 30 percent. The charge for $1 million of insurance is currently $225 a year for up to three rooms and $50 a room for more than three. This insurance has a $250 deductible and does not cover elevators or chair lifts. Liability insurance on an individual host home without this group policy could easily cost over $1,000.

## SELECTING A RESERVATION SERVICE

There may be only one reservation service that covers your region, or there may be many. You may not have to choose only one. Very few services are exclusive, and each understands that it may not be able to send you guests as often as you would like. Not all reservation services are equal. To decide whether a service can really help you function more efficiently and/or increase your business, ask some questions of the director before having a representative slate you for a home visit and interview. To help you do this, see the sample questionnaire on the following page.

If the answer to many of these questions is yes, you may be ready to apply for host status. (See the sample host application shown on pages 189–191. It was used by Bed & Breakfast U.S.A., Ltd.)

## Reservation Service Questionnaire

|                                                                                                  | Yes | No |
| ------------------------------------------------------------------------------------------------ | --- | -- |
| Does the service inspect all member homes?                                                       | ___ | ___ |
| Does the service promote each B&B?                                                               | ___ | ___ |
| Does it maintain a business office with regular hours for telephone service and an answering machine? | ___ | ___ |
| Does the service help you determine the price to charge for your rooms?                          | ___ | ___ |
| Does it set and enforce a cancellation policy?                                                   | ___ | ___ |
| Is the reservation service quoted often about B&B in favorable press coverage?                   | ___ | ___ |
| Does it collect money (deposits) from guests?                                                    | ___ | ___ |
| Does the service share knowledge about pertinent B&B regulations in your state and area?         | ___ | ___ |
| Does the service offer a group liability insurance policy for members to purchase?               | ___ | ___ |
| Does it sponsor events for members to meet and to improve their hosting skills?                  | ___ | ___ |
| Does the service encourage networking by publishing newsletters or other communications?         | ___ | ___ |
| Does the service belong to Bed & Breakfast Reservations Services Worldwide, the trade association that sets standards for the industry? | ___ | ___ |
| Does it have a computer hookup so that travel agents can gain access to all its listings, including your B&B? | ___ | ___ |
| Does the service have a reputation of consistent, courteous treatment of hosts and guests?       | ___ | ___ |
| Will the service provide you with the names and telephone numbers of two or three current hosts as references? | ___ | ___ |
| Does the service revise its directory of host homes often enough to keep up-to-date with new listings and new developments at established homes? | ___ | ___ |
| Does the service check with the host before booking each guest?                                  | ___ | ___ |
| Does the service offer special purchasing plans for linens and other items necessary for doing business? | ___ | ___ |
| Does the service offer member hosts a waiver of fees for booking reservations at other B&Bs of similar courtesies? | ___ | ___ |

## Sample Host Application

NAME _____

PHONE (_____) _____-_____

Street Address _____ City _____ State ____ Zip _____

Mailing Address (if different) _____

Members in household (if any children, include ages) _____

Will you accept children?  Y  N  Smokers?  Y  N  Do you or any member of your family smoke?  Y  N  Do you have pets?  Y  N  If yes, what kind? _____ How many? _____ How long have you lived in this home?_____ the area? _____ Where did you hear about us? _____

DESCRIPTION OF HOME: TYPE (e.g., Victorian, Colonial, etc.) _____

Year built _____ Describe (include unique features) _____

_____

_____ (Attach photos)

Circle extras in home (not guest rooms): PIANO, AC, TV, CABLE TV, VCR, POOL TABLE, POOL JACUZZI, FIREPLACE, OTHER _____

LOCATION OF HOME BY CAR: Mins. to heart of nearest city? _____

What city? _____ Mins. to nearest restaurant? _____

How long to airport? _____ Train station? _____ Blocks to city bus? ____

Do guests need car?   Y  N

List attractions nearby within drive time: _____

_____

HOST INFORMATION

Host Occupation _____ How long? _____

Company? _____ Work phone _____

Spouse occupation _____ How long? _____

Occupation _____ How long? _____

Company? _____ Work phone _____

If retired, please give former occupation and write "retired" next to it.

What are your hobbies and interests? _____

_____

Have you traveled B&B?  Y  N  Where? _____ Breakfast you'll serve:

Full or Continental (circle one) Sample menu _____

---

USE THE FOLLOWING ABBREVIATIONS TO FILL IN THE CHART BELOW.

SIZE OF BED:  K (king),  Q (queen),  TBD (twin bedded double),
      S (single bed).

TYPE OF BED:  M/B (mattress & box spring),  Sofa (sleeper couch),
      P (platform bed),  WB (waterbed),  C (canopy),  4P (four-poster),  B (bunks),  T (trundle),  H (highriser).

BATHROOM:  PA (private attached),  P (private access in hallway),
      Semi (share with one other room),  SB (share w/other guests),
      SF (share w/family).

BATH:  S (shower),  T (tub),  C (combined shower and tub).

PLACEMENT OF ACCOMMODATION:  1 (lower level—stairs down),
      2 (first floor—no stairs),  3 (upstairs 1 flight),  4 (apartment
      building—indicate which floor and E if elevator building), also
      indicate DM if doorman building,  5 (3rd floor and private home).

AMENITIES:  AC (air conditioning),  TV (black-&-white TV),  CTV
      (color TV),  K (kitchenette),  suite (includes sitting room),
      R (rollaway),  crib (laundry facilities), canoe or boat,  HT (hot
      tub),  S (sauna),  D (deck),  PE (private entrance),  UnH
      (available unhosted),  FP (fireplace in bedroom),  LK (lock on
      bedroom door),  J (Jacuzzi),  P (pool).

| ROOM | SIZE BED | TYPE BED | BATHROOM | BATH | PLACEMENT | AMENITIES |
|---|---|---|---|---|---|---|
| A | | | | | | |
| B | | | | | | |
| C | | | | | | |

If you have more than three rooms, please indicate above information on a separate sheet.

ADDITIONAL THOUGHTS: Will you have complimentary beverages (coffee, tea, etc.) available for guests?  Y  N

Do you currently belong to any reservation service that sends paying B&B guests to you?  Y  N

If so which? _____ On a separate sheet of paper, please provide a detailed description of how to get to your home from the nearest highway or airport (if applicable). Locate your home on a map (hand drawn is OK or use a phone book map of the area). Be on time for interview (circle preference) Weekdays/Weekends  AM/PM

I understand that this application is only part of the information the service requires to evaluate my request for host membership. A visit by a member of the staff will take place before an agreement is authorized. My $20.00 nonrefundable interview/application fee is enclosed. This fee will be applied toward my first year's membership fee if accepted as a host. The balance of my year's membership is due when the host contract is signed if accepted at the host visit. I understand that thereafter the service will be entitled to a 20 percent commission on all guests it sends.

Signed _____ Date _____

## THE HOME VISIT

To prepare for the home visit, the first thing you should do is relax. Bed and Breakfast hosting is a two-way street. Reservation services want good new hosts; they need the hosts' hospitality as much as the hosts need the services' marketing. The purpose of the home visit is for the reservation service to meet you and see what you've done with your home so that it can represent you accurately to prospective guests. You will be providing a very personal service, after all, as a joint venture with your reservation service. Both parties should feel comfortable with each other and be fully informed about what each will provide. Your house should be clean, pleasant, and ready to receive company. Set the table for breakfast for two, and make it attractive. Welcome the interviewer as you would a guest. The interview gives you a chance to ask questions and clarify day-to-day operations with the service representative. The goal always is to keep alive the personal-referral aspect of this business that has made it so successful. Enjoy your chat.

The reservation service representative will check the information you have provided in the host application and help you set rates. Together, you will write a listing describing your B&B and detailing your house rules for the reservation service to use in material they publish about your place. They may also photograph your home so that the staff members who will be talking about it to travelers will be able to speak almost firsthand.

## PREPARING YOUR LISTING

Your listing is a written description of your B&B. It should include the style of your home, what places of interest you are near to, a little about your family, details of the accommodations, and the rates. Any special features or restrictions should be included so that prospective guests can easily get a sense of what it will be like to visit your home. Here are some sample descriptions.

**Host #17.** WALTON (New York, a rural location about 3 hours to New York City)—A chalet-style home on 200 beautiful acres with a large pond. A rowboat, pedal boat, and canoe are available. Fishing for rainbow trout, turkey hunting, and bow hunting. Host is retired but busy with gardening, making toys, and producing maple syrup. Hostess does tole painting, canes chairs, and makes quilts. Hostess will gladly baby-sit. This place is a nature lover's paradise. In December, guests can cut their own Christmas trees; and in spring, they can help sugar the maples. When snow is plentiful, guests can cross-country ski right on the property, then come inside to get warm in front of the huge fireplace. The wooded area is a bird-watcher's delight, and the fall leaves are breathtaking. Hostess is a wonderful cook (from scratch) and enjoys using her imagination. This B&B is only 15 minutes from Delhi State College. Accommodations include: (a) large room with a double bed, three single beds, TV; (b) large room with a double bed, two single beds, one cot, TV. Guests share a bath. Smoking outside only. No pets. Children are welcome if well supervised (because of pond). Rates: Single $30, double $45 daily; single $150, double $210 weekly. Children under 2, free; extra persons in room, $10 each.

**Host #006.** THE ENCHANTED COTTAGE (Gold Medallion) (Amish Country, Bally).
GUESTHOUSE for 2: $100 per night. 2-night minimum stay.
CORPORATE MID-WEEK for 1 or 2; $80 per night.
CORPORATE LEASE for 1 or 2: $900 p/mo; $6,300 p/yr.
RELOCATION 31-NIGHT RATE for 1 or 2: $1,150.
    Escape to a childhood dream: In a clearing in a dark wood there is a two-story Cotswold cottage straight from the pages of *Hansel & Gretel* (but with all the modern comforts), charmingly furnished with antiques and hand-made pieces. Meant just for two, downstairs there is a living room with antique wood-

burning stove and an efficiency kitchen; upstairs the bedroom with full-size bed and bath.

Find a welcoming *Tea and Tasties* or *Cheer and Cheese* downstairs on your arrival. Your kitchen larder can be stocked for breakfast or you may have breakfast served in the "Woodcutter's House" nearby, before an open fire or al fresco, depending on the season.

Dinner can be found nearby at a first-class inn—a short walk down a winding narrow country road that passes by pastures, fields, and woodlands.

Historic sites nearby include Daniel Boone's Homestead, Hopewell Village (an authentic restoration of an ironmaster's compound), and Victorian St. Peter's Village on the spectacular French Creek. There is antique and flea market shopping in many nearby villages. Skiers will be 10 minutes away from Doe Mountain Ski Area.

**Host #44.** LEE, MA—An 1854 Victorian home in top-quality condition. Fireplace in living room, outside garden, patio, located two blocks from the town square, 8 miles to Jacob's Pillow, cross-country skiing 5 miles, 4 miles north of the Rockwell Museum, 5 miles to Tanglewood. Accommodations include 4 double-bedded rooms with shared bath. Continental breakfast, children over 9 welcome. Smoking limited to certain rooms. No pets.
RATES: 6/1–10/31 weekday $65, weekends $85; 11/1–6/1 weekdays $45, weekends $65.

**Host #38.** NEW YORK CITY—E. 47th St. (Near 3rd Ave.). A luxury studio apartment in a doorman, elevator building. Queen bed, queen sofa, antique dresser, table and chairs in large room along with color cable TV, phone with answering machine, fully stocked kitchen, and private bath with Jacuzzi. Close to U.N., walk to theater, museums, shopping, and public transportation. No smoking or children.
RATES: $125 daily.

Although your reservation service representative can write the description for you, your input will make it better. The important thing is to include enough to give the reader the right impression, yet be concise. Always make sure to include the size of the beds and the type of bath. If you have a piano, pool, tennis courts, or any other special features, put them in capital letters so that a reader skimming for such items will notice them. This type of description will be needed for your service, directories, and your brochure, so take your time with it. Ask someone who writes well to edit it. If anything changes at your B&B, make sure to let your service know so that the change can be reflected in your listing.

## THE HOST CONTRACT

Once you have been accepted by a reservation service, you will be asked to sign a host contract that spells out your legal responsibilities and those of your service. It should define your roles, indicate whether or not your approval is needed before bookings are made, and spell out commissions expected, the cancellation policy, host family responsibilities, guest responsibilities, telephone policy, rates, key policy, return bookings and referrals, and conditions for terminating the contract. Usually, written notice by either party is enough to cancel the contract, but commitments to take guests hold until the visit is past.

## DAY-TO-DAY RELATIONS

In general, your reservation service is working every day to promote your B&B. A staff member will inform you that a particular guest is interested in staying with you and confirm that you are willing to accept this individual (and members of his or her party). If the reservation is for quite some time in the future, you may hear from the service by mail, but this is increasingly uncommon as B&B becomes better established.

Requests for reservations are considered pending by the service until a host accepts them. Guests are usually told to call back in a day or two to find out if the reservation has been approved by the host. At that time, a deposit is requested. At each stage until the check has been received and the confirmation sent out, the staff monitors the status of the reservation. It follows through on guests who fail either to call back after requesting a reservation or to send their deposit. Staff members know that it is very costly for a host to hold a reservation for someone who may not come. On rare occasions, especially during the busy season, an incomplete reservation can fall through the cracks because answering a ringing phone always takes priority over checking through files. If you are not certain that a reservation is definite, alert your service that you haven't received your confirmation. The staff will appreciate it.

Guests want to know fairly soon if their reservations have been confirmed, so much of the reservation service's business is done by telephone. You should let the service know the best times to contact you to save time and expense all around, and an answering machine is a must.

If you are going to be closed for a period of time for any reason, notify the service as far in advance as you can. You will not be penalized for taking breaks from hosting as you choose.

## GET TO KNOW THE STAFF

The staff members are people whom you should know personally. If you live close enough, stop by to introduce yourself. The better each person knows you and what type of B&B you have, the better he or she can represent your interests. Understand that there may be turnover. As new people come in, it behooves you to get to know them, too. Invite them to spend a free night at your house.

## IN CASE OF EMERGENCY

Emergencies do happen once in a while. Guests understand that they are coming to a private home, and they are unlikely to want to visit a house that has become a full-fledged infirmary. In such cases, your service will try to find a substitute B&B for your guests, and you will forfeit any money received or promised for this booking. If they are touring and cannot be reached in time, the reservation service may ask you to direct them to the alternative B&B when they call you for directions. However, this would be highly unusual.

Cancellations on the part of the guests are also handled through the service. A statement of the cancellation policy should be included with the written confirmation notice sent to guests when reservations are made. Reservation services realize that you have gone to some expense and effort to freshen the guest rooms and have made plans for or already purchased the food to serve for breakfast. Therefore, you and the service split the cancellation fee according to the normal commission percentage. If the fee for last-minute cancellation is one night's cost, you will get this amount minus your service's percentage. If you have already been paid for the stay by the reservation service, you will have to send the money back to the service so that it can send the guest the appropriate refund.

If a guest arrives and finds your place unacceptable because something is not as it should be (your pool is not functioning; your children have chicken pox), this is a just cause for cancellation, and the guest's money will have to be refunded.

Sometimes the situation is not so clear. For example, one of my hostesses lived in a historic home with a small cottage on the property. She rented the cottage to year-round tenants but also took B&B guests in two beautiful bedrooms in the main house. The guests arrived Friday night and could not take a shower because there was no water. In the morning, there was still no water. They liked the hostess but during breakfast said they had to leave because it was not acceptable that they had a private bath but no water. It turned out that the tenants had gone away for the weekend and left a toilet running. This was taking all the water from the old well system, leaving insufficient pressure in the line to get the water up to the second floor of the main house. The guests called our service and asked for a refund of the entire weekend because they had to make other, more costly and inconvenient arrangements at the last minute. We felt they were justified and hoped to persuade them to try B&B another time, so we asked the hostess to return the full amount. This was a judgment call; the service felt that the situation was one the hostess would have to resolve before we sent other guests. The hostess could have insisted on being paid for the night they stayed because they used the room and ate breakfast, but she agreed with us and refunded the money. When you work with a reservation service, such problems must be resolved as they arise. However, you must agree in principal to refund or not as the service sees fit; otherwise, the service will stop representing you.

Sometimes a guest's stay will be cut short by a family or work emergency. In these situations, the guest is expected to pay for one more night than he or she has stayed. For example, a guest who had to leave on the third day of a five-day stay would pay for four days and get one day's refund. If the guest is someone who stays with you often, you may prefer to give him a rain check for another visit. Offering a credit at the same B&B usually appeases an irate guest who claims not to have known about the cancellation policy or gives a host a way to offer something in lieu of refunding the additional nights. When a guest wants to use this credit, it must be a time when the host has the room available. It is important to put a time limit on a credit so that it expires if not used within twelve months.

At special times of the year, certain places enforce no-refund policies without exceptions. This is especially true of locales with one very active season or a few major events, such as college graduations or an annual festival.

Remember, the reservation service does double work for cancellations and loses money on them, too. The service does all it can to prevent them, but they are part of doing business with a growing clientele.

❖❖❖❖❖❖❖

**Question:** If the reservation service lists my B&B in its directory, won't that make my place open to the public?

**Answer:** *No. The listings are never identified by name or street address. A reservation service's directory is usually available only by subscription or to those travelers who are members of the service. The only way anyone can contact your B&B is through your service. That contact sets in motion the screening and matching process that is the service's function. You benefit by having the attractions of your B&B (and your own interests)* *highlighted without having to leave promotional materials in public places. Of course, any errors or changes in your listing should be communicated to the service at once to avoid disappointments.*

❖❖❖❖❖❖❖

**Question:** If I wanted to offer a special Singles Christmas next year, how should I go about having my reservation service promote this?

**Answer:** *Write up a description of what you are offering. It should appear in service newsletters up to six months ahead of time to give guests a chance to make their holiday plans. Realize that this type of event is best done annually so that people who find out about it this year but can't attend can plan for next year. Here is a sample description written for just such a weekend:*

*A host is offering her home for a Singles Christmas. It begins Christmas Eve with a buffet supper and caroling by the piano or pump organ in front of the fire. Each guest is asked to bring a gift suitable for someone of either sex (value under $10). Gifts are opened on Christmas morning after a hearty breakfast. Then enjoy sports, games, or reading before Christmas dinner, which will be served with all the trimmings. A fix-it-yourself supper will be available from leftovers in the kitchen. Breakfast the next morning is included. The complete cost is $200 per person for two nights. Up to fourteen can be accommodated if people are willing to share rooms. The property is an 1865 farmhouse on 100 acres, ten minutes to Cornell and Ithaca College. Skate on Cayuga Lake. Ski Greek Peak or Song Mountain thirty minutes away. Two cats are in residence. To reserve, call the reservation service.*

# 9

# Operating Smoothly

## TAKING RESERVATIONS

**Y**our phone is a key element in the reservation process. Good phone manners, a pleasant phone voice, and an organized questionnaire kept by the phone are required. DeeDee Marble of Governor's Inn in Ludlow, Vermont, gave a wonderful seminar at the Philadelphia PAII conference entitled "Turning Every Telephone Call into a Reservation." When I returned from the conference, I typed up my notes about telephone tips and put the sheet in the front of my reservation book by the phone so that any of my family or staff would answer properly. One tip that I thought made a lot of sense was never to seem disorganized. If you don't have a pen by the phone when it rings, don't say, "Hold on. I'm looking for a pen." Say, "Could you please hold on for a second while I get my pies out of the oven?" or some equally graphic image conjuring up illusion. I will never forget the day I came in the door to find my eleven-year-old telling the guest to hold on while she took her pies out of the oven. I picked up the phone and the guest asked about the pies.

Make a reservation sheet similar to the sample shown on the following page that will leave room for all the guest information you will need.

## YELLOW PAGES

If you plan to do any of your own marketing, it is important to make sure you have a business line so that you can be listed in the Yellow Pages. It is surprising how many calls we get from the Yellow Pages. Just by having a business line, the phone company gives you a free listing. Make sure they put it in the Bed and

### Barbara's Phone Sheet

Date _____

Last Name _____ First Name _____

Address _____

Street                Apt.    Town              State      Zip

Telephone _____ Home _____ Work

Price Range _____ Date of Arrival _____

Date of Departure _____ Arrival Time _____

Car or Train    # People _____    # Rooms _____

How heard about us  _____

---

Type of Bed:  K  Q  DB  TT  S  Suite  Other _____

Special Needs _____

Ages of Children  _____ Bath:  P  SH

Smoke:  Y  N  (Smoking outside only)    Pet Allergies  Y  N

---

Entered in Reservation Book _____ Date Confirmed to Guest _____

Guest Will Call Back:  M  T  W  TH  F

Told Cancellation Policy: Y  N **(if you cancel less than 7 days before the stay is to begin, one night's lodging will be deducted from your refund for each room booked.)**

---

Cost: Rm #1 _____ + Rm #2 _____ + Rm #3 _____ = Cost per night _____

Number of nights x _____

Room cost $ _____

Tax (AHH) 6.75% or (NYC) 8.25% _____ x Room Cost $ _____

Occupancy tax 3% _____ x Room Cost $ _____

Total Due $ _____

---

Total Payment

Amount Deposited _____ Date Received _____

Balance Due _____ Date Received _____

Type of Payment: Check _____ Visa/MC # _____

Exp. Date _____ Approval # _____

Breakfast section. Consider also paying for an ad in the Yellow Pages serving the nearby area that you find is home to most of your guests. (For me this would be Manhattan.)

## ANSWERING MACHINES

No one at a small inn can answer the phone every minute. Please make sure your message conveys the flavor of your place as well as a positive attitude and asks the potential guest to leave his or her name, phone number, and convenient time to be called back. When you return the call, be apologetic for being unavailable when they called and happy to assist with their travel planning. Always offer to send a brochure even if they are looking for a different type of accommodation or location for this trip. You want to include them in your next mailing and interest them in your place for their next trip.

In New York State, and, I imagine, most other states, the phone company has an answering service you can subscribe to. The monthly fee is small, but there is an additional small charge for retrieving your messages. I have mine set to pick up on five rings; meanwhile, my answering machine will pick up after three rings. What the phone company service does for me is to answer when I am on the phone. The caller doesn't hear any ringing; instead, my voice comes on to say that I'm on the other line and will call back shortly. I have chosen this because I hate call waiting, whether I'm the caller or the one being interrupted, and I don't want callers to get a busy signal and decide to try another inn. I am able to get right back to them and not miss any reservations. I have been surprised at how many of these messages I get. I hate to think about the business that was lost before this service became available.

## 800 NUMBERS

The decision is still out on 800 numbers. Certainly, the prices have gone down and the innkeepers who have them think that they distinguish their inns from the competition. Most innkeepers in areas that are not highly competitive don't see the need for an 800 number. Remember, with an 800 number the inn pays for the phone call. Since many guests are only window shopping, the 800 number encourages less-than-serious inquiries.

## KEEP THE EXPERIENCE REWARDING

You can keep B&B a rewarding experience for you and your guests by avoiding the most common pitfalls that can short-circuit a good time for all. Guests report dissatisfaction to reservation services when their reasonable expectations go unfulfilled in three basic ways:

- Confusion about arrival time and directions to the B&B

- Cleanliness of the bedroom, bath, or kitchen

- Advertised features that were not functional at the time of the visit

## AVOID CONFUSION ABOUT
## ARRIVAL TIME AND DIRECTIONS

Once guests have committed to a reservation, it is important to decide on a mutually agreeable arrival time and to make sure that they have clear directions to your place. It is reasonable to expect a two-hour window during which guests plan to arrive. It is usually necessary to explain to guests why the arrival time is so important to you. We let guests know that we need to be able to do things such as run out to the market and don't want them to arrive when no one will be there to greet them. If they are running very early or very late, they need to call from the road to let us know. Alas, guests who forget to do this often leave you waiting for long hours, and it is hard to greet them with a happy face when they have had no regard for the value of your time. Brenda and I try to alternate weekends now that we have trained a small staff of teenagers to clean rooms on Saturdays, Sundays, and school vacations. We have a two-night minimum on the week-ends, so our Saturday or Sunday check-ins are rare. This being the case, off-season, we ask Saturday and Sunday arrivals to check in around noon or after 6:00 P.M. This actually leaves us a few hours to enjoy life. Most guests understand and cooperate. Under unusual circumstances, such as planes or trains arriving in mid-afternoon, we make accommodations. In season, we get too many drop-ins wanting to look at the inn to leave it unattended.

## Tips on Giving Directions

When giving directions, be exact. Go out and drive the route(s) into your town from the major thoroughfare(s), and write down the mileage for each portion of the drive. Remember, you are giving directions to people who are probably unfamiliar with your region, so give the simplest route rather than the fastest. But try to send guests along scenic routes whenever possible. Watch for landmarks a stranger might be able to identify at first glance, and mention them in your directions. Indicate when the guest may have traveled too far or made an incorrect turn at a difficult intersection. For example, if you get to the Taconic Parkway, you have gone too far. Drive the route both during the day and at night, and note any differences for the benefit of late-arriving travelers. Tell people where it's okay to park, and make sure your parking area and walkway are unobstructed and well lit.

Directions may be mailed, faxed, or given over the phone for last-minute reservations, but unless the directions are very short, it is most time-effective to mail or fax them.

Post a train or bus schedule near your business telephone so that you will be able to answer questions about service when guests call. Keep the numbers of the taxi and car rental companies there, too, and be able to give guests an idea of how far you are from the station and what the taxi fare should be.

Remember, if you are not home, another family member may answer the phone. So make sure that everyone is briefed on giving directions, answering questions, and getting an approximate arrival time from the guests. Put the guests' name and arrival time on your calendar so that someone is home to welcome them.

Remind guests to phone in case of delay so that you will not be worried about them.

In major cities with good public transportation, guests may want to use it. Keep a transit map handy, and use the system yourself often enough to know the basics of getting to major attractions in town from your B&B.

## Arrival Times

If your schedule is such that no one is home during the day, it is fine to set specific hours for arrival, but be sure to make it clear that it won't be possible for your guests to get into the house prior to this time. If you are delayed, or if the guest is late and you must leave to keep another commitment, you should have a standby system worked out with a neighbor or friend so that someone will be on hand to greet the guest. Lateness should be rare if your directions are good and your guests are motivated to arrive at the agreed-on time.

Even in an unhosted B&B, someone is usually present to show the guest where things are and handle any financial business at the outset of the stay. Of course, if other members of your family are willing to do the greeting, the guest will not be left waiting, regardless of whether you have a cooperative neighbor. This is one situation you need to work out ahead of time with your family. When your guests arrive, you will also have to give them their key and explain your home's security system (if there is one). One kind of excitement that no one looks forward to is an uninformed guest mistakenly tripping an alarm and being mistaken by the police for an intruder.

## PROVIDE CLEAN, ATTRACTIVE ACCOMMODATIONS

There are simple daily procedures for running your B&B that will keep things on an even keel no matter what your scale of operation. These are the very things that, if neglected, are sure to spoil the fun of your business. With B&B offering such enrichment and enjoyment, it makes sense to take timely care of those routine matters that mean so much to guests. You may find that you want help from other people to keep everything in ready-for-guests condition all the time, or you may find that maintaining your home in top condition is exactly what you like to do yourself because it brings you great pleasure to invest your time and personality in your B&B activities. You may also find that concentrating your attention on your home (if you have been accustomed to working away from home or haven't really looked at your home as a place of business in the past) leads you to follow pursuits that turn out to have a direct, positive impact on your business. Gardening, flower arranging, gourmet cooking, taking courses in interior design, woodworking, restoring antiques, or upholstering, or studying another language may become fringe benefits that make you a more versatile host and contribute to the beautification of your home.

Arriving guests expect to find a clean room with fresh sheets and towels, a fully equipped and sparkling bathroom, and clean and attractive public rooms and yard. In the vast majority of cases, your guests want to consider your B&B their home away from home and expect to do basic cleanup themselves, providing the articles to do so are at hand. Many hosts feel that for a stay of less than a week, there is no reason to enter the room at all until a guest has departed unless a guest room has special maintenance requirements such as a fireplace. Guests make their own beds (or not) as they see fit, take fresh towels and place used ones in the hamper or laundry room, and clean the tub and washbasin after they are finished in consideration of others who are also using the bathroom. All these are tasks most people would consider usual to do in their own homes. I personally prefer to make up beds, dry towels, check to see if there are empty glasses or dishes to be brought down, and give the bathrooms a wipe-down whenever I pass by. I also check to make sure that there is soap in the dispenser, tissues in the tissue box, enough toilet tissue, and so forth.

To some extent, what guests expect is determined by how costly your accommodation is. If you are offering luxury accommodations in the $100-plus range, you will be expected to provide more extras and certainly do all daily maintenance.

Another factor to be considered is how long the guests are to be with you. Guests who stay more than a week expect that you will clean their room, change the sheets and towels, and perhaps add some fresh flowers or a fruit basket (a nice thank-you for a lengthy booking). Cleaning includes both dusting and vacuuming. The guests should be told a day ahead of time that you will need to be in their room for an hour or two (enough time to wash the sheets and air the beds) in order to accomplish this. This will give them a chance to tidy up personal belongings and let you know what they might need.

We once had a couple come from overseas for the birth of their daughter's third child. They stayed three weeks and four days. We found them wonderfully amusing individuals and enjoyed their stay with us very much. On the second day, I popped my head into their room and saw a large suitcase propped open on my Victorian sofa. I told them that once they were unpacked, I would be happy to place their luggage in the attic so that they would have much more living space. Well, they lived out of that suitcase for their entire stay, never hanging anything in the closet or utilizing the dressers' considerable drawer space. Personal things were spread all over the marble-topped dressers, and even though I told them each week about my cleaning day, I was never able to clean off the furniture. Vacuuming and changing the linens were the best that could be done. These people were on vacation and chose to live this way. Forcing them to be neat would have been an invasion of their privacy and would have made them feel uncomfortable. Sometimes, the best you can do is close the door and your eyes. Other guests are so neat that they make their beds even on the day they leave. You know that this is just what they do at home.

Always clean up and change sheets immediately after guests leave so that the room is ready for new guests. Do this even when you are not expecting new guests. Often on a Sunday after a houseful of weekenders have departed, I am tempted to leave the mess till Monday. It almost never fails that someone calls from within the community to discuss their daughter's upcoming wedding and to have a look at our rooms to see if they will want to place wedding guests here. The frantic race to get the house in order reminds me always to be company-ready.

## LONG-TERM GUESTS

Eventually, you will get a request for a long-term guest— perhaps an executive on temporary assignment for three months, a teacher brought in to finish the school term for someone who is on leave, or a couple waiting for their house to be completed. Long-term guests often become part of your extended family. They will want laundry privileges, may help out with the dishes, walk the dog, baby-sit for your child, or barter some of their professional services for a reduction in room costs. Any experienced B&B host can recount numerous stories of antique clocks restored to working condition, family portraits photographed, a quilt made, or cooking lessons given in exchange for lodging. These very personal reminders of guests-become-friends are treasured long after the visit has ended. For many hosts, these encounters with other interesting and talented people are the major reason for their involvement with B&B.

## CONTINUAL UPKEEP

If you have lived in your home for years, take a good look at it from the outside as well as the inside. What do you see as you drive up the street? Does your house need a new coat of paint? Are your bushes overgrown? What impression will your guests get as they follow your directions to the parking area and step inside your home? Remember that you are trying to get some distance from your personal perspective and see your home as a stranger would. Day-to-day cleaning and making breakfast never stop, but certain routine maintenance or freshening up must be done seasonally or as needed. Pretend that you have just bought your home. Evaluate what needs to be done to bring its general condition up to snuff.

## Saving on Maintenance

When we moved to our home in Croton-on-Hudson, B&B was part of our strategy to make living in our dream house a reality. We had an energy audit, insulated our attic floor, put storm windows on our sun porch, and installed insulating draperies. My ex-husband was good with his hands, and between us we could take on many of the projects that others hire professionals to do. Saving on the cost of outside labor was tremendously helpful to our budget, but projects took longer because they had to be completed on weekends and in the evenings. Needless to say, you have to enjoy the work as well as the results and have a great deal of commitment and determination to keep up the momentum. We found that it was necessary to work on a project for no longer than three months at a time and then take at least a month off before doing anything else on the house. Schedule vacations and times when you have no house responsibilities to give you a breather and renew your strength before tackling a new project.

We began by making a list of maintenance jobs such as cleaning the gutters, caring for the lawn, and draining the radiators. Then we decided which chores we would hire help for. We decided lawn care was more efficiently done by a gardener, leaving us free to tackle the jobs where very skilled labor would cost us dearly. We put regular tasks on our calendar so that they wouldn't get lost in the shuffle.

Then came the list of special projects. It is always necessary to start by making a list of the projects you want to complete, estimating their cost and the time needed to complete them, and setting priorities. Remember, best estimates for cost and time are usually wrong but nonetheless help you make plans and execute them.

Once the work is completed, your home will require constant maintenance. Paint needs to be touched up; sheets need to be replaced before they become frayed or shabby.

Before you open your B&B, your public rooms should be finished, the outside of your home should be appealing and well maintained, and the guest rooms should look warm and inviting.

If your goal is to fix up three rooms for guests, it may be wise to start with one. Then, as your business grows and you get the feel of this way of life, you can finish additional rooms. Some of the hosts I have met have photographed their homes during restoration and transition and keep this album both for their own enjoyment and sense of accomplishment and to show to interested guests. Many guests are in the process of restoring their own homes and enjoy exchanging solutions to problems encountered along the way. Don't, however, assume that all guests want a blow-by-blow description of everything you have done.

## DECORATING OR REDECORATING

Like maintenance, decorating or redecorating your house to make it a more attractive B&B is an ongoing process (see the following pages). In choosing a decorating style, turn again to your reservation service for guidelines about what travelers in your region expect. Within the boundaries of what qualifies any room as a standard accommodation, you should aim for something distinctive that reflects your own personality and interests or something unique about your home or area. Emphasize comfort and convenience, the former for your guest's benefit, the latter for yours. If you have a collection of something lovely, the guest room may be the place to display it. If you are interested in upgrading a simple room into a higher category, review the characteristics of an executive accommodation on pages 50–51, and spend your money on those features that will return your investment sooner, such as a small private bath, a set of sliding doors to a small patio, a pullman kitchenette across one end of the room, a sauna or hot tub. The room may need something as simple as new bedspreads and curtains or something as elaborate as a complete architectural renovation. The hosts I know run the gamut from people who just added a few items to their ordinary rooms to those who purchased faded mansions and restored them to resplendent condition specifically to open a B&B. (For some of their stories, see Chapter 14, "Interviews with Successful Hosts.")

The Alexander Hamilton House exterior

## Garage Saling, or I Can't Believe I Filled the Whole House!

I would like to share with you the suggestions that I followed in finding the treasures that make guests ask me if my family has lived here for generations.

A seven-foot couch for $100, a carved Victorian dresser for $25, a service of fine china for ten for $150—these are just a few of the things I have found at garage and estate sales. You, too, if you have some weekend mornings to spare, a list of your furniture needs, and an adventurous spirit that enjoys the thrill of the hunt, can acquire many one-of-a-kind items at a fraction of their retail prices to make your B&B very special, indeed. Here are a few tips, the results of many an enjoyable weekend.

1. Shop in the best neighborhoods. Get a good map, and use it to explore expensive areas. People with a lot of money often don't know the value of what they have to sell. They will often price things according to whether or not they like them.

The master suite at the Alexander Hamilton House

Alexander Hamilton House sunporch breakfast room

Alexander Hamilton House pool

The bridal chamber at the Alexander Hamilton House

Alexander Hamilton House living room

2. Favor places that are run by the owners rather than pro-fessional salespeople. Professionals hike the price by 25 percent. But it is also worth getting to know the profes-sionals because they can look out for certain things that you've had trouble finding.

3. Set limits for yourself in advance so that you will know if something is in your range and then you won't be tempted to overspend. This is especially important for auctions.

4. Certain things are easy to reupholster using a staple gun; others need professional attention. It is wise to know the retail cost of a new piece of furniture and what reupholstering will cost before you bring home a bargain sofa and find you need to spend $1,000 plus fabric to reupholster it.

5. Take some risks. For example, if you think that no one else will want or have a place for some item, submit a low bid (a final offer that you will pay), and ask the

owner or salesperson to call you if it is still available and he or she is interested in selling at your price. Sometimes this gets you a real bargain.

6. If you don't see what you are looking for, ask. Sometimes this will remind the seller of a piece that was too awkward to bring downstairs.

7. Sellers seldom expect to get their asking price. Don't be afraid to offer less and negotiate.

8. Dealers try to get there early. If you are serious, emulate them. They can't afford to pay what you can because they have to mark up the items for resale.

9. Garage sales are not consistent. Realize that you often go to ten bad ones for every terrific one. When you find yourself at a bad one, just count that as one step in your quest. As in any treasure hunt, there are many detours and dead ends on the way to the trove.

Good luck!

## HANDLING SPECIAL FEATURES OF YOUR BED AND BREAKFAST

You will probably include certain special features of your home in your B&B description. If you do, guests will expect to have access to them. Therefore, if something prevents the use of a special attraction, it is very important that guests be told about the problem in advance. Understand that they may choose to make other plans, in which case you will owe them a complete refund because cancellation policies do not apply when a host home cannot offer what it claims to. If an attraction is seasonal—for example, your swimming pool—make sure to specify when it is open. Guests visiting during a hot Indian summer weekend in late September may be disappointed to find that your pool closed on Labor Day. It will protect you to be able to show that the Labor Day closing date is listed in your printed description.

Of course, use of special features may require special rules for guests, rules that you are responsible for telling them as well as posting for consultation if you are not at home. Do not assume that guests will know how to use your facilities. Special instructions will be required for use of your fireplace, pool, hot tub, sauna, spa, weight training equipment, sound system, VCR, laundry facilities, microwave, office machinery, and the like.

A welcoming letter in each guest room letting guests know which facilities in your house are available for their use and if there are any limitations or special precautions th~t must be taken is very useful and will be appreciated. Because every B&B is different, what you will include in your letter may be very different from what I put in mine. A farm B&B might need to give a map showing the walk down to the paddock to meet the horses and tips about which horses like apples and how to offer the apple with the hand open, so the horse takes only the apple, not a nibble of fingers, too. You might set a one-apple limit for each horse so your guests don't overfeed them while trying to be nice.

A host with a VCR and a collection of old movies will want to provide instruction for using the machinery as well as how the films are arranged. Directions and the phone number of a nearby video store might be included so that guests can take advantage of a rainy afternoon to relax and catch a film they have wanted to see.

## Fireplaces

The romance of a crackling fire on a cold night is an unbeatable attraction for many getaway-weekend guests. If your fireplace is in a public room, have the fire ready to start, and let your guests know how to open the flue and light the fire. If guests are arriving in the evening, it is very welcoming and cozy to greet them in front of a toasty fire.

If the fireplace is in the guest room, assume your guests will want to use it. Lay the first fire yourself, and leave extra wood close enough so that guests can keep it going without disturbing their privacy or yours. Show guests where the fire extinguisher is located (preferably in the guest closet). Ask them to call you immediately if there's the slightest problem with the flue or any other aspect of the fireplace (such as the screen not closing properly or smoke in the room). If guests are staying more than a day or two, show them how to clean out the ashes, or ask them to let you know when you can go into the room to take care of it. Ashes can impair the draw of your fireplace if the buildup is considerable, and their smell can permeate the entire house very quickly.

### FIREPLACES RENT ROOMS

If ⏶ romantic setting is what your guests crave, a room with its own fireplace is highly desirable. Until recently, the cost of a masonry chimney made installing a fireplace in the bedroom too costly to justify return on investment. The advent of the zero-clearance fireplace makes it possible to add fireplaces to many of your guest rooms. The fireplace can be wood-burning or gas and is very inexpensive, only a few hundred dollars, depending on size. Rather than a masonry chimney, zero-clearance fireplaces use an insulated metal cylinder that is boxed in and made to match the exterior of your home. This mock chimney starts at the fireplace level and goes to ten feet above your roof line. It does not start at ground level. If you select an antique mantel, understand that most bedroom-size mantels have only a thirty-six-inch opening. You will need a certain distance between the opening of the fireplace and the mantel. A company called Superior makes a small fireplace that will fit this, and you can get great discounts here if you are a member of the B&B Collection. For larger places, a company called Majestic is good. You can also check your local fireplace stores to see these products.

### WHAT ABOUT WOOD?

Plan to have your chimney sweep service the fireplaces each year, and think through your policies on wood. In my opinion, it is bad form to expect guests to arrive with firewood in hand, yet I have heard from guests about innkeepers who do just that. When guests arrive at the Alexander Hamilton House, they find their fireplace set and ready to go. There is enough extra wood to make a second fire or keep the first one burning for several hours. Each day wood is replaced. This is included in their room rate. Should they need additional wood beyond what we provide, we charge $10 for an extra wood delivery. When ordering wood, shop around. You want it to be seasoned (not freshly cut) so that it will burn easily. Make sure to provide kindling as well as some newspaper. We have also included fire-starting bricks, which make even the most inexperienced fireplace user an instant success. These are available at your warehouse buying club at very reasonable cost.

### THE DRAWBACKS

In-room fireplaces do cause some problems. Number one is dust. Fireplaces create lots of ash, which, once blown into your guest room, looks like dust. It is necessary to check rooms more often; the room you dusted and vacuumed this morning may need to be cleaned again this afternoon.

In addition, you need to give very detailed instructions to guests to prevent them from doing very stupid and potentially dangerous things. Should a guest fail to open the flue, you may have smoke detectors going off at 2:00 A.M. Guests need to be told not to remove burning logs from the fireplace under any circumstance and to call you should anything look wrong. Always get wood for guests yourself. Do not let them go get it. You would increase your liability if they tripped carrying an armful of wood. Needless to say, they also think that if you let them get wood once, they can do it any time and as often as they like. Wood is not free in most parts of the country. Don't be stingy with wood, but don't let all your profits go up in smoke.

## Pool Safety

As long as you have a private-home B&B that does not fall under special state or commercial regulations, you usually do not need a lifeguard at your pool. Check your state and local regulations. If there is no lifeguard, it is up to you to ensure safety at poolside by establishing rules and providing life preservers and life jackets for young children and nonswimmers. It would be wise for someone in your family to know cardiopulmonary resuscitation (CPR), lifesaving, and how to give mouth-to-mouth resuscitation. Any course you take will be both practical and tax-deductible.

During the swimming season, establish a routine for testing the pool water and adding chemicals to it. Try to do this at a time when few people would want to swim. Let parents know that children are not allowed at poolside without a responsible adult present. Make sure any nonswimming child wears a life jacket at poolside, even if the youngster is not planning to go in the water. Make sure anything served near the pool is served on plastic plates or in plastic glasses. Glass can shatter by a pool, and even though you sweep up carefully, a stray piece of glass could become lodged in someone's foot.

Keep a first-aid kit handy and an extra bottle of suntan lotion in case guests forget theirs. It's very thoughtful to have some sun-block lotion, especially for babies, and make sure that there are some shady umbrellas for adults to sit under while they supervise the children.

Most locales have rules about fencing around a pool. Few, though, have rules about pool covers. Make sure that your pool is safe in the winter as well as summer by having a safety cover, keeping your gate closed, and telling parents that no one is allowed near the pool when it is closed.

## Laundry Facilities

As an innkeeper, you decide whether laundry will be done in-house or sent out to a commercial laundry. Most small inns do the laundry on-site. Commercial washers and dryers are not necessary, but having large-capacity machines is essential, and having two dryers makes it possible actually to finish your laundry at a reasonable hour.

Even guests who stay only a day or two may need to wash out something. Guests who stay longer will need access to a washer and dryer. It makes it very comfortable for guests if the hosts provide information about what they are free to use. If guests are sharing a bath, it would be embarrassing to hang stockings or undergarments over the tub to dry. Let guests know that they can hang up a few articles in your laundry room, or offer to include some of their things with the family wash.

I have instructions posted next to my washer and dryer, but I try to be there the first time guests use the machine so that I can answer questions and make sure they understand how to clean the filters. Because I do so much laundry on a routine basis, I make sure guests understand that household laundry has priority. In the case of long-term guests, I expect them to purchase their own laundry soap and bleach; otherwise, I do not. I keep the iron and ironing board in the extra linen closet on the guest room level of the house and happily set it up for guests who need it.

Other hosts set up their laundry rules differently. A hostess who has a number of relocating executives as long-term guests does their laundry and is paid extra for the service. How you handle laundry is up to you. The important thing is to realize that many guests have laundry needs and that you should be the one to initiate the discussion. The last thing you want is for a guest to wash out undergarments and hang them to dry on your antique wooden headboard.

## MAINTAINING YOUR SATISFACTION

Hosts become dissatisfied when guests' expectations are unreasonable. Most commonly, this happens when guests fail to sense the line between the kind of service they can demand in a hotel and the attention to which they are entitled in a private-home B&B. In general, the more expensive your accommodation, the more hotel-type service people tend to expect. Even when you do not bill yourself as a luxury B&B, you may find yourself being asked to cross this line.

### Setting Limits

Along with making guests aware of what they may do, it is always necessary to make any limits clear. For instance, if you permit smoking but restrict it to certain parts of your home, these limits must be spelled out. In addition to including this information in any literature about your B&B, you will want to be very clear about it in your welcome letter. You may want to mention your breakfast hours, how much notice is required for candle-light dinners, or anything else that a guest needs to know.

## Telephone Use

Guests need access to a telephone. In small B&Bs this usually means a phone that guests may use in a spot offering some privacy. One way to provide this phone without worrying about guests running up long-distance bills is to provide a courtesy phone. It is best if this phone has its own line, so that your guests don't tie up your incoming line and keep other important calls from getting through. The Courtesy phone is provided free of charge to innkeepers by a firm in Texas. They surcharge the user for long-distance calls paid for by their credit card, and you receive a 40-cent commission for each call.

At larger inns, providing in-room telephones is becoming more and more important. It is essential if you hope to have business guests and will save you countless experiences of having to pad down the hall in your robe and slippers because someone's baby-sitter needs to get through in the middle of the night.

We made the decision to install in-room phones two years ago and have not regretted it. We earn about one-third the monthly cost of the phone lines from the courtesy phone people. The rest is an expense that is more than justified by our increase in weekday business, not to mention the decrease in wear and tear on the innkeeper. I'm much cheerier in the morning after getting a full night's sleep. Should you be interested in this phone system please call me at (914) 271-6737, and I'll be happy to refer you to the supplier.

AT&T also has a program for inns whereby they pay a commission to the innkeeper. The advantage of the AT&T system is that they don't surcharge the caller. The disadvantage is that you must purchase the phones.

If you go the route of giving each guest room a phone, I suggest also providing an answering machine. If you buy them on sale, they are inexpensive, under $30 for each room, and they are very much appreciated by guests. Remember also to give each guest the number of their direct line when confirming their reservation. This way they can leave their private number with important people at home who will contact them directly should the need arise.

## YOUR HOME OFFICE

Whether your home office is an entire room or just a desk in the corner of your family room, it should be the one place where you keep all your business-related things. It should include:

- Your guest book.

- Receipts.

- Checkbook specifically for this business. Keep your personal account separate so that you can keep good track of your B&B expenses and income.

- Sales tax form folder.

- Envelope or cashbox for receipts for business expenses.

- Manila envelopes for reservation information and other communications with your reservation service (saves extra telephone calls).

- A calendar to mark the dates you are booked, the number of people in each party, and which rooms they will be staying in.

- Business cards.

- Business stationery for letters to guests or media.

- Correspondence notes with business logo or name for short notes to upcoming guests or thank-yous to others who help you with your business.

- Christmas cards or other holiday cards to send to former guests.

- Postage scale and stamps.

- Telephone answering machine.

- Scratch pads, pens, pencils, tape, eraser, mailing labels, scissors, and stapler.

- Typewriter (makes correspondence look professional when you enclose a cover letter with your press kit). But avoid typing personal notes to guests; a handwritten note is a nice touch in these days of electronic everything.

- Home computer for financial record keeping, recipe storage, and so on.

- Floppy disks and software.

- Books, periodicals, course outlines, and notes dealing with running a B&B or small business in general. A set of reference cookbooks is also a good idea to help you enliven your breakfasts.

- Copying machine—not essential, but handy.

- Fax machine. This is not essential, as you can send and receive faxes through your local copy store. If or when you can afford it, fax machines are more and more useful for everything from sending out directions and confirmations to making it more convenient for business and international guests to receive information from colleagues.

## THE RARITY: A TROUBLESOME GUEST

If you accept only guests who have been screened by your reservation service and have prepaid for their stay, most of them will cause you no problems. But on rare occasions, you will have a troublesome guest. When this happens, you must evaluate the problem. A guest whose personality is not to your liking but who is not disruptive to your home or interfering with the enjoyment of other guests is just someone who will be there a short time and then easily forgotten. If a guest disrupts your home or interferes with the enjoyment of other guests, you must handle the situation immediately. Take the guest aside, and speak to him or her about why what they are doing is disruptive. If necessary, ask this guest to stay somewhere else. It is up to you under these circumstances to determine whether it is appropriate to refund the payment for the balance of the stay. Certainly, if a guest is violating house rules by smoking or has smuggled in a pet, you are under no obligation to refund anything. If guests have become intoxicated, are having a loud argument with each other, and have awakened other guests, ask them to quiet down. Under no circumstances should you get involved with a drunken, hostile person. In such a case, wait until morning, and ask the guest to leave. Rest assured, however, that most hosts have never had occasion to do this.

## LANGUAGE PROBLEMS

If your B&B is attractive to foreign guests, you will eventually have folks staying with you who understand little or no English. One such booking occurred at my B&B this winter. A young Italian man staying in town with relatives called to book a pair of his friends who were coming in from Italy the next day for an indeterminate stay. The friend living here spoke a little English. The new arrivals spoke none, but carried a dictionary. Business was very slow, and we were happy to have guests coming.

Once they arrived, we found out how difficult they were going to be. They were young men who preferred to play until the wee hours of the morning, sleep most of the day, expecting breakfast served close to noon or beyond at a moment's notice before their ride came to take them out for the next evening's revelry. Although we painfully worked with the dictionary and charades and the use of their friend as interpreter, it was difficult to convey house rules, and we felt that they were purposely pretending not to understand us so that they could continue to smoke in the bathroom and annoy other guests with noisy late-night arrivals.

The last Saturday night they were here, the guests in the next room were so annoyed at having been disturbed by the rude behavior at 3:00 A.M. that they turned on their radio at 7:00 A.M. and went down to breakfast, leaving the radio on facing the room of the loud young guests. I think the boys finally got the message. Unfortunately, it was at the expense of really nice guests who didn't deserve being awakened in the middle of the night.

This was perhaps more an example of the rare, difficult guest, but communication with those who speak a foreign language must be addressed. Try to build into your library some paperback foreign-language dictionaries and phrase books. French, German, Spanish, Italian, and Japanese should certainly be the core. Even if you can't pronounce the foreign-language equivalent, having the dictionary or phrase book allows you to point at the English and have them read in their own language the translation. If one particular nationality frequents your B&B in increasing numbers, consider having your confirmation form translated and putting down house rules in that language also. Many tourist attractions now print their literature in other languages. Have these on hand. Last but not least, enlist your friends who are fluent in other languages. Speak to them about helping out if you are having trouble communicating.

## SEPARATING HOME FROM WORK

Burnout is common in the service industry when people become too involved in their businesses. It is important when you work at home to make time for privacy, family activities, and visiting with personal friends. Sometimes, especially during your busy season, the outside stimulation of meeting so many interesting people may make you forget to maintain your relationships with friends and the community. Don't allow this to happen to you. Schedule vacations. Plan activities out of the house, and enjoy them. Although you may become very involved in your B&B-related activities and in being a pioneer in a new industry, don't let B&B become the only thing you talk about. Remember, the most successful hosts are interesting to guests because they lead rich and exciting lives.

❖❖❖❖❖❖❖

**Question:** What about house rules for pets? Our two dogs are pretty accepting of others, and we have a fenced-in area for them. They sleep outside in a dog house except on the coldest winter nights, when we put them on a screened-in porch. Our town strictly enforces a leash law; the first offense costs the owner $25, the second is $50, and every one after that goes up to $100, plus the costs of having the animal boarded at the local police station impoundment area ($15 a day). Also, there is a local ordinance requiring owners to clean up streets, sidewalks, and green spaces after their pets. Will I be responsible for pets of guests staying with me? What if a visiting pet damages furnishings in my home or, worse yet, damages a neighbor's garden or menaces a child? I know my dogs very well and have spent a great deal of time training them well. How can I be sure visiting pets will behave? Am I responsible for providing pet food?

**Answer:** *If you want to take pets, you will have a large clientele. Consult with your attorney and insurance company about correct clauses to put in your guest contract covering the situations that you have mentioned. Accepting pets will probably increase your potential liability. Have a frank discussion with the owner before the pet arrives. The guest may decide that the regulations will interfere with other plans for the visit and choose instead to board the animal or hire a sitter to care for it at home. Ask about the animal's training. It is wisest for owners to bring their animal's customary food along rather than switch its diet on a trip. Guests need to know that they are fully responsible for seeing to the care of the pet unless you arrange otherwise in advance.*

*Establish a relationship with a good veterinarian in your area in case a pet should fall ill during its stay with you. Think carefully about where you will allow the guest to bring the pet on your premises, and tell the guests exactly what you allow. Many people traveling with pets fully expect that the animal will be allowed to sleep in the guest's bedroom, perhaps in the bed. Many people with pets allow them the full run of their own homes and do not realize that others would never dream of allowing a cat on the beds or upholstered furniture.*

*Finally, realize that other guests will be coming during the same period. If they have allergies and have chosen your B&B because you have no cats of your own and you allow a cat to come, it may spoil their whole vacation. Remember, you have agreed to provide for the comfortable hospitality of all your guests.*

*For these reasons, most hosts, even true pet lovers, seldom permit guests' pets.*

# 10

## Increasing Profitability

This chapter is intended for innkeepers who need to take a fresh look at their operations and marketing techniques. It is easiest, of course, to continue to operate the way you always have, but it is often necessary to reexamine your ways if you want to increase revenues or decrease costs.

Income at the Alexander Hamilton House has increased over 850 percent since 1982. This doesn't happen by accident. So before you decide that none of these techniques will work at your inn, read them carefully with an open mind.

To increase profitability, it is necessary to increase revenue, decrease costs, or both.

### INCREASING REVENUE

### Increase Occupancy

#### HONE YOUR MARKETING PLAN

Review your current marketing plan. Most computers allow you to enter referral information on each guest. Even if you do record keeping by hand, keeping track of where your reservations come from is essential.

*Where Do Your Current Guests Hear about You?* I was surprised by the results. Close to 12 percent of my guests came from the AAA and another 14 percent came from local referrals and past guests. Twenty-seven percent came from the various guidebooks. Two percent each came from local restaurants, the historic sites, travel agents, computer bulletin boards, other inns, town government, and local businesses. Four percent each came from paid advertising and publicity. Eight percent came from B&B reservation services, 6 percent came from our county B&B association, and 5 percent didn't know where they heard about us. Under 1 percent each came from gift certificate sales, brides, brochure, outside promotions (like Nabisco), airline computers, our state association, tourist map, and drop-in traffic.

I realized that although this information tells me a lot about where our guests hear about us, it only gives the number of reservations. I needed more information to refine my marketing techniques further. For example, I needed to know how much income was generated from each source. Because my rooms range in price from $95 to $250 for a double, a few nights in one of the more expensive rooms may generate more money than a week in one of the less expensive ones. I need to know what kind of business each referral source generates. Toward this end, I spoke to the folks at Forster & Associates who provide Kozyware, my computer system. Their newest update will allow me to get just this kind of information.

*What Does This Information Tell You?* Just looking at the referral information we already have tells us a lot. Certainly, the AAA is a very important source of referral. I have spoken to a number of small innkeepers lately who decided not to join or stay with the AAA because of the new lock requirements. Certainly, my experience is such that doing this would cut sharply into my business. If the AAA wants dead bolts on the doors, dead bolts we shall have, even if it costs me $100 a door to have bolts that fit with my decor. Doing a more detailed analysis of my AAA referrals, I found that they generated $16,820, close to 13 percent of gross income for the year.

*Using Promotional Gifts.* The 14 percent of my reservations that came from past guests and friends in the local area tells me that I need to make sure that each guest leaves with a brochure or something with our name, address, and phone number on it. I want to make it even easier for them to send their friends to us. For years, I have had the idea to have recipe cards made up for some of our favorite breakfasts, with our contact information on the back. My sense is that guests will put these cards in their recipe files and know where to find them when they want to refer someone, whereas I'm not too sure whether guests save brochures for any length of time.

*Use Your Marketing Information to Plan Better.* I certainly want to continue my efforts to have local meetings at the house and be on historic house tours. So far, all these efforts have required very little out-of-pocket expenditures and reap colossal benefits to my bottom line.

*Create a Reason for Locals to Visit Your Inn.* A few months ago, one of my neighbors started a women's network in town. The idea of the group is to have meetings once a month to network, meet other people, promote their businesses, get support for political causes, start a book club, or anything else that you want. Just a small article in the local paper sparked considerable interest. At the first meeting, thirty-five women showed up. The home of the woman who hosted the meeting was jam-packed. I immediately offered to have future meetings at the Alexander Hamilton House.

*Newcomers Need to Know about You.* I have lived in Croton for fourteen years. I was shocked to find that twenty-five of these women were strangers. At subsequent meetings I have treated newcomers to a tour of the house while everyone gets comfortable over cake and coffee that I have waiting for them. This kind of group is especially attractive to newcomers to the area who want to meet others and get involved in the community. Some told me that they came to the meeting just to see the B&B. (Little did they know that I would have shown them around had they just rung the doorbell.) Two of the women offered to help out at the inn should I need someone to cover for me, and many more are just dying to spend the night in one of the Jacuzzi rooms when they can get a baby-sitter. All are now telling their friends and neighbors what a great place we have to put up out-of-town guests.

*Don't Become Complacent!* It is very important to remember that change happens all the time. Communities change as well. When you have been somewhere a long time, it is easy to become complacent and think that everyone in town knows about you. They don't. Even the ones who know about you need to be reminded. Those who haven't been inside since you redecorated think of your place as it was. If you have spent substantial time, money, and energy making the place better, don't forget to show it off.

*Evaluating the Guidebooks.* Because 27 percent of my guests that came from various guidebooks, I needed to see which books really give me a return on my investment. A more detailed look showed the following:

| Book | Number of Reservations | Yearly Revenue ($) | Cost ($) |
|------|------------------------|--------------------|----------|
| AAA Tourbook | 48 | 15,635 | 0 |
| Annual Directory of B&Bs | 3 | 860 | 25 |
| B&B Guest Houses | 2 | 530 | 130 |
| B&B USA | 16 + 3 America Online | 3,355 + 850 | 35 |
| Best Places to Kiss in New York | 18 | 5,420 | 0 |
| Chesler books, B&B in the Mid-Atlantic States and Coast to Coast | 12 | 1,740 | 75 |
| Christian B&B | 1 | 130 | 25 |
| Country Inns Magazine | 12 | 3,170 | 834 |
| Inspected, Rated, and Improved | 1 | 1,135 | 350 |
| Mobil Travel Guide | 2 | 555 | 0 |
| Complete Guide to B&Bs, Inns, and Guesthouses | 7 + 4 CompuServe | 1,700 + 970 | 35 |
| National Trust | 4 | 955 | 105 |
| Nonsmoker's Guide | 5 | 745 | 25 |
| Official Airline Guide | 3 | 95 | 0 |
| PAII | 1 | 780 | 150 |
| Rand McNally | 1 | 95 | Library, not in print |
| Yellow Pages | 12 | 2,240 | 0 |
| Unknown | 28 | 5,955 | ? |

Total books: $46,915, 24 percent of gross sales

Unfortunately, 25 percent of the money earned from book referrals came from people who couldn't remember which book they read about us in. This certainly tells me that I don't know enough to make a decision about which books to continue with or drop for next year, and I will need to be more diligent in getting this information in the future.

*Return on Investment.* In our industry, commercial lodging establishments spend 5 to 10 percent of their gross sales on marketing. New places may spend up to 30 percent. Certainly, when gross sales are large, you have a great deal to spend on marketing. When your gross sales are smaller, you have a lot less to spend, and each dollar spent must really perform. When evaluating the performance of your various marketing tools, a successful ad or promotion is not one that pays for itself, but one that pays for itself at least five to ten times over.

Looking at the return from my guidebook advertising, there was not a single one that didn't return at least three times its cost. *Bed & Breakfast USA* paid for itself 120 times, Pamela Lanier's book, *The Complete Guide to B&Bs, Guest Houses and Inns,* paid for itself 76 times; *The Nonsmoker's Guide* returned 31 times its cost; *The Annual Directory of B&B Inns* 34.4 times its cost, and Bernice Chesler's books 23 times their cost. Certainly the *AAA Tourbook* took the award for single most effective listing and *The Best Places to Kiss in New York* took second as they cost nothing and produced the most money.

The analysis of the guidebooks hasn't convinced me to drop my ad in any of the books because I have close to $6,000 worth of unaccounted-for guidebook-referred income, but I have certainly seen how valuable the guidebooks are to my business.

*Read Your Listings.* I also noticed that although my listing in the *AAA Tourbook* won top honors, my listing in the *Mobil Travel Guide* brought only two reservations, even though our rating was the same. I thought, "Could this just be due to much less use of the *Mobil Guide?*" On vacation in London this spring, I saw the *Mobil Guide* in a bookstore. I'm embarrassed to say that I had never seen it before. I looked up our listing and was horrified to find that Mobil doesn't list each town. They list large cities and put you under the nearest one. We are four miles south of Peekskill and ten miles north of Tarrytown. Most of the historic sites that people visit are in Tarrytown. Van Cortlandt Manor, which is right here in Croton, is also listed under Tarrytown. No sites are listed under Peekskill. When I returned home, I called the *Mobil Guide* and asked that we be placed under Tarrytown. They said, "No problem, but this won't take place until the next edition in 1996." Shame on me for not finding out sooner. Moral to the story: Make sure to read all your listings.

*Donate to Local Libraries.* A visit to a few of the libraries near your home to peruse the B&B section will convince you that they are understocked and that most of their guidebooks date from when Lassie was a puppy. Most of us receive a new guidebook each year from many of the publishers who list our ads. Donate last year's to a library near by. You can take the tax deduction while helping to get the word out about B&B. This idea comes from my partner, Brenda, who is often a wealth of interesting information and good ideas.

### FILL YOUR ROOMS DURING THE WEEK

At the same time we changed to all-private baths, we made the decision to add separate phone lines with answering machines and color cable TV. In most rooms we are able to do this discreetly, so as not to change the ambiance. This has made it possible to add business travelers to our target market of romantic couples and tourists. Although we are not big enough to go after conferences, we are in a location convenient to a number of businesses. Businesspeople are repeat customers. Reach out to them. They appreciate personal attention without intrusiveness. Bend your cancellation policies for them. We have a weekly rate that gives the seventh night free. For cost-conscious businesspeople who stay here regularly, I often offer the seventh night free even if it's three days one week and four the next or one night a week for many weeks.

*There Are More Weekday Nights than Weekend Nights.* Some of the more rural inns have added additional buildings containing bedrooms, baths, and meeting rooms to go after the small meeting and conference market. They rent equipment as needed and pass along the charges to the company meeting there. Outside caterers are always happy to provide other meals for your business meetings and will give you a commission on them.

*Use Your Imagination.* Create a reason for people to come to your inn midweek or off-season. Donny Smith at the Maine Stay in Camden, Maine, has a stitchery week. She hires someone famous for sewing and advertises in needlecraft newsletters. The first year, she filled a few rooms. Now she fills her place, as well as two other inns, and the participants look forward to each yearly outing.

I recently returned from a three-day cooking school experience at the Clifton Inn in Charlottesville, Virginia. Chef Craig Hartman has twenty-five years of experience that he graciously shares with others. Although he has offered individual classes for locals in the past, he decided this year to use the cooking classes to fill some weekday rooms at the inn during his off-season. Although this was very time-intensive for Craig, the experience was a good one. He will offer classes again, but he found that he needs to market them much earlier. People need time to decide to take this kind of learning vacation. If you think you might want to offer other meals at your inn and want to get some firsthand experience, contact the Clifton Country Inn, Rte. 13, Box 26, Charlottesville, VA 22901, (804) 971-1800.

While I was at cooking school, Craig shared with me a marketing secret of another Virginia inn. They get a renowned gardener to come to the inn in early spring to teach classes. They publicize this event in gardening club newsletters and fill the inn with gardeners who clean out the inn's flower beds while the master gardener instructs. Obviously, this type of marketing takes thoughtful, advanced planning, but fueled by your creativity, it is as limitless as your imagination.

## PIGGYBACKING ON YOUR PUBLICITY

If you work hard at getting, or are lucky enough to have, a wonderful write-up in a quality publication, have reprints made and use them in your marketing. *Country Inns Magazine* did a beautiful article about our renovations. They made it possible for us to have reprints of the article made with additional color photos on the front and back. The reprint is an excellent promotional piece to send out to travel agents, prospective brides, corporate travel departments, and others who have the opportunity to send many guests. The six-page reprint cost a little more than $1 a copy for 2,000 copies. It is not something I can afford to send out routinely to guests, but it is very impressive and certainly gives the impression we want to project. At the inn, we have to hide them as all the guests want to take them as souvenirs.

## Grow the Inn

Another way to increase revenue is to have more rooms to rent. If you have started small with the feeling that the business will grow in time, ask yourself if the time is right. Certainly, awareness and use of B&Bs have skyrocketed since the 1980s. I've been shocked to read a best-selling book and find the hero looking for a B&B to stay at or turning on the TV and hearing the characters talk about a B&B. When we opened this B&B, we had one room. This quickly grew to four rooms that shared two baths. As the idea of B&B caught on, I took the risk of adding a bath to my library and sitting room and turning that into my first suite. It is important, while walking around the house and looking at each room, to ask yourself, "Is this the best use of this space?"

In 1991, I hired a contractor to turn most of my attic into the Bridal Chamber, and in 1993, I added a master suite over a one-story sunporch. These two luxury rooms with Jacuzzi, in-room fireplaces, and fine furniture and decor were a big investment but now account for close to 45 percent of our income. We could see that our clientele was changing. Whereas people were content to share baths ten years ago, we were losing reservations in the four rooms that shared the two hall baths. We needed to have all private baths. I opted to turn one of the bedrooms into two bathrooms, so that the two rooms on either side would each have a private attached bath. This left one room with a private hall bath, but gave us a total of seven guest rooms, all with a private bath. I don't want to say much now about construction. See the next chapter for that, but know that although construction is hell, the results are worth it. We've put in four fireplaces, added five bathrooms, and lived to tell about it. It has changed the quality of the inn, increased our occupancy, and made it possible to earn a living from innkeeping.

## Reflect Your Upgrading in Your Rates

Take a good look at your rates. Compare them to other places in your area, and honestly evaluate what you have to offer. Although I always advise new innkeepers to enter the market somewhere in the middle range, as your reputation grows and you upgrade your facility, your room prices should reflect what you have done. You certainly don't want to price yourself out of the marketplace, but you don't want to give away the store. If you don't charge enough, potential guests will think you don't have a nice place.

### FLEXIBLE RATES

I am always leery of prospective guests who try to bargain with me on the phone. Last-minute callers often think that you will reduce their rate rather than let a room go empty. If they start this type of conversation, I soon end it. If, however, a guest can't afford the more expensive room that is open, I will often sell them the less expensive room that is already booked. Then, I have the choice of upgrading the new guest or the other guest who had previously booked the room. During the week, it's a way to reward my regulars with a stay in one of the Jacuzzi rooms while still allowing them to stay within budget.

### MAKE MORE MONEY FROM EXISTING RESERVATIONS

Adding more rooms to your inn is very costly and eventually comes to an end. The telephone and your phone skills can easily add up to 10 percent on the money generated by a single reservation while providing a real service to harried guests. I usually ask if this is a special occasion. If the guest says, "Yes, it's my girlfriend's birthday," I respond, "Oh! Would you like us to do anything special as a surprise for her?" This starts them thinking. I pause only a few seconds and start naming things that we could do that would be a special treat. "We can have a bottle of champagne chilled and waiting or a vase of special flowers, balloons, chocolate-covered strawberries, whatever you want. Just tell us what to get and what to spend, and we'll happily do the running around for you." Don't forget to ask what they want to say on the card. Men especially want someone else to do the running around for them and gladly avail themselves of your kind offer. When women make the reservation, I often ask them to have their husbands or boyfriends call so that I can discuss dinner reservations or directions. This gives me the opportunity to talk to the men and sell our extra services.

I always explain that I don't have a liquor license, and that if I pick up alcohol, I am only being reimbursed for the actual cost of the liquor. In some states, if you have a liquor or a wine license, you can use this method to generate income that I cannot. I do, of course, buy my flowers and balloons from a florist who gives me a 25 percent discount on my shopping. The guests don't pay any more than they would have had they stopped at the florist themselves, but I make 25 percent on their order. If I make chocolate-covered strawberries or a picnic basket, I charge the cost of the food times 3, as a caterer would (one-third materials, one-third labor, one-third profit).

## Use the Inn for Events

Innkeepers who have inns with a lot of land and adequate parking should consider hosting events: storytelling days for children, art exhibits, cooking contests, and the like, not just weddings. These events usually not only fill guest rooms but also act as a wonderful way to publicize your inn and to give others a chance to see it firsthand.

## Be More Professional

### DRESS THE PART

As you take your business more seriously, upgrade your inn, add more services, and don't forget that you are part of the decor. No, this doesn't mean coming to the door in costume or doing the gardening in fancy dress. However, it is important when expecting guests to be clean (no plunger in hand or gardening dirt under the nails), professionally dressed, and company-ready. Sure, we all get caught scrubbing or digging by unexpected guests or potential guests who are stopping by to see if this is the appropriate place for the out-of-town wedding guests. Smile graciously, and apologize for your attire.

### TAKE RESPONSIBILITY FOR PROBLEMS

Problems sometimes occur at the best of inns. Guests will respect you and be willing to meet you more than halfway if you shoulder responsibility. Never try to explain your way out of, or blame someone else for, problems, be it that your cleaning help missed their bathroom, the city's sewer system backed up into the guest bathroom, or that the ten days of record heat and humidity have turned the pool green. If you can fix it, do so immediately. Thank the guest for bringing this problem to your attention. Make up for their inconvenience in some way. This may mean sending them to lunch while you fix the toilet, changing the room to a better one at no extra cost, refunding a night's stay, or, in a worst-case scenario, finding them some other place to stay and paying for it. Admit responsibility. "I'm so sorry. This is our fault. We want your stay here to be wonderful. What can I do to make this up to you?" A fruit basket, a plate of cookies, or any little extra often makes up for a lot.

### GO TO CONFERENCES HELD IN STATE AND NATIONALLY

We learn from the ideas and mistakes of each other. Conferences are a way to network, learn, share, and renew excitement about what we do. If you think you are too old or experienced to learn, you are ready to sell.

## DECREASING EXPENSES

### Get Organized

Numerous trips to the market are a waste of time and money. Keep a running list for each store.

## HONE YOUR PURCHASING SKILLS

Join a warehouse club such as Sam's Club, BJs, or Price Club, and learn what are the best values there. Investigate discount buying through your state and national association or discount buying clubs. Stock up when essentials are on sale, but remember to use what's in your freezer before it needs to be tossed.

You will be routinely solicited by long-distance services. Although your first reaction is to say nicely, "Go away. Don't bother me," hear them out. The cost of switching is usually free and the savings may be significant. If you like what you hear, but don't want to switch, go back to your phone company and tell them that you'd like to stay, but can't afford to pass up the savings you're being offered by the other company. They will very likely match it or offer a premium that is equivalent.

Use basic cleaning supplies. We find that the basics—a good bleach, a nonbleaching disinfectant, a good spot cleaner, Windex, and a heavy-duty lime remover for shower stalls—are usually adequate for most cleaning. It is too easy to be suckered into a variety of fancy cleaners that may not mix with each other and create toxic fumes, as well as being ridiculously overpriced disguised bleach, disinfectant, or spot cleaners.

## SHOP YOURSELF A VACATION

Get a credit card that gives you frequent-flyer miles, and use it for food, cleaning supplies, and other business expenses that you usually pay for by cash or check. However, be religious about paying these bills promptly every month. By the end of the year, you'll undoubtedly have enough frequent-flyer miles to get away next year, which prevents burnout and makes you a better innkeeper. Having these expenses on your card helps you keep track of them for tax purposes. (Don't throw away your receipts. You still need them.) But understand that paying high interest rates on your unpaid credit card balance will defeat the whole purpose. Many phone companies also have programs that give you frequent-flyer miles. Take advantage of them.

## Watch Those Interest Rates

Keep an eye on interest rates. Understand that refinancing your home or inn can often save you thousands of dollars over the life of a mortgage. Get an amortization schedule. Prepay something extra each month. Even a small extra payment, as little as $25 a month, will decrease the price of your loan by thousands.

Credit card debt is exorbitant. Don't use credit cards for big-ticket items unless you can pay them off in a month or two. Take advantage of interest-free installment plans, or try to negotiate a lower price for paying up-front.

## Be a Jack of All Trades

Learn the basics of how to fix a toilet and other such tasks, but also know your limits and when to call for an expert. You can save lots of money by doing your own wallpapering, small painting jobs, and simple plumbing or carpentry repairs. But only do them if you can do them right. Sometimes your partner is better at this than you. Recognize your strengths and shortcomings.

## Research Your Needs Before Buying
## Big-Ticket Items

My computer was one of the first on the market. I was very proud of it. It had twenty megabytes of hard disk. It word-processed and carried my reservation program and even my accounting program. Although considered hopelessly out-of-date by my computer-savvy, sophisticated friends and acquaintances, it worked fine until the fall of 1995 when I wanted to change accounting programs and the new program wouldn't fit my memory bank. Everyone told me to get a new computer. Brenda, with her fancy new laptop, laughed at me and teased me mercilessly about computing in the dark ages. However, I found a man who could update my computer to a 386, give me 160 megabytes of memory, and make it possible for me to enter the 1990s. This cost under $200. The point here is that I didn't need the bells and whistles that would have cost me $2,000 or $3,000 more. Best of all, my computer is still PHS (you know, "Press here, silly"), just my style. Understand that I've used the computer as an example. It is very easy to be seduced by the latest upgrades on any product when you rarely need them and can save substantially by buying items with only the features you really need.

## Appliance Service Contracts

One of the single largest consumer rip-offs on the market is the service contract. You wind up paying large sums to cover things that are most often covered under your warranty in the first year. The service contract cost over the life of a product is usually considerably more than the cost of occasional repair or replacement. Put the cost of service contracts on your appliances into the cookie jar instead. Take the repair costs from it, and treat yourself to a few new appliances with what's left over.

## Saving Time Is Saving Money

Reviewing procedures and distribution of duties between partners should be done on a regular basis. If your inn has grown and changed over time, you may need to rethink who does what. You may need to add extra staff to do some of the mundane chores to free up yourself or your partner to do more administrative tasks and to have time left over to enjoy your life. All work and no play is still unbearably dull. Success may be defined in many ways. Make sure your success is not at the expense of your happiness. Learn to delegate and manage. Your inn will be more profitable and your life more enjoyable.

## SHARE YOUR IDEAS

If you have found any of these ideas useful, they are yours to use with my blessings. If you have other ideas or want to share with others techniques that have worked for you, please write to me, and I will pass them along.

# 11

# Specialty Bed and Breakfasts

## BIG-CITY BED AND BREAKFAST

In most large cities, Bed and Breakfast is flourishing partly because of the big savings to the traveler and partly because business travelers have "discovered" B&B. Certainly, the demand on a city B&B is usually seven days a week compared to the weekend desirability of most tourist locations in the country. Consequently, there is also less seasonal variation.

Although most city B&Bs are apartments, others are houses, brownstone buildings, or small owner-occupied apartment houses. It is easy to understand the differences between city B&Bs by looking at the following categories:

**Hosted.** This is a large apartment or house, owner-occupied, where guests rent an individual bedroom or suite. Some have shared baths, others private. The host makes breakfast much the same as in the country B&B, except that breakfast is usually early as travelers are often on their way to work.

**Unhosted.** A studio or one-bedroom apartment, stocked with breakfast food, with kitchen and private bath. The host is not present but makes sure the place is clean and stocked before each guest arrives. The host is usually available to the guest by phone. A package of information on restaurants, shopping, museums, maps, transportation, and the like is compiled for the guest's use.

**Unhosted apartments in owner-occupied building.** In this situation, the host family owns the structure and lives on one or two floors while the rest of the building offers small individual apartments for guests, each with its own kitchen, private bath, and entrance. For guests, this is often the best of all possible worlds because they have total privacy with direct access to the hosts.

Hosted city B&Bs are the type most similar to B&Bs outside of big cities. In this situation hosts have direct contact with the guests and can closely monitor the care of their home. In unhosted accommodations, the only contact is usually by phone when the guest calls to give an arrival time and get entry instructions. This is a good time to share with the guest any of the idiosyncrasies about your place.

After my divorce, I had money to invest and preferred to invest it in something I knew about—B&B real estate. I bought a studio apartment in midtown New York City. In looking for the apartment, I had a number of issues to consider:

1. The apartment had to be a condo, not a co-op, because I did not want to have to fight for board approval. I preferred to be totally up-front about my use for the apartment so that I wouldn't have troubles with management later on. I selected a building with studio and one-bedroom apartments close to the United Nations so that there would be less likelihood of trouble with the neighbors, and the building's tenants would be individuals rather than families. It turned out that the proximity to the United Nations worked well, not only because it is a safe, convenient neighborhood, but also because more than 50 percent of the apartments are owned by foreigners who use them for only a short time each year and rent them the rest of the time to offset their cost.

2. I needed a twenty-four-hour doorman building. This makes the guests feel safer, and I call the doorman with the name and arrival of the guest to protect my investment as well.

3. I needed a housekeeper who could change sheets, clean the apartment, and restock the refrigerator in response

to my call. The superintendent of the building helped me find such a reliable person.

4. I was lucky. When I saw the apartment, it was gutted, and ready for renovation, so I was able to have it finished to my specifications. I wanted a Jacuzzi, French doors from the foyer into the living/bedroom, and recessed lighting. If you select an apartment that needs work, you must consider the cost of improvements when you calculate the return needed on your investment.

5. Since this is an investment, it is necessary to calculate your cost of purchase, refurbishing, decorating, monthly maintenance, and so on. In figuring maintenance, include your building maintenance payment, housekeeping, taxes, gas and electric, phone, cable TV, and tipping the doormen and the superintendent a few times a year. Keep good records. All your expenses will be tax-deductible because this is a business in which you are actively involved. Before you proceed, figure out how much money you will have to make to break even and how much to make a profit. Remember, you are also building equity, and although real estate is not a very liquid asset, it is an important one. If you buy at the right time and the market goes up, when you sell the apartment, the profit may be enough to justify a small negative cash flow. Certainly, it would be better to make a profit from B&B and another at sale.

6. Since I don't live in the city, I didn't want to worry about keys. The solution was a combination lock that I can change whenever I feel like it. This way, once the reservation is confirmed and the money received, I give the guests the current combination, and they can come and go at will.

I have found that my break-even point is about fourteen days a month. Every additional night per month the apartment is taken is profit. It has been a good investment, since I'm averaging close to 20 days a month and steadily building equity.

## SHIPBOARD BED AND BREAKFAST

A number of yachts are offering Bed and Breakfast these days. Appropriate insurance and a licensed captain are mandatory. For example, Guesthouses, a Pennsylvania-based reservation service, offers yacht B&B on the Chesapeake. Some yacht stays are just overnight on the ship; others include a full-day's sail and meals from picnic lunches to fancy dinners.

## FARM BED AND BREAKFAST

Farm B&Bs are particularly exciting to families with young children. Whether the attraction is just being able to look at the animals, feed the chickens, milk the cow, or have a ride on a big piece of farm equipment, the opportunity to sample a different way of life is very tempting. The icing on the cake is the traditional big farm breakfast. Farm B&Bs don't try to give luxury; instead, they promote the unique experience.

## HISTORIC BED AND BREAKFAST

Historic B&Bs are usually at least fifty years old and have either historical or architectural significance in the community. Hosts are proud of their authenticity and usually have many pieces of period furniture. Some hosts of historic B&Bs have done considerable restoration and keep a photographic record to share with interested guests. Most historic houses are located in areas of historic interest. Guests who come to tour historic homes, battlefields, and so forth also are thrilled to stay in a historic house.

## HAUNTED BED AND BREAKFAST

Yes, use your ghost to market the inn. Some guests want to stay in a haunted house.

## BED AND BREAKFAST WITH A CAT

There are even B&Bs that offer rooms with or without a cat. It costs more with the cat, of course.

Let your imagination run wild. I've had mail from a B&B where guests stay in *teepees*, and even one that offers an original jail cell.

# 12

**❖❖❖❖❖❖❖❖❖❖❖❖❖❖❖❖❖❖❖      ❖❖❖❖❖❖❖❖❖❖❖❖❖❖❖❖❖❖❖❖**

# Construction

Construction, whether it's total renovation, a major addition, or just work limited to one room, is a task that most innkeepers face sooner or later. Like delivering a baby, it becomes your total focus for an intense period during which you often wonder, "How did I get myself into this?"

## GET ORGANIZED

Planning is the key to successful construction. No facet of the job is too small to be worthy of your careful scrutiny. Decide whether you will hire a contractor to do the job or be the general contractor yourself. In either case, you will be hiring people who have possibly not worked for you before.

Speak to both an architect and a structural engineer about your project. A structural engineer may be able to produce the plans for your job at a fraction of the price of using an architectural firm. Make sure that whichever way you go, it is understood that the price includes a few visits to the site to check on things during construction as well as anything unforeseen that should occur during construction.

Make sure that your plans are permitted by your town's building code. Don't forget about conforming to requirements of the Americans with Disabilities Act whenever possible. Give yourself enough time. Remember that getting permissions and financing can take longer than expected.

## GENERAL CONTRACTOR

The person who hires and insures all the workers at the job site is the general contractor. Contractors usually give you a set price that will cover everything. They are responsible for their own work as well as for the work of those they hire, and they will stand behind all the workmanship and return to fix anything that is not up to standard. If your skylight starts leaking in the middle of the night on a holiday weekend, you want to be confident that your contractor will send somebody to handle this pronto. General contractors usually procure materials and fixtures, and you need to be very clear should you want to sign off personally on the products used for your job. Specify in your contract anything out of the ordinary, and some of what you think should be ordinary but may not be.

If you decide to take on the responsibility of being a general contractor, understand that there is a built-in cost, as well as many advantages and disadvantages. You will still be hiring electrical, plumbing, and other contractors. A contract spelling out all expectations works best. Even something so simple as cleaning up at the end of each day, which is essential to having any prayer of doing business while construction proceeds, needs to be in writing. Although you will be buying many of your own materials with your credit card and getting your frequent-flyer miles by the thousands, you may not be getting the best price from suppliers. Contractors who are recurrent users usually get the best rates, but they also make a percentage for their trouble. If you have the time and energy to shop around and use discount buying clubs to get great buys, you can make up for this. You will have final responsibility and control. If you estimate incorrectly the amount of materials you need, you will be the one paying for more because you're the general contractor.

## TAKE BIDS AND CHECK REFERENCES

Even if you have used a particular contractor, electrician, or plumber before, take bids from at least three other reputable professionals. Before you do this, figure out exactly what you want done and how much you can realistically afford to pay for this project. If you have to arrange financing, do this before the job begins. Remember, the lowest bids may cost you money in the long run should you fail to check references and the person you hire takes longer to do the job than promised or displays less-than-adequate workmanship. Go look at other jobs that have been completed by these people, and talk with the owners of the properties. Understand that no one is perfect and no job ever comes off without some slight crises. Find out how quickly any problems were attended to during the job and after the dust had settled.

## DUST IS EVERYWHERE

Understand that even if you think the work will be localized, there will be more extra dust around than ever before. Workers going in and out of the building in all kinds of weather track in the weirdest things. Sheetrock dust is insidious, and you will be finding it everywhere for days after the work is done. Keep dusting and vacuuming often during the day.

## SIGN A CONTRACT

It should be clear from the outset who will do what, on what time schedule, and at what price. Understand that should you make changes during the course of the job, the cost will go up as will the time necessary to get the job done. This is unavoidable, so at least in your mind know that the job will take longer than planned. Expect 25 to 100 percent longer.

## STAY ORGANIZED

If it is your job to select the wallpaper, the lighting fixtures, the furniture, or the like, don't wait to make these decisions. Having workers on the job to install anything while you make decisions about what you want, or waiting for delivery of items you did not order far enough in advance, delays the completion of the job and costs you big money. Supplying the plumbing or electrical fixtures yourself can be a double-edged sword. You may save money on the purchase price, but you are also responsible for any damage they cause. For example, a pinhole defect in a shower body can easily cause a great deal of water damage to your newly tiled wall and ceiling below. You will have to pay for the replacement of the shower body, labor, the tiler, and all repairs.

## DUST IS STILL EVERYWHERE!

Plan to keep vacuuming. Never permit guests to make reservations while you are under construction without telling them and giving them the option to stay elsewhere. Bump them up to a more expensive, out-of-the-way room should you find that conditions are worse than you anticipated.

## GET EVEN MORE ORGANIZED!

Be clear about what are to be acceptable working hours. Noisy work cannot begin before 8:30 A.M. on a weekday and 10 A.M. on a weekend or holiday. You do not want your guests unduly disturbed. Nails or other debris left in the driveway or parking area are not acceptable. If there is to be some demolition and a dumpster is required, make sure that it is parked as far out of the way as possible. This may be less convenient for the workers but necessary for the safety and comfort of your guests. See that the full dumpster is removed from your property as quickly as possible.

## FINANCING YOUR PROJECT

If you don't have the capital required to finance your dreams, try to get a home-equity loan so that at least the interest will be deductible. If you purchase materials with credit cards—for those frequent-flyer miles—don't run a balance from month to month.

## AGAIN, DUST IS EVERYWHERE!

Getting this job done as much on time as possible seems more crucial each day. Vacuuming three times a day and feeling that you are getting nowhere fast becomes immensely stressful. Feed and water (or coffee) your workers daily. Make extra muffins at breakfast so that you will have enough for their coffee break. Volunteer to go out to pick up sandwiches at lunch time, so the workers stay on the job site and get the job done sooner. Once a week, make lunch to show your appreciation. Friday works best. Keep them coming back for more. The quicker this job is completed, the sooner you can reduce your dusting.

## BE YET MORE ORGANIZED!

Know that certain processes, such as applying polyurethane to wood floors, create fumes that may be dangerous and make it impossible to do business for a few days. Turn off pilot lights on your stove, and in your water heater and furnace, as these fumes are potentially explosive. This way, you can prevent possible explosions.

## MAKE SURE YOU GET YOUR C OF O

Don't forget to follow through and get your certificate of occupancy (C of O). You need to make sure that everything done on your property is done above board with the appropriate paperwork because the inn is your biggest asset. Should you ever decide to sell, you will need to produce all the C of O documents, or the sale will not go through.

## CONSTRUCTION IS STRESSFUL!

There have been days during construction when Brenda and I have argued like raving banshees ready to slit each other's throat over some unimportant issue, all because of construction stress. One day, we had nineteen workers on the property. We were tripping over them, answering their telephone calls, running around with food and coffee, and thinking this chaos would never end. We couldn't express frustration at them, so we expressed it at each other. The contractor finally came over and said, "You girls need to take a trip to the mall." We immediately stopped screaming, burst into laughter at the ridiculousness of the argument, and headed for the stores. Unfortunately, as with any other extended period of stress, relationships with your family or colleagues suffer. Eating and spending money seem to give temporary relief, but nothing cures this malady like the completion of your construction project. Humor works best. Construction, like writing a book, can make you laugh or cry. I prefer to laugh.

# 13

# Best Breakfasts

F or B&B guests, the best breakfasts are those that suit their schedules and give them a chance to get to know their hosts a little better. Obviously, weekdays, when everyone is trying to get out to take care of the day's business, require one approach, and lazy Sundays on the terrace, with everyone in a relaxed and expansive mood, require another. So, your breakfast style will vary depending on who the guests are, what their food preferences are, how much time you have to share, and how much fun you get out of food preparation. For many hosts, providing a unique breakfast is a real high point of a visit; for others, the simpler, the better.

If you aspire to running a deluxe B&B, excellent food beautifully served is an integral part of what you need to plan for every time you have guests. If you have a garden, no ingredients can surpass what is truly fresh and ripe. This chapter gives sample recipes and includes a list of cookbooks to explore when you feel yourself falling into a beginning-of-the-day rut.

Are your guests tired of cereal out of the box? Unable to face another road stand name-brand doughnut? Then they're ready for your best breakfasts!

## WHEN TO SERVE BREAKFAST

Whether you have rigid breakfast hours or a flexible schedule according to your guests' needs should be determined by your lifestyle. Discuss the options with your family. Some hosts who have many outside demands on their time opt for fixed breakfast hours: 7:00 to 8:00 A.M. or 9:00 A.M. on weekdays and 8:00 to 10:00 A.M. or 9:00 to 11:00 A.M. on weekends. This is a way to limit the time expected of you in the kitchen. Make sure to include these breakfast hours in any written material you prepare or in a guest's confirmation notice. If you decide to be flexible, it is necessary to touch base with your guests each night before so that you will know what time to have breakfast ready the next morning.

## PLANNING AHEAD

When planning your menu, first take into consideration how many guests you will serve. Serving a romantic breakfast for two guests and serving to a family of five who will shortly be followed at your table by two adult couples require different planning. You have spoken to your guests the night before, so you have a good idea whether they will be in a hurry or ready for a leisurely breakfast of something special.

In Europe, a continental breakfast of a croissant and coffee is the rule. Not so in America. Most guests really look forward to this first and most important meal of the day.

## PRESENTATION

Sometimes, guests arrive at the table at different times. In such cases, it is easier to serve a buffet-style meal. That way, guests can help themselves and take a seat at the table. Whether you serve buffet-style or serve each guest once he or she is seated, follow the same basics of setting a pretty table: an attractive centerpiece or floral arrangement (seasonal changes add interest; silk flowers are sensible in winter), spotless glassware and silver, candles (collect an assortment of holders), cloth napkins, tablecloths or place mats, and napkin rings. Some hosts collect table accents of all types (from butter molds to interesting vases, vintage dishes and cutlery, or curio salt and pepper shakers) to make each day's breakfast setting different. Others assemble vintage linens to create exceptionally nostalgic settings for special occasions. And remember, all such acquisitions used for B&B are tax-deductible.

Breakfast in bed, if you offer it, should be served on lovely trays with fine china, crystal, a fresh flower, cloth napkins, piping-hot coffee, and wonderful food. A morning paper is a nice extra.

## TIMESAVING TIPS

1. Learn to make the best use of your freezer and microwave. (If you don't have a microwave, plan to purchase one. It's a true time-saver for your B&B needs.)

2. Whenever you bake, prepare a double batch, and freeze the extras. (Always mark the date and item description on the wrapper so that you will use the food while it is still good.)

3. Arrange fresh berries on cookie sheets and freeze them whole; then bag them to enjoy when the season is past in pancakes and mixed into fruit cups and fillings.

4. Wrap things individually for the freezer so that you can prepare enough for one guest or several without thawing more than you need.

5. Don't feel locked into classic breakfast food. Freeze cooked chicken to use as a filling for crepes, cooked beans for Mexican burritos, or a pot of thick soup or chili for skiers who may need a heartier breakfast.

6. As you use up the last of the orange juice, make more. If your pitcher is always full, you won't have to keep guests waiting while you make more.

7. There are many coffee makers with timers that allow you to prepare the pot the night before and set it to go on before you get to the kitchen. Another advantage to having the coffee ready early is that often a guest will awaken very early and wander into the kitchen. It is nice to find coffee waiting.

8. If breakfast is to be served early, you may also want to set the table the night before.

## OTHER TIPS

1. Keep your kitchen clean, even when cooking. Don't let garbage accumulate. Throw away eggshells and plastic wrap instead of leaving them on the counter.

2. Try to incorporate some regional specialties in your menus, but have some standby alternatives in case not all your guests are adventurous eaters. For example, most people enjoy their first taste of real maple syrup, but not everyone can survive Mexican hot chillis.

3. Do most of your breakfast preparation before the guests get to the table so that you will be able to join them if that is appropriate. Make sure the condiments are on the table. You will of course have to go back into the kitchen to take away the first course and bring in the second or get more coffee, but you should still be the gracious host. And it should look easy. Don't give the appearance of being a jack-in-the-box.

4. Most guests enjoy it when you join them at the table. They like the personal attention and the chance to ask questions about the region, restaurants, local events and places of interest, and so on. Whether you dine with them, chat, or just serve is your decision. Keep in mind that a romantic couple or four friends who haven't seen each other in a long time may have little interest in getting to know you better. In such cases, it is best for you to give them their privacy.

5. Don't start clearing the table the minute your guests have finished their last mouthful. Often, they will enjoy relaxing and getting to know each other better over another cup of coffee. Once you start to take dirty dishes

away, it may be perceived as a signal that breakfast is over and that you are anxious for them to leave.

# SPECIAL CONSIDERATIONS

## Children

Most children will be less than excited by the opportunity to sample your breakfast specialties. Consequently, it is a good idea to have your pantry well stocked with breakfast cereals, juice, milk, and peanut butter (if all else fails). Have a high chair and bib available if you accept little ones. A supply of plastic plates, bowls, and cups will also serve you well. The ones with famous cartoon characters painted on them are especially well received by youngsters, and your fine china and stoneware will be protected. Speak to the parents about the child's tastes before planning to serve your gourmet offering to him or her. If there is more than one child present (even if they are from different parties), they are often much happier to be served on a little table of their own near the TV. Saturday morning cartoons are likely to be preferable to the sophisticated conversation of adults trying to get to know each other. However, before you separate parents and children, speak to the parents so that they don't feel you are trying to exclude the child.

## Vegetarians

Vegetarians are usually quite easy to plan for because some eat eggs, and French toast or pancakes are enjoyed by everyone. If they don't eat eggs, try yogurt, fresh breads, and jams. If you are a vegetarian, include this information on any description of your B&B so that the lack of meat won't be a surprise.

## Health Problems

Whether your guests have health problems or are just concerned with preventing them, many people today prefer to avoid fat, sugar, salt, or caffeine. Stock up on decaffeinated coffee and teas. Herbal teas may or may not be caffeine-free, so read the label. It is usually not too difficult to plan menus around these requirements. You can easily offer an alternative to someone who has a restricted diet and still serve your main breakfast selection to the rest of your guests. People with severe allergies may bring their own food. Don't be insulted; be thankful, and do your best to serve it as attractively as possible.

Dorry Norris gave a wonderful seminar on "Breakfasts for the Food-Sensitive" at the 1990 PAII conference in Philadelphia last spring. Thanks to Dorry, I am able to share this handy list with you:

## The "I-Can't-Eat-That" Emergency Pantry

   Oatmeal—regular rolled oats
* Barley flour
   Cornmeal
* Arrowroot powder
   Egg whites
   Egg substitutes
   Low-sodium rice cakes
* Gluten-free bread
   Cereal-free, salt-free baking powder
   Nondairy oleo—safflower or soy oil
   Decaffeinated coffee and teas
   Lemons
   Artificial sweeteners
   Apple juice—frozen concentrate or bottled
   Low-fat cottage cheese
   Low-fat yogurt
   Crushed pineapple in its own juice
   No-salt herb mixtures
* Soy cheese

*Usually available in health food stores

## Kosher Food

If your guests keep a kosher kitchen at their home, they may not be able to eat breakfast at your home. Keeping a kosher kitchen is a way of life, not something you can do for a weekend to accommodate a particular set of guests. In such cases, it is best to ask what (if anything) they can eat and whether they would prefer to be served on paper plates if your dishes are not kosher. They may choose to bring their own food or not eat. Again, don't be insulted. However, if you keep a kosher kitchen, make sure to mention this in any material about your B&B. You will, of course, be able to offer an array of wonderful foods, but because there are certain limitations, it is best for guests to know in advance.

## WIDEN YOUR CULINARY HORIZONS

Develop the habit of browsing through cookbooks for new ideas. Recipes in books from major publishers are kitchen tested, so you will waste less time (and ingredients) on recipes that fail. Try out new recipes on your family before offering them to guests. Here is a list of cookbooks dedicated to the first meal of the day; they will give you a sense of the vast array of recipes from which to choose. You may also find wonderful things in more comprehensive books.

Durand, Pauline W., and Yolande Languirand. *Brunch: Great Ideas for Planning, Cooking, and Serving.* New York: Barron, 1978.

Janericco, Terence. *The Book of Great Breakfasts and Brunches.* New York: Van Nostrand Reinhold, 1983.

Jester, Pat. *Brunch Cookery.* New York: Dell, 1981.

Phillips, Jill M. *The Good Morning Cook Book.* New York: Pelican, 1976.

The following books emphasize entertaining and use of specialized food groups.

Gorman, Marion. *Cooking with Fruit.* Emmaus, PA: Rodale, 1983.

London, Sheryl, and Mel London. *The Herb and Spice Cookbook.* Emmaus, PA: Rodale, 1986.

Norris, Dorry. *The Sage Cottage Herb Garden Cookbook.* Boston: Globe Pequot, 1991.

Sass, Lorna J. *Christmas Feasts from History.* New York: Metropolitan Museum of Art and Irena Chalmers Cookbooks, 1981.

## SAMPLE MENUS

An asterisk (*) indicates that the recipe is included in this chapter.

❖❖❖❖❖❖❖

### *HONEYMOON BREAKFAST ON A YACHT*

Strawberry Gateau De Crepes*
Whipped Cream
Champagne

❖❖❖❖❖❖❖

### *BUSINESSWOMAN'S BREAKFAST WHILE OVERLOOKING THE HUDSON*

Baked Apples or Pears in Crust*
Home-baked Biscuits*
Van Wyck Baked Eggs*

❖❖❖❖❖❖❖

### *BREAKFAST BEFORE VISITING THE ZOO WITH CHILDREN*

Orange Juice
Phyllo Blintzes*
Assorted Jams
Egg and Cheese Casserole with Herbs*

❖❖❖❖❖❖❖

### *BREAKFAST PICNIC ON VENICE BEACH*

Bran mixed cereal,* Barbara's mixed cereal,* Muesli*
Fruit Curry*
Yogurt

### FIFTH AVENUE APARTMENT BREAKFAST WITH SUNDAY TIMES

Lox and Bagels
Capers, Cream Cheese, Raw Onion, Tomatoes
Vegetable Zip*

❖❖❖❖❖❖❖

### 10-BELOW SKI BREAKFAST

Roasted Pancakes*
Peach Topping*
Canadian Bacon
Hot Chocolate

❖❖❖❖❖❖❖

### PRE-SIGHTSEEING BREAKFAST

Broiled Grapefruit*
Stuffed French Toast*
Maple Syrup
Coffee or Selection of Teas

❖❖❖❖❖❖❖

### COLLEGE INTERVIEW BREAKFAST

Raspberry Shake*
Shredded Wheat Bread*
Coddled Egg*

❖❖❖❖❖❖❖

### CLASS REUNION BRUNCH

Confetti*
Novelty Breads and Rolls
(Chapatis, Poppy-Seed Rolls, Rye Crescent Rolls, Potato Bread,
Whole-Wheat Sunflower Seed Bread, Croutons)*
Welsh Rarebit*
Rhubarb Fizz*

❖❖❖❖❖❖❖

### LOW-CHOLESTEROL BREAKFAST

Orange Juice
Snow Eggs*
English Muffins

❖❖❖❖❖❖❖

### BREAKFAST BEFORE HOLIDAY SHOPPING

Grapefruit-Avocado Cup*
Egg Burritos* or Cheese Strata*
Coffee

❖❖❖❖❖❖❖

### SINGLES WEEKEND OMELET BREAKFAST

Assorted Muffins
Omelets by the Dozen*
Green Tea

❖❖❖❖❖❖❖

### HEARTY WINTER BREAKFAST

Apple Tart*
Homemade Sausages*
Green Tomato Pie*

❖❖❖❖❖❖❖

# RECIPE TREASURY

### STRAWBERRY GATEAU DE CREPES (Serves 2)

6 small vanilla crepes
2 cups whole strawberries
2 cups strawberries, slightly mashed and sweetened to taste
Strawberry jam
1 cup confectioners' sugar
Shredded coconut

*Place each crepe on a decorative individual serving plate. Spread small amount of jam on crepe; then spoon on sweetened mashed strawberries. Repeat this process twice. Arrange whole strawberries around edge of gateau. Sprinkle with confectioners' sugar and shredded coconut. Serve with whipped cream.*

### VANILLA CREPES (Makes 32 to 35 crepes)

3 eggs
½ teaspoon salt
1½ cups flour
2 cups milk
1 tablespoon sugar
2 teaspoons vanilla extract
2 tablespoons melted butter

*In blender combine eggs, flour, milk, salt, sugar, and vanilla. Blend on low for a minute. Scrape batter down sides with rubber spatula. Add melted butter and blend again for fifteen seconds. Refrigerate for at least 1 hour. Stir batter before cooking. Cook on upside-down crepe griddle or in traditional pan.*

*Once made, crepes can be stored two to three days in the refrigerator if wrapped tightly in foil or plastic bags. They will store in the freezer for up to four months sealed in freezer bags. Thaw them before trying to separate them. Putting a sheet of waxed paper between each crepe before freezing makes them easier to separate when you are ready to use them. Heat in microwave oven before filling.*

## BAKED APPLES OR PEARS IN CRUST

Small apples or pears, one for each person
1 pie crust for every three apples or pears (Ready-made crusts available in refrigerated department of supermarket work fine.)
Raisins and raspberry jam mixed together (Or substitute a variety of other sweet fillings.)
Granulated sugar

*Core each apple or pear from the top. Do not go all the way through, but carve out a pocket 1 inch across. Spoon filling into pocket. Cut pie crust into four quarters. Cover with quarter of pie crust rolled thin. Use a little extra from the fourth quarter of crust to fill in any gaps. Make a simulated stem; if you want to be fancy, add a pastry leaf as well. Sprinkle with sugar. Bake in preheated 375-degree oven for 30 minutes or until golden brown.*

## HOME-BAKED BISCUITS (Serves 4 to 6)

1¾ cups unbleached flour
¼ cup soy flour
1 tablespoon baking powder
½ teaspoon salt
⅞ cup heavy cream
½ tablespoon honey
⅓ cup butter or margarine, melted

*In a medium bowl, combine dry ingredients. Add cream and honey, stirring only until dough forms a ball. Knead for 1 minute on a lightly floured surface. Roll dough out to ½-inch to ¾-inch thickness. Cut into round biscuits approximately 2 inches in diameter. Dip each biscuit in melted butter before placing it on a greased cookie sheet. Bake in middle of preheated 450-degree oven for 10 to 12 minutes or until golden brown. Serve at once.*

### Variations

*Here are a few suggestions for extra-flavorful biscuits. Just stir in listed ingredients before adding liquids. For bite-size party appetizers, roll dough to the same thickness to fit a straight-sided baking pan. Cut to desired shape after cooling for 5 minutes, but still serve warm.*

**With Cheddar and Bacon** Add ½ cup grated cheddar cheese and ¼ cup bacon bits.

**With Chives** Add 2 tablespoons chives.

**With Curry** Add 3 tablespoons curry powder.

**With Herbs** Add 1 tablespoon of your favorite dry herb, such as sage, savory, tarragon, or thyme.

**With Garlic** Add 2 tablespoons very finely minced garlic.

**With Onion** Add 3 tablespoons very finely minced onion, ⅛ teaspoon pepper, and ½ teaspoon caraway seeds.

**With Parsley** Add 4 tablespoons minced fresh parsley.

**With Stuffed Olives** Add 3 tablespoons finely minced green olives stuffed with pimento.

## VAN WYCK BAKED EGGS (Serves 1)

Vegetable cooking spray
Italian seasoned bread crumbs
1½ strips bacon, cooked until crisp and drained
2 eggs
1 tablespoon cottage cheese
½ slice Swiss cheese
1½ tablespoons Cheddar cheese, crumbled
½ fresh cherry tomato
1 sprig fresh parsley or other fresh herb

*Spray vegetable cooking spray into an individual cassolette. Coat sides and bottom of cassolette with seasoned bread crumbs. Break bacon into bits and place in bottom of cassolette. Gently break both eggs over bacon bits. Place cottage cheese on top of eggs. Cover with Swiss and Cheddar cheeses. Garnish with cherry tomato half. (Do not substitute any other variety of tomato because they will run.) Baked in preheated 350-degree oven for 30 minutes. Serve with fresh parsley garnish or a sprinkling of fresh herbs. You can prepare a number of these eggs at once and pop them into the oven half an hour before you expect each guest for breakfast.*

## PHYLLO BLINTZES (Serves 8 to 10)

1 pound phyllo pastry
½ pound butter, melted
2 cups ricotta cheese
1 egg
Pinch of salt
¼ teaspoon vanilla extract
2 tablespoons sugar
1 tablespoon melted butter

Thaw phyllo according to the directions on package. Mix ingredients for filling with a spoon until smooth. Take 2 sheets of phyllo dough, and lightly brush top sheet with butter. Cut sheets into 4 long strips. Place 1 tablespoon of filling on bottom of each strip. Fold corner of phyllo over filling; then fold like a flag, alternating left to right to shape a triangle. Place seam down on buttered cookie sheet and brush again with butter. The blintzes can be baked at once or frozen for later use.

Bake at 375 degrees for 20 minutes or until golden brown. If you turn the oven off and open the door slightly, the blintzes will hold for up to a half hour. Serve with preserves.

Thaw frozen blintzes overnight in refrigerator. Before baking them, brush them again with melted butter. Bake in a 250-degree oven for 15 minutes. (Heating them in the microwave makes them soggy.)

## EGG AND CHEESE CASSEROLE WITH HERBS (Serves 4 to 6)

8 eggs
½ cup milk
½ cup cottage cheese or ricotta
2 slices Swiss cheese, torn into small pieces
2 tablespoons of your favorite herb (such as chives, oregano, dill)
Vegetable cooking spray
½ cup crumbled Cheddar cheese

Whip eggs and milk with a wire whisk. Add cottage cheese, Swiss cheese, and herbs, and mix with wooden spoon. Pour into a deep pie dish sprayed with vegetable cooking spray. Sprinkle with crumbled Cheddar. Bake at 375 degrees for 45 minutes to 1 hour. Top should be lightly browned.

## BRAN MIX CEREAL (Makes 1 quart)

2 cups banana chips
1 cup rye flakes
½ cup slivered almonds
½ cup honey
1 teaspoon vanilla
2 tablespoons vegetable oil
½ cup warm water
¼ teaspoon salt
½ cup blond raisins
1 teaspoon vegetable oil

In large oiled baking dish, place banana chips, rye flakes, and almonds. Combine honey, vanilla, oil, water, and salt in small saucepan, and heat just to boiling point. Pour mixture over dry ingredients, and stir well until everything is moistened. Make layer even in pan. Bake in middle of preheated 300-degree oven for 15 minutes or until fragrance is first noticeable. Then continue to bake mixture, stirring it well every 5 minutes until it is toasted to your taste. Cool in the baking pan. Add raisins, and store in 1-quart glass jar with tight lid.

### BARBARA'S MIXED CEREAL (Makes 1 quart)

1 cup rolled oats
½ cup wheat germ
½ cup dried apples cut in small pieces
½ cup dried figs cut in small pieces
½ cup crushed soy nuts
½ cup chopped peanuts
¼ cup sunflower seeds
¼ cup raisins
¼ teaspoon salt

*Combine all ingredients, and store in 1-quart glass jar with tight lid. This is the simplest of all cereals because no other preparation is required. Tastes special with ice-cold buttermilk and a sprinkling of maple sugar.*

### MUESLI (Serves 1)

4 tablespoons rolled oats
¼ cup light cream
1 apple, washed and grated with the skin on
Juice of 1 lemon
1 tablespoon honey
2 tablespoons finely ground nuts (such as hazelnuts, cashews, almonds)

*Soak oats in milk for 5 minutes. Stir in grated apple and lemon juice. Top with honey and nuts. This Swiss classic is one of the quickest fresh breakfasts ever. Vary it by using fruits that are in season.*

### FRUIT CURRY (Serves 4)

2 pears, sliced
½ honeydew melon, cut in 1-inch pieces
1 banana
½ cantaloupe, cut in 1-inch pieces
2 navel oranges, cut in sections
10 dates, halved
1 cup white grape juice
1 teaspoon mild curry powder

*Combine all ingredients in mixing bowl. Refrigerate at least 2 hours.*

### VEGETABLE ZIP (Makes 1⅓ cups)

1 fully ripe tomato
½ cup clam juice
2 tablespoons lemon juice

2 shakes Tabasco sauce
½ cup cucumber slices

*Place all ingredients in blender, and spin for 10 seconds. Serve over ice.*

## ROASTED PANCAKES (Serves 4)

1 tablespoon unsalted butter
2 eggs
1 cup milk
1 cup unbleached flour, unsifted
¼ teaspoon salt
¼ cup confectioners' sugar
Fresh seasonal fruit topping (See recipe for Peach topping.)

*Preheat oven to 450 degrees. Place butter in 10-inch quiche pan, and warm for 5 minutes or until it melts. Coat pan completely with melted butter.*

*In a mixing bowl, beat eggs and milk. Add flour and salt, beating with wire whisk until batter is smooth. Or place eggs, milk, flour, and salt in blender, and spin for 15 second on medium speed.*

*Pour batter into quiche pan, and bake for 15 minutes. Reduce heat to 350 degrees and bake an additional 7 minutes. The pancake should be puffy and golden brown. Remove from oven and sprinkle with confectioners' sugar. Serve in quiche pan with a selection of fresh fruit toppings.*

### Peach Topping (Serves 4)

½ stick butter or margarine
4 cups fresh ripe peaches, sliced
Juice of 1 lemon
½ cup maple sugar
½ teaspoon cinnamon
¼ teaspoon nutmeg
½ cup slivered almonds

*In medium saucepan, melt butter, and add all ingredients except almonds. Stir over medium heat until peaches are soft and well coated with sugar mixture. Serve over pancakes or ice cream. Top with almonds.*

### Variations

*Variations for sauces include blueberries, raspberries, strawberries, or any sweet preserve.*

## SNOW EGGS (Serves 1)

3 eggs whites
3 teaspoons vegetable oil
2 tablespoons low-fat cottage cheese
1 teaspoon fresh chives, minced, or an equal amount of minced scallions
¼ teaspoon arrowroot powder

*Combine all ingredients, beating lightly. Add 1 teaspoon vegetable oil to nonstick pan at medium heat. Add egg mixture; allow to cook without stirring until edges set, then stir from outer edges to center. Too much stir-ring or too high heat will make the eggs watery. Serve garnished with fresh chive blossoms, orange, kiwi, or other bright fruit.*

## BROILED GRAPEFRUIT

1 grapefruit for each two guests
Maple or strawberry syrup
A strawberry or cherry to garnish

*Slice grapefruit in half. Use grapefruit knife to separate sections. Pour a tablespoon of strawberry or maple syrup over exposed side. Place in broiler and broil for 5 to 6 minutes or until edges start to brown. Garnish with berry and serve hot.*

## STUFFED FRENCH TOAST (For Each Guest)

4 pieces of cinnamon-raisin bread
Cream cheese
Slivered almonds
Batter—1 egg beaten with a tablespoon of milk and ½ teaspoon of vanilla

*Spread cream cheese on all slices of raisin bread; sprinkle two with sliv-ered almonds. Close sandwiches with the other two pieces of bread. Dip in batter and prepare like normal French toast in a well-heated pan and 1 teaspoon melted butter or margarine. Turn over as the first side browns lightly. Serve with heated maple syrup (the microwave works very well for heating the syrup).*

*Stuffed French Toast can be kept warm in the oven for a short time while you prepare enough to serve all the guests.*

## RASPBERRY SHAKE (Serves 4)

1 cup plain yogurt
2 cups raspberries (frozen or fresh)
½ cup sugar
1 teaspoon vanilla
1 tablespoon vegetable oil
⅛ teaspoon salt
1 cup low-fat milk

*Place all ingredients in blender, and spin 20 to 30 seconds or until mixture is of uniform texture and color. This is delicious with strawberries, too.*

## SHREDDED WHEAT BREAD (Makes 2 loaves)

5 shredded wheat biscuits
2 tablespoons butter
¼ cup molasses

2 teaspoons salt
2 cups whole milk, scalded
½ cup warm water mixed with
1 package dry yeast
3 cups whole-wheat flour
½ cup unbleached flour
Vegetable cooking spray
Melted butter

*Crumble shredded wheat biscuits in large mixing bowl. Add butter, molasses, salt, and milk. Combine well, and allow to cool to room temperature.*

*Stir in yeast mixture, blending well. Add flours gradually, stirring with spoon or hands until dough leaves sides of bowl. Place dough on floured surface, and knead gently for 3 to 4 minutes. Return dough to bowl, cover it with a damp cloth, and let it rise in a warm spot until it has doubled. Punch dough down, divide it in two, and shape each half into a loaf.*

*Spray two loaf pans with vegetable cooking spray. Place each loaf into a pan. Cover, and let rise until three-quarters of the way up the sides of the pans. Bake in preheated 375-degree oven for 45 minutes or until golden brown. Remove from oven, and brush with melted butter.*

## CODDLED EGG (Serves 1)

Vegetable cooking spray
½ strip bacon, cooked and drained
1 tablespoon shredded mozzarella
1 tablespoon shredded Cheddar cheese
1 egg
½ piece of Swiss or Sweet Munchee cheese, torn into small pieces

*Spray the inside of the ceramic portion of a coddler with vegetable cooking spray. Drop in bits of bacon. (You can substitute corned beef, pastrami, ham, or salami.) Sprinkle half of the Cheddar and mozzarella, crack in egg, sprinkle with three cheeses, and screw on top of coddler tightly. Place in boiling water up to level of the top of the coddler. Allow to cook for 10 minutes at slow boil. Remove top, and serve. Coddled eggs are wonderful because you make up as many as you need for the day and then wait until your guests appear at the table before you put them in the water to cook.*

## CONFETTI (Serves 8)

2 cups rice, cooked and chilled
1 cup green seedless grapes, halved
½ cup blond raisins
1 cup pineapple chunks
¾ cup walnuts, broken into small pieces
½ cup maraschino cherries, halved
Juice of 1 lemon
¼ cup mayonnaise
¼ cup plain yogurt

1 avocado, sliced thin
1 orange, sliced thin

*Combine all ingredients except avocado and orange slices in mixing bowl.
Refrigerate at least 2 hours. Transfer to serving dish. Garnish with avocado and orange slices.*

### CHAPATIS (Indian Flat Bread) (makes 1 dozen)

2 cups whole-wheat flour
½ teaspoon salt
2 tablespoons vegetable oil, melted butter, or margarine
½ cup to ¾ cup cold water
⅓ cup clarified butter (or melted unsalted butter or margarine)

*In large mixing bowl, combine flour and salt. Make a well in the dry ingre-
dients, and pour in oil. Mix thoroughly until texture is even. (Your fingers
are really the best tools for this because you can feel the little lumps
better than with a fork or spoon.) Add ½ cup water, and keep working the
dough with your hands until it begins to form a ball. Add additional water,
1 tablespoon at a time, until dough mass is no longer crumbly, but is not
sticky.*

*Turn dough out onto a very lightly floured surface. Knead 8 to 10 min-
utes or until glossy and elastic. Form dough into 12 even-sized balls, and
roll each out into a pancake 7 inches in diameter. (The pancakes will be
very thin.)*

*Brush each Chapati lightly with clarified butter, and cook in a heavy skil-
let over medium heat for approximately 1 minute. Turn, brush second side,
and repeat until Chapati is lightly browned. The Chapati should be flat, so
press it down with a spatula if it starts to swell in the pan. Serve hot, or
stack and wrap in foil before placing in preheated 200-degree oven for 10
to 15 minutes to hold until you are ready to serve.*

### POPPY-SEED ROLLS (makes 1 dozen)

1 package dry yeast or 1 yeast cake
1¼ cup warm water
½ teaspoon honey
1 egg, beaten
1¾ cup unbleached flour
¼ cup soy flour
½ cup butter or margarine, softened to room temperature
¼ cup sugar (optional)
1 teaspoon salt
1 cup sautéed onions
½ cup plus 3 tablespoons poppy seeds
Melted butter

*Dissolve yeast in warm water and honey. Let mixture sit until bubbles form
(called* proofing*).*

*In large mixing bowl, combine egg, half the flour, ½ cup warm water,
¼ cup butter, sugar, and salt. Beat vigorously for 2 minutes (an electric*

*mixer is a help); then add remaining flour. Mix well. Cover tightly, and refrigerate overnight.*

*Soak poppy seeds for 1 hour in cup warm water. Remove dough from refrigerator, and punch it down. Roll out on a floured surface into an oblong no more than ½ inch thick. Coat surface with butter, spread onions and drained poppy seeds evenly over the surface, and roll up into a jelly-roll shape (the longer end toward you). With a very sharp, nonserrated knife, cut the roll into 1-inch-thick rounds. Arrange in greased 2-inch muffin cups or a shallow baking pan, with edges of rolls barely touching. Cover rolls with damp towel, and let them rise until doubled in bulk. Brush tops with melted butter, and scatter extra poppy seeds over the tops. Bake in middle of preheated 400-degree oven for 12 to 15 minutes.*

❖❖❖❖❖❖❖

### RYE CRESCENT ROLLS (Makes 2 dozen small rolls)

1 package dry yeast or 1 yeast cake
¼ cup warm water
½ teaspoon honey
1½ cups rye flour
2¾ cups unbleached flour
¼ cup soy flour
¼ cup wheat germ
¾ teaspoon salt
¼ cup sugar or honey
2 eggs, beaten
⅔ cup melted butter
1½ cups sour cream

*Dissolve yeast in mixture of warm water and honey. In large mixing bowl, combine all dry ingredients and half the unbleached flour. Make a well in the mixture, and pour in yeast mixture, eggs, ⅓ cup butter, and sour cream. Stir thoroughly; then add remaining flour to form a somewhat sticky dough. Turn dough out onto a floured surface, and knead it until elastic, about 8 to 10 minutes. Return dough to bowl, and cover it with damp towel. Let dough rise until doubled, about 1 to 1½ hours. Punch dough down, and divide it into two pieces. Roll out each piece on a floured surface into a thin circle about the size of a small pizza pan. Cut each across the diameter of the circle 6 times, forming 12 triangular wedges. Brush remaining melted butter over wedges. Roll each wedge from the outer edge toward the center of the circle to form a crescent. Bake on foil-lined cookie sheets in middle of preheated 400-degree oven for 20 to 25 minutes or until browned*

### POTATO BREAD (Makes two 10-inch round loaves)

2 packages dry yeast or 2 cakes yeast
3 cups warm water (approximately)
1 teaspoon honey
1 pound potatoes, peeled, boiled, and mashed
10 cups unbleached flour

2 teaspoons salt
2 tablespoons olive oil

*Dissolve yeast in ½ cup warm water. Proof with honey (let it sit until it bubbles). In large mixing bowl, combine mashed potatoes, flour, salt, and yeast mixture. Add enough warm water to make a smooth, workable dough. Turn dough out onto a very lightly floured surface, and knead it for 10 minutes. Divide dough into two equal pieces. Roll out to fit two 10-inch round baking pans. Oil the pans liberally with olive oil. Transfer dough to pans, and brush light coating of oil on top.*

*Cover dough with damp cloth, and let it rise 1½ hours or until at least doubled in bulk. Bake in the middle of preheated 400-degree oven for 40 minutes or until golden brown. Cool to room temperature before cutting. This is an old-fashioned Italian peasant bread. Pureed garbanzo beans may be substituted for the potatoes.*

## WHOLE-WHEAT SUNFLOWER SEED BREAD (Makes 3 loaves)

4½ cups whole milk
¼ cup molasses
¼ cup honey
⅜ cup butter or margarine
2 packages dry yeast or 2 cakes yeast
½ cup warm water
1 cup wheat germ
½ cup sunflower seeds
1 tablespoon salt
12 cups whole-wheat flour

*In large saucepan, combine milk, molasses, honey, and butter. Warm over medium heat until butter melts, stirring so that molasses and honey blend in. Remove from heat, transfer mixture to very large mixing bowl, and let it cool to lukewarm.*

*Dissolve yeast in warm water with 1 teaspoon sugar or honey; let it rest until bubbles forms. Add to milk mixture. Stir in all other ingredients and 10 cups of the flour. Mix well until dough comes away from the sides of the bowl. Use the remaining 2 cups of flour during the kneading process. Whole wheat requires at least 20 minutes of vigorous kneading in order to develop a fine grain. Butter the mixing bowl, and return dough to it, cover with a damp cloth, and allow it to rise until doubled. Punch dough down. Let it rise again. Punch it down again, and knead it for 5 more minutes. Form dough into 3 loaves.*

*Butter 3 loaf pans (9 by 5 by 3 inches), and transfer loaves to them. Brush tops with melted butter. Cover with a damp towel, and let dough rise until it nears the top of the pan sides and is rounded on top. Preheat oven to 425 degrees. Place loaves in the middle of the oven, and bake for 15 minutes. Reduce temperature to 350 degrees, and bake another 30 minutes. Bread is done when it recedes from the sides of the pan and sounds hollow when tapped. Turn out of the pan onto rack to cool.*

### CROUTONS (CHEESE, HERB, AND SWEET)
### *(Makes about 2 cups each)*

1 loaf white bread
1½ cups melted butter or margarine
½ cup finely grated Romano cheese
1 teaspoon parsley flakes
1 teaspoon sage
1 teaspoon garlic powder
½ teaspoon paprika
¼ teaspoon salt
⅛ teaspoon freshly ground black pepper
¼ cup sugar
½ teaspoon cinnamon
½ teaspoon finely grated candied ginger

*Cut bread into slices about ½ inch thick. Remove crusts (if desired), and save them for making crumbs. Cut bread into cubes no more than ½ inch on a side. In a large skillet, swirl cubes around in melted butter until all are well coated. Roll a third of cubes in grated cheese. Roll the second third in herb mixture. Roll remaining third in sugar, cinnamon, and ginger. Arrange each variety in a single layer on its own cookie sheet. Bake in middle of preheated 250-degree oven 20 minutes, stirring occasionally to ensure even browning. Store in plastic bags or airtight tins. Use for garnish or in stuffing.*

### WELSH RAREBIT (Serves 6)

1 tablespoon butter
1 pound sharp Cheddar cheese, grated
1 cup beer
1 teaspoon dry mustard
Water
Pepper to taste
2 egg yolks

*In a saucepan or chafing dish, melt butter and cheese. When cheese is partially melted, add beer, and stir until well combined.*

   *Mix mustard with a small amount of water to form a soft paste. Add to cheese mixture along with pepper.*

   *When mixture is slightly thickened, remove from heat, and stir in egg yolks. Serve with hot rolls, bread, or over toast points or English muffins.*

### RHUBARB FIZZ (Makes 2 quarts)

4 pounds pink rhubarb
6 cups water
1 cup superfine sugar
1 quart ginger ale, chilled
Strawberries or chamomile blossoms
6 sprigs mint

*Rinse rhubarb, and cut it into 2-inch pieces, but do not peel it. Place pieces in large pot of water, and bring to a simmer. Cover, and cook over medium heat until very tender, about 30 minutes. Drain liquid into punch bowl, and stir in sugar. Discard pulp.*

*Chill thoroughly. When ready to serve, add ginger ale. Decorate with strawberries or chamomile blossoms. Pour into frosted, tall glasses over ice cubes, and garnish with mint.*

## GRAPEFRUIT-AVOCADO CUP (Serves 4)

1 avocado, sliced
1 grapefruit, sectioned
1 cup grapefruit juice

*In small serving cups, combine ingredients. Serve chilled.*

## EGG BURRITOS (Serves 4)

4 eggs, scrambled
4 flour tortillas
1 ripe tomato, sliced
1 ripe avocado, sliced
Salt and pepper to taste

*Arrange eggs, tomato, and avocado slices on tortillas. Season to taste. Roll in edges of tortilla to seal. Place on cookie sheet, and warm in 350-degree oven for 5 minutes. Serve hot.*

## CHEESE STRATA (Serves 6 to 8)

Vegetable cooking spray
1 large loaf of white bread, crusts removed
6 ounces crumbled Cheddar cheese
6 ounces crumbled Mozzarella cheese
4 large slices Swiss cheese, torn into small pieces
8 eggs
2 cups milk
½ stick butter, melted
½ teaspoon dry mustard

*Spray a 9-by-12-inch roasting pan with vegetable cooking spray. Line pan with one layer of white bread. Sprinkle half of the three cheeses over the bread. Add a second layer of bread and the remainder of the cheese. In a medium-size bowl, mix the eggs, milk, melted butter, and dry mustard well. Pour mixture over the bread and cheese. Cover pan with plastic wrap, and refrigerate overnight.*

*In the morning, remove plastic wrap, and bake in preheated 350-degree oven for 45 minutes to 1 hour. Top should be lightly brown.*

*This is a wonderful recipe for a large group who all want breakfast at the same time. It needs to be served immediately; once it starts to cool, it will fall and lose its visual appeal.*

❖❖❖❖❖❖❖

## OMELETS BY THE DOZEN

You may vary your omelets by incorporating cheeses, vegetables, potatoes, grains, or pasta; by making them folded (French), puffed (Spanish), or served in wedges (Italian); and by serving them with sauces. The combinations could keep you experimenting in the kitchen for weeks. Here are a dozen variations to begin with.

### Basic French Omelet (Serves 2)

4 eggs (Use no more in a single omelet, or it will be difficult to handle.)
½ cup water
2 tablespoons butter
Salt
Pepper

*Beat eggs gently in medium-size bowl. Add water, and stir until mixture is of even consistency. Melt butter over low to medium heat in 8-inch skillet, tilting pan so butter coats sides about halfway up. Pour in egg mixture. When eggs begin to set, lift up edges all around with a spatula and tilt pan so uncooked mixture runs beneath the cooked. Eggs should not stick to the bottom of the pan. If this starts to happen, reduce heat, and slide a bit more butter into the pan when you lift eggs from the bottom. High heat makes eggs toughen, so treat the omelet very gently.*

*When the bottom of the omelet is a golden brown and the top is almost set but not runny, slide spatula under one half, and flip it over on top of the other half. Ease the folded omelet onto a heated plate, season to taste, and serve at once.*

### Omelet with Herbs (Serves 2)

Choose one of the following combinations:
1 teaspoon fresh parsley and 1 teaspoon fresh chives
1 teaspoon dill and 1 teaspoon prepared mustard
¼ teaspoon garlic powder and ½ teaspoon oregano
¼ teaspoon sage and ¼ teaspoon thyme
¼ teaspoon rosemary and ¼ teaspoon nutmeg

*Mince fresh herbs, or crush dried. Add one combination to Basic French Omelet just before folding. Serve at once.*

### Omelet with Cheese (Serves 2)

4 ounces of your favorite cheese

*Grate cheese, and add to Basic French Omelet about 1 minute before you fold it. Cheese should be melted but not running out of the edges of the omelet. Serve at once.*

### Omelet with Onions (Serves 2)

1 Bermuda onion
2 tablespoons butter

*Slice onion very thin, and sauté in butter in separate skillet over medium heat. Do not use high heat, or butter and onion will scorch. When onion slices are transparent, remove skillet from heat, and set aside while you prepare eggs. Add onions to omelet about 1 minute before folding. Serve at once.*

### Omelet with Mushrooms (Serves 2)

4 ounces fresh mushrooms
3 tablespoons butter
1 tablespoon fresh parsley, chopped
½ cup yogurt

*Slice mushrooms very thin, and sauté in butter in a separate skillet over medium heat for 5 minutes. Remove from heat, and fold in parsley and yogurt. Return skillet to heat until yogurt is warmed through, but do not allow mixture to bubble because excessive heat destroys many nutritional factors in the yogurt. Add mushroom mixture to Basic French Omelet as eggs begin to set. Fold, and serve at once.*

### Omelet with Fried Peppers (Serves 2)

2 cups sweet or hot peppers
¼ cup olive oil
¼ teaspoon garlic powder

*Slice peppers into thin rounds, and sauté in olive oil in separate covered skillet over low to medium heat until peppers are soft. Stir occasionally to prevent scorching. Sprinkle garlic powder on peppers. Add peppers to Basic French Omelet just before folding. Serve at once.*

### Omelet with Green Beans (Serves 2)

1 cup green beans
Juice of 1 lemon
¼ cup slivered almonds

*Steam green beans until they are fork-tender. Squeeze lemon juice over the beans. Fold in almonds. Add mixture to Basic French Omelet as eggs begin to set. Fold, and serve at once.*

### Omelet with Marinated Artichokes (Serves 2)

4 marinated artichokes (Spanish, in jars)

*Add artichokes to Basic French Omelet just before folding. Serve at once.*

### Omelet with Spinach and Feta Cheese (Serves 2)

½ cup fresh spinach, cleaned
¼ cup Feta cheese, crumbled
¼ cup toasted bread crumbs
¼ teaspoon nutmeg

*Steam spinach until just softened. In mixing bowl, combine spinach, cheese, bread crumbs, and nutmeg. Add to Basic French Omelet as eggs begin to set. Fold, and serve at once.*

### Omelet with Potatoes (Serves 2)

1 large baked potato
1 tablespoon minced fresh parsley
2 tablespoons olive oil

¼ teaspoon vinegar
2 tablespoons Bakon (tastes like bacon but is made from nutritional yeast)

*Cut potato into ½-inch cubes, leaving skin on. In mixing bowl, combine potato and other ingredients. Let rest for 15 minutes before putting in omelet. Add to Basic French Omelet just before folding. Serve at once.*

### Omelet with Olives and Pimento (Serves 2)

¼ cup black or green olives (Greek, Spanish, or Italian)
2 pimento pods (in jar)
2 tablespoons freshly grated Romano or Parmesan cheese

*Cut olives into slivers, discarding pits. Slice pimentos into thin strips. In mixing bowl, combine olives, pimentos, and cheese. Add to Basic French Omelet as eggs begin to set. Fold, and serve at once.*

## *APPLE TART (Serves 6)*

### Crust

2½ cups unbleached flour, sifted
1 tablespoon baking powder
1 teaspoon salt
1 cup butter, chilled
¼ cup lard, chilled
½ to ¾ cup ice water

*Place flour, salt, and baking powder in large mixing bowl. Cut in butter and lard with fork or pastry cutter. (Do not use your fingers because that warms dough.) Add half the ice water as necessary to make dough come cleanly away from the sides of the bowl. Roll out on a lightly floured surface to be just slightly larger than a 12-inch tart pan.*

### Filling

6 medium McIntosh or other tart apples, peeled and sliced
2 eggs
1¼ cups sugar
½ cup whipping cream
½ cup whole milk
⅛ teaspoon salt
2 egg whites
1 cup slivered almonds

*Arrange apple slices in circular pattern, their sides just touching, to cover the bottom of crust. Bake in preheated 350-degree oven for 20 minutes.*

*In mixing bowl, combine 2 eggs, ¼ cup sugar, cream, and milk. Pour over apples after baking 20 minutes. Return tart to oven for another 20 minutes until top is golden brown and knife inserted comes out clean. Cool to warm.*

*In small saucepan, mix egg whites, almonds, and 1 cup sugar over medium heat. Stir continuously until mixture starts to congeal. Pour over cooled tart, and spread evenly over top.*

❖❖❖❖❖❖❖

## HOMEMADE SAUSAGE (Makes 6 pounds)

6 pounds lean pork
6 teaspoons salt
3 teaspoons freshly ground black pepper
4 teaspoons sage
½ teaspoon thyme
1 teaspoon paprika

*Run all ingredients through a meat grinder twice. Shape into patties, and freeze until needed. Bake on a cookie sheet at 450 degrees for 20 to 25 minutes or until cooked completely through. By making your own sausage meat, you will avoid the preservatives so widely used in commercial sausages.*

## GREEN TOMATO PIE (2 pies, each serves 4 to 6)

4 pie crusts (Frozen will do nicely, once thawed.)
8 to 10 very hard green tomatoes
2 very large onions, sliced and sautéed in ½ stick sweet butter
Italian seasoned bread crumbs
Coarse salt
Freshly ground pepper
2 tablespoons brown sugar (approximately)
1 pound Swiss cheese
1 pound Muenster cheese
Wine vinegar

*Prepare two crusts. Into each, sprinkle bread crumbs. Layer tomato slices, cheese, and sautéed onions. Sprinkle each layer with coarse salt, pepper, and brown sugar. Repeat until pie shells are full. (Depending on size of tomatoes and onions, this may even fill a third pie shell.) Top with more bread crumbs and a sprinkle of wine vinegar. Put top crust on each pie. Crimp edges and slash. Bake at 375 degrees until brown. Brushing top with milk as pie starts to brown will glaze it nicely. This pie freezes very well. It can be made all summer into early fall when green tomatoes are in your garden, frozen, and served all winter as a very hearty main dish for a skier's or hunter's breakfast.*

# 14

Interviews with
Successful Hosts

**W**hen I say that a host is successful, I don't mean that he or she makes a lot of money from Bed and Breakfast. Some do, of course, but what makes for success in this business is satisfaction. Successful hosts are people for whom the B&B lifestyle is enriching and satisfying. Guests find them gracious and hospitable. Reservation services get rave reviews for feedback and find working with these hosts a pleasure because they are cooperative, respond promptly, and always follow through on their commitments.

The following is a very brief glimpse into the wide variety of people who have become small innkeepers over the last ten years. These innkeepers are a sample of the many who were gracious enough to share their time and ideas at the PAII conference in Reston, Virginia, in the spring of 1994. These cameos paint pictures of the diversity from which folks come to enjoy lives as innkeepers. In addition, I asked folks to share their best tips, biggest mistakes, or most successful marketing strategies. Many of these are included.

## JOAN SUTTER, THE INN AT HARBOR HEAD, KENNEBUNKPORT, MAINE

Joan is in her tenth year of running a five-room inn. She is open all year, but is busiest May through October. She started with two rooms and expanded over time. She had already lived in the house for fifteen years with her family. As the family dwindled, the inn took over the rooms.

*Best tip:* "I found I can do a lot of things that I never knew I could do. I make all my own drapes, and I'm not a seamstress. Also, shared baths don't work in my area."

## MARGUERITE SWANSON, DURHAM HOUSE, HOUSTON, TEXAS

Marguerite also started from scratch. She bought a house on the historic register in her area. She rents her six rooms from $60 to $85 and reports an approximately 75 percent occupancy rate.

*Marketing:* She believes in advertising in guidebooks and in *Texas Monthly.*

*Biggest mistake:* "Some very expensive listings in *Innview*, a magazine geared to travel agents, and in the *Reed Southwest Guidebook.*"

## MERI FOUNTAIN, FOUNTAIN'S B&B, GIG HARBOR, WASHINGTON

Meri and husband Bruce lived in their waterfront island home before taking guests. They had always enjoyed traveling and meeting people. Their one guest room had been built for Meri's Dad before he died. When Bruce suffered a stroke and they could no longer travel, they decided to become a very small B&B. They still enjoy meeting people. However, the people now come to them.

*Marketing:* Only through her local chamber of commerce.

## JUNE KLEMM, BOXWOOD INN, AKRON, PENNSYLVANIA

June has four rooms with private bath in the main house and a carriage room over the barn with fireplace and whirlpool tub. She and husband Dick bought this home specifically to make into a

B&B. They added a wing to make private host quarters. They wanted a unique, historic property and lived in the house until their wing was finished six months later.

*Marketing:* Through the local tourist bureau and a quarterly newsletter.

*Biggest mistake:* Underpricing: "We rationalized to ourselves that we needed to do this to stay competitive, but we offer so much more than the other Lancaster County B&Bs." They charge $75 to $95 for a room in the house and $125 for the carriage house.


## KATIE GODMINTZ, CAPITOL HILL INN, SEATTLE, WASHINGTON

This 1903 Queen Anne inn with five guest rooms, two private baths, and two shared baths was once a "pigsty boarding house for young men," said Katie. It was in a great location, only seven minutes from the convention center. She knew she wanted to start a B&B, so, along with her daughter, she bought the house and began restoration.

*Biggest mistake:* Sinking $30,000 into building bathrooms. Katie admits to being "totally ignorant." She paid by the hour and never had a contract or put the job out for bids. The job was over budget and late. If she had to do it over again, she would get recommendations, sign a contract, and put in a penalty clause for finishing late.

*Marketing:* She gets her best results from the AAA, her visitor's bureau, marketing to groups, *Innplaces* by MaryAnne Ferrari, and America Online.


## VLANNE MYDLER, BOONE'S LICK TRAIL INN, ST. CHARLES, MISSOURI

Vlanne has five guest rooms, all with private bath. He's been in business for seven years. He purchased the building specifically to make a B&B and spent seven years totally renovating it.

*Marketing:* The community, working at the Visitor's Center, and the Lewis & Clark Trail office.

*Biggest mistakes:* His private space is too small and there's no place to expand. There was a building next door, but it's no longer available. "I wish I had six to eight rooms." With five rooms he has part-time staff. He prefers not to advertise for help. "My best help knocks at my door," states Vlanne.

## JUDY CLEMMER, THE LEADVILLE COUNTRY INN, LEADVILLE, COLORADO

Judy's nine rooms with private bath opened six years ago. The Clemmers relocated from Texas after selling a family business. They had been coming to ski for many years, and a friend in the ski business said he needed lodging space. They had never been to a B&B as a guest. They bought the building in August, started renovating on Labor Day, and were open for business December 7.

*Biggest mistake:* Not having her brochure and advertising in place before opening.

*Marketing:* She feels that her 800 number helps her compete. She has no question that her state association membership and participation in the state guide are her best marketing tools. The guidebooks and her Denver Yellow Pages ad are also very helpful. Newspaper advertising has not worked.

## HELEN ADAMS, CAPTAIN DIBBEL HOUSE, CLINTON, CONNECTICUT

Helen's been in business for eight years. She and her husband retired and came to Clinton with no family. They had no practical knowledge about innkeeping, but felt that with their pensions they didn't need the inn to survive. They opened with three rooms and one bath and soon discovered that this would not do.

*Biggest mistake:* The first contractor they hired gave them two-and-a-half baths. Within a year they had taken them out and hired a creative contractor, plumber, and electrician. They now have four rooms, all with private bath.

*Best tip:* Do as much as you can yourself. Also, warn guests about construction.

*Most successful marketing:* Word of mouth and the guidebooks.

## NANCY HOFFMAN, RYAN HOUSE, SONOMA, CALIFORNIA

Nancy bought an existing business after burning out in her past job. Her husband continued to work, so she felt that she didn't have to really support them with the B&B. Although they had previously lived in the Bay area, they had vacationed in Sonoma. They now offer four rooms with private bath. The inn income supports the house, pays the taxes, and provides a few extras. They did a lot of renovation, remodeling the kitchen, rebuilding falling-down porches, and converting the attic into a suite.

*Best advice for construction:* Have a sense of humor. Be upfront and explain to guests beforehand.

*Biggest mistake:* Spent too much money. "Also, I made the mistake of assuming that all B&Bs were legit. I referred people to places I didn't know, and they were dissatisfied."

*Best tip:* Plan well ahead. Stay well stocked. Market cooperatively. Nancy finds her 800 number very important. Her ad in *Country Inns Magazine* really pulls, as does the AAA and her state association guide.

## DENNY BECKER, A TEETON TREE HOUSE, B&B INN, WILSON, WYOMING

Denny built his dream house from scratch over the last twenty-one years, and it is now a six-guestroom B&B. He was an outfitter river and mountain guide; his wife was a teacher. Denny sold his business and went off to South America for six months. When he returned, they decided to have children. At his wife's suggestion, they decided to turn their house into a B&B. His wife still teaches but helps out in the summer. Their kids are now teenagers. He warns other innkeepers that problems can develop if the family perceives that the guests are more important than they are. You need to make sure they always know where your true priorities lie.

*Biggest mistakes:* "I priced myself too low in the beginning. I also wanted to please everyone and found myself promising more than I could deliver. I once overbooked and had not only to refund the guest's money but also pay for their lodging elsewhere."

*Best tip:* Make a minimum of rules that are clear and well spelled out.

*Marketing:* Guidebooks are number one. Best guide: Doris Kennedy's *Wonderful Little Inns and Hotels Under $100.* Denny also explained that being in the Jackson Hole area creates special marketing needs. It is a far-out destination point. Most people who plan this trip start by requesting the *Wyoming State Travel Guide.* He uses its list to send out a folded postcard. One part describes his inn. The other is addressed to the inn with a check-off list of nearby activities and on the reverse side has a reservation request form. The description of the inn begins with "A gem of an inn that is way out on a forest mountainside in the quiet solitude and only 3/4 mile from town. Add the opportunity to retreat up 95 gentle steps . . . ." He makes sure that anyone pursuing reservations with him is in good shape and sees the remoteness of this home as an asset rather than a liability. For those who return the card, a second mailing goes out with a four-color flyer and some excellent press about the inn.

## JULIE HENEGHAN, IDAHO COUNTRY INN, SUN VALLEY, IDAHO

Julie and her husband were living in Sun Valley and wanted to stay there. There were no inns to buy or older homes to fix up. Five years ago, they built their ten-room, private-bath inn in an area that was already zoned "tourist." They included an innkeeper apartment on the other side of the kitchen.

*Biggest mistake:* The innkeepers' quarters are too small. They now want to move off-site.

*Best tip:* Add a second dryer. Now that they have a second dryer, the laundry actually gets done. Also, computerize.

*Biggest challenge:* The inn was built prior to the ADA. They can't find a way now to provide easy wheelchair access as there are a number of steps to the first level. They have installed vibrating alarms, however.

*Marketing:* They find guidebooks with ads that cost under $50 to be the best return on investment. Their ad in *Country Inns Magazine* performed far better than the one they placed in *Ski Magazine.* Local advertising and the chamber of commerce also work well for them.

## SALLIE CLARK, HOLDEN HOUSE, COLORADO SPRINGS, COLORADO

Sallie and her husband were living in San Diego. They had grown tired of southern California and wanted to live in Colorado. They originally planned to have a twelve-room inn, but found out at an innkeeping course that they didn't have sufficient capital. Her husband opted to work outside the home while Sallie ran the inn. Colorado Springs had a good economic base, centering around business, tourism, and education (the Air Force Academy). Alas, there were no inns for sale. They bought a large Victorian House and renovated it. Originally, the house had an unstable foundation and no plumbing or heating, and no bank would provide a mortgage. The City of Colorado Springs helped out. Once the building was up to code, they refinanced. They opened in June of 1986. They have three rooms with private bath in the main house and two suites in the carriage house. The neighbor's dog was causing a problem, barking at guests, so they bought the neighbor's house and got the zoning approval to have three more rooms there. This provides them with a handicapped-accessible room.

*Biggest mistakes:* "I wish I had learned more from others. I didn't have my initial brochure ready and didn't market enough prior to opening. I had failed to plan a marketing budget." This cost them considerably in lost revenue in the beginning.

*Tips:* "Learn the fine line between rigid and flexible. Also, once you're established, get help." Sallie now has three staffers, two part-time and one full-time.

## PAULINE MEDHURST, QUEEN ANNE INN, SOUTH BEND, INDIANA

Pauline described herself as a college teacher who was suffering from burnout when she turned to innkeeping. She and her husband had the first B&B in South Bend. They have seven guest rooms, five with private bath. They have been running the inn for eight years.

*Mistakes:* "We started with too little capital and not enough business background. I had to go back to teaching part-time for a while to make up the difference and felt split in half." Pauline has now retired from teaching and devotes herself full-time to the inn. She and her husband have their eye on the property next door and want to expand to twelve rooms.

*Tips:* She has one full-time staff member who also helps bake for teas, which she offers one day a week and one Saturday a month. She recommends a good business plan and a computer system.

*Marketing:* Guidebooks, a sign on the toll road, and her 800 number seem to be her best sources.

## PETER HOLLADAY, HOLLADAY HOUSE, ORANGE, VIRGINIA

Peter opened five years ago by taking over an old family home. To renovate what became a six-room inn he couldn't get a traditional mortgage, so he negotiated an investment loan that was converted after three years to a conventional home loan. During those three years, the interest rate was very high and burdensome.

*Mistakes:* Peter feels that he has made a number of costly mistakes. Mistake number one certainly was the investment loan and not setting enough capital aside before starting this project. He also did a tremendous amount of construction without storing the furniture, which would have made working so much easier.

*Marketing:* Cooperative marketing with several neighboring inns has been his best return. His worst marketing effort was the direct mail piece he once sent to people from a wine enthusiasts' mailing list. He got no business from it.

## BAMBI ARNOLD, THE MANOR, HOLDERNESS, NEW HAMPSHIRE

I met Bambi on the telephone a few months before the conference because of a direct mail piece she did to promote her twenty-seven room lakeside country inn. Their inn is quite large and has a restaurant with four dining rooms. The success of her direct mail piece was interesting to me as I have often wondered about this type of marketing. The piece was truly wonderful: an over-sized postcard with three glossy full-color pictures on one side and terrific handwritten (really printed, but looked like real handwriting) copy on the other side. It began with "Greetings from Golden Pond" and went on to describe their wonderful place. The handwritten look made me think that it was indeed a personal postcard written from a friend. I read it rather than tossing it out immediately, as I was enthralled. The card wasn't sent to me, but to a friend who was on the mailing list Bambi bought. She paid 6¢ a name for the list, which came on mailing labels and was allowed to be used only once. (The mailing list people seed the list with false names. Should you use the list again, you will be caught and charged.) Her postcards cost 12¢ each plus printing and 29¢ for postage at the time for first class. Bambi figures the cost of this mailing to be about 50¢ each for 5,271 cards mailed out. Big mail order companies estimate a 3 percent return. Bambi had 110 phone calls and seven letters in the first month. A few months later, when I actually met her at the conference, she was up to 150 calls and twenty-five written responses. Two mailmen who saw the card when delivering it called to request a brochure. Although she has not figured out how many reservations resulted from this mailing, she considers it a success. During my last phone call with her, over a year since the mailing, Bambi remarked that people are still walking in to the inn carrying the card.

## DIANNE LEGENHAUSEN, APPLEGATE B&B, PETERBOROUGH, NEW HAMPSHIRE

Diane and her husband were ready to retire on their pension. They moved to New Hampshire and opened a four-room, private-bath inn five years ago. She feels that it is manageable and would like to add another room or two.

*Biggest mistake:* They lived in the house during renovations.

*Best tip:* "We went to a lot of B&Bs to see what we liked or didn't like."

*Marketing: New Hampshire State Travel Guide, Weekending in New England,* and the Yellow Pages produce the most business for them. Dianne feels that her 800 number pulls, as does sending postcards to past guests.

## MARY HOCKETT, SALSA DEL SALTO B&B, TAOS, NEW MEXICO

Mary was divorced. She decided on the spur of the moment to open a B&B with her new partner, a French chef. They have now married. He had been in the hotel business, but they soon learned that his wealth of knowledge didn't always apply to an eight-room B&B. The clientele was very different. They have two homes right next door to each other. One contains six guest rooms; the other two guest rooms and their living quarters. They have been in business for seven years. Mary says that although they'll never have a lot of money, they live in a beautiful part of the country and get to do what they enjoy.

*Biggest mistake:* Not knowing the market. They wasted a lot of money.

*Tips:* Don't take negative feedback personally. Use it to get better.

## BARBARA CAMPBELL, WAIMEA COTTAGE, KAMUELA, HAWAII

Barbara had a little washhouse on her property. At her daughter's wedding, everyone who saw it called to ask if their friends or relatives coming down to visit could use it. Barb knew of B&B from abroad and decided this was for them. That was fourteen years ago, and four years ago she built a second cottage. She stocks the fridge and provides food baskets and flowers.

*Marketing:* Guidebooks, press releases to traveler writers, ad in *Country Inns Magazine.*

*Mistake:* "Doing all my own cleaning almost burned me out."

*Tip:* Only do construction between 8:00 A.M. and 4:00 P.M.

## GARY GOSSELIN, INN AT BLUSH HILL, WATERBURY, VERMONT

Gary and his wife bought a working B&B eight years ago. He was in the hotel business and was tired of moving around so much. They wanted to settle down with their children. They thought that they would do this for about ten years, but now they have decided to continue. They offer six guest rooms (four with private bath, two with shared bath) and have private quarters for themselves and their two children.

*Biggest mistake:* Shared bath.

*Marketing:* Word of mouth, Bernice Chesler's guides, and cooperative ads in the *Boston Globe* and *Vermont Magazine.*

## DEBORAH MOISIMANN, SWISS WOODS, LITITZ, PENNSYLVANIA (AMISH COUNTRY)

Deborah moved here from Switzerland ten years ago so that her whole family could be together. They built a house for the family plus an annex. They offer seven rooms with private bath. Although her husband used to work outside the home, he is now employed full-time at the inn. They have four children. Deborah has a number of part-time helpers to do housekeeping, as well as a Sunday morning kitchen assistant who can take over completely if the need arises.

*Biggest mistake:* Not taking the business seriously enough at first and having to learn from her mistakes.

*Tips:* Be very organized. Utilize your freezer. Hire enough help. Keep your debt as low as possible.

*Marketing:* Guidebooks, local tourism promotion, and involvement with the local tourist agency.

## YOU OF YOURTOWN, U.S.A.

Once you've used this book to open your home to B&B guests, I'd like to hear your story. Who knows, the next edition may include your tips and anecdotes. Write to Barbara Notarius, Alexander Hamilton House, 49 Van Wyck Street, Croton-on-Hudson, NY 10520.

❖❖❖❖❖❖❖

**Question:** I plan to retire in a few years and was thinking of moving to Texas to be closer to my married children. I've always dreamt of being an innkeeper. Is this a good second career for retirement?

**Answer:** *Some call innkeeping the stewardess fantasy of middle age. Speak to a handful of friends, and at least one couple will confess their desire to abandon the rat race and open an inn. The fantasy includes a wonderful old house with views or gardens and the creation of mouth-watering food for interesting people who will flock to the door as paying guests. For many, this is just a pipe dream, but for an increasing number of people, it is a dream becoming a reality.*

*Innkeeping as a lifestyle change works for many in retirement. They have start-up capital and usually a pension or some other outside income to keep them going until their inn turns a profit. Because they are not totally reliant on the inn for their livelihood, they can run small inns with only a few rooms and give each guest special attention. Experience from past careers, coupled with maturity, is a distinct advantage. Older innkeepers know how to make visitors feel welcome. In retirement, the goal* is no longer to amass wealth. For some, it is a way to move to a new location and quickly become part of the community. For others, it is a way to remain in the cherished home, utilize the extra bedrooms, supplement retirement savings, and ensure a social flow so often missed when they become cut off from the traditional workplace.

Bed and Breakfast is the fastest growing segment of the travel industry in America today. It will undoubtedly continue as the baby boomers age, and it will make innkeeping a realistic fantasy as part of retirement planning.

At the Professional Association of Innkeepers International conference in Reston, Virginia, in April 1994, I spent four days interviewing innkeepers and prospective innkeepers as part of the research necessary to update this book. I was not aware until this conference of how many people are looking toward innkeeping as a way to change their lifestyle while making a career change as retirement approaches.

The stories of Pam and Don McMurray, Jack and JoAnne Warmoth, and Ray and Sandy Tool illustrate very different paths to just such retirement careers.

Pam and Don McMurray, proprietors of the Norris House in Leesburg, Virginia, came from corporate America. They were both doing marketing for large utilities in California. After more than ten years, both were burning out. Don started his own business, and Pam changed companies to head a division of another utility company. Both traveled often, and they realized that they had accumulated over a million-and-a-half frequent-flyer miles between them. They began taking weekend trips all over the country. One Labor Day weekend, in Bar Harbor, all the traditional hotels and motels were full, and they were forced to stay at a B&B. They had such a wonderful time that they began to seek out B&Bs and small inns when they traveled, and kept thinking of different couples they knew who would make great innkeepers. Finally, they looked at each other and said, "Actually, we would make great innkeepers."

They started looking at properties and doing their home-work, talking to innkeepers and watching what they did. They were told that it was a "risky" business and that they would probably not make a lot of money, but their entrepre-neurial spirit was ripe and they decided that they had two houses to sell in California and had made other good real estate investments, so they were in a good financial position to take the gamble.

Meanwhile, they selected their own criteria for a location: (1) near a major city; (2) near a major airport (Don still would need to travel); (3) another B&B in town; and (4) restaurants and other attractions that would augment business.

Both were amateur genealogists, and their weekend travel-ing also gave them an opportunity to trace their roots. Although both grew up in California, it turned out that both families came from Virginia to California during the gold rush. Tracing her family back to Louden County, Pam felt very much at home in Leesburg, and when, on route from Washington, DC, she spied a Nordstrom (California department store), she knew she could survive there.

Neither felt that they could afford to purchase a going concern and fully expected to buy a rambling old home that needed much renovation. They were in luck, however, because the market was in a slump and the innkeepers at the Norris House had been unable to sell and had left the inn in the not-very-capable hands of some college students. Originally on the market for over $700,000, the inn sold for under $400,000. It needed a lot of work, so Pam and Don began by stabilizing the building and then started to work on the interior room by room.

They currently have six guest rooms that share three baths. They also rent the house next door, in which they have a tea-room and their quarters. A partner runs the tearoom, and the lovely landscaped area between the two houses is the site for weddings twice a month. Pam brings in an outside caterer for the weddings. She uses the tearoom kitchen, and the bride and groom guarantee all six guestrooms for the weekend.

*Pam and Don have adjusted very well to a new place and lifestyle. They have plans to expand the inn in the future. They have made lots of new friends, and although they are kept very busy with their innkeeping duties, both feel that it was the right move and one that keeps them feeling young and vital.*

*JoAnne and Jack Warmoth came to see innkeepers in a very different way. They don't own the inn. It is the former home of Ralph Teetor, founder of Perfect Circle Corporation and inventor of cruise control. Teetor House in Hagerstown, Indiana, offers four guest rooms, each with private bath.*

   *JoAnne worked for the Teetors for many years, and when both died, their daughter in Indianapolis wanted to keep the home, but did not want to relocate there. Friends advised her to make it a B&B. She did this and asked JoAnne and Jack to run it. Jack, who worked in a foundry for thirty-four years and faced a forced early retirement, now takes care of the grounds and maintains the house. JoAnne's territory is the interior. She does the cooking, and together they enjoy hosting the guests who stay here. They love to tell the story of Mr. Teetor, who was blinded at age five and despite his disability went on to establish a successful business and invent numerous things in his basement workshop. They earn a salary as innkeepers, enjoy living on this beautiful estate, and meet many interesting people. The business generates enough to pay their salary and keep up the house. For ten years, the Teetors' daughter has rested easily knowing that her childhood home is well cared for and that she can stay there whenever she visits Hagerstown.*

*Ray and Sandy Tool had not opened their inn yet when I first spoke with them. They were fifty-five and fifty-six years old, respectively, married for two years, and had just closed on the home in Saint Augustine, Florida, that was to become their inn, Casa de Sueños (House of Dreams). Sandy has worked for a large hotel chain creating recipes and menus for their restaurants and has given five-years' notice. Ray has begun his innkeeping career while continuing his consulting and sales business. When they bought it, the inn was still a large Spanish-*

style structure housing four legal offices. The last owner renovated the structure and did considerable work, including new
wiring and plumbing. Ray and Sandy have done their home-
work. They plan to have six guest rooms with private baths as
well as innkeepers' quarters. The inn is right across from the
historic district, located between two other B&Bs.

Saint Augustine, America's oldest city, has an active B&B
association that works cooperatively to market the B&Bs to travelers. At present, all six rooms are open and guests are very
welcome at the Casa de Sueños. Although Ray projected 35
percent occupancy to start, he has enjoyed between sixty and
seventy-five percent occupancy since opening in May 1995. Ray
has additionally hosted a number of weddings at the inn and
one renewal of vows in celebration of a couple's twenty-fifth
anniversary. He's proud to have officiated at two of the weddings—all that is required in Florida is that you be a notary.

These couples share with you a desire to make their retirement
years rich and lively. They are outgoing, enjoy meeting people,
creating and sharing good food, and making their visual environment attractive. They plan ahead and give attention to small
details. They are not unlike many others who are taking seminars, reading books, or just plain trying out inns to see if
innkeeping will be a part of their future.

# Appendix A

# Bed and Breakfast

# Reservation Services

*ALABAMA*

**Lincoln, Ltd., Bed & Breakfast**
PO Box 3479
Meridan, MS 39303
(601) 482-5483    Fax: (601) 693-7447

This service covers from Natchez to Memphis, Mississippi, statewide, and selected areas of Louisiana and Alabama.
*Annual fee:* Yes
*Commission:* Based on property
*Director:* Barbara Hall
*Member:* TNN and Worldwide

*ALASKA*

**Alaska Private Lodging**
Stay with a Friend
PO Box 200047
Anchorage, AK 99520-0047
(907) 258-1717    Fax: (907) 258-6613

This service markets B&Bs throughout south-central and south-east Alaska.
*Annual fee:* None
*Commission:* 20 percent
*Director:* Mercy Dennis
*Member:* TNN and Worldwide

## ARIZONA

### Mi Casa Su Casa
PO Box 950
Tempe, AZ 85280-0950
(602) 990-0682 or (800) 456-0682
Fax: (602) 990-3390

This service specializes in Arizona, New Mexico, Utah, and Nevada.

*Annual fee:* $50

*Commission:* 20 percent

*Director:* Ruth Young

*Member:* TNN and Worldwide

## ARKANSAS

See **Missouri,** Ozark Mt. Country B&B

## CALIFORNIA

### Bed & Breakfast San Francisco
PO Box 420009
San Francisco, CA 94142
(415) 479-1913    Fax: (415) 921-BBSF (2273)

This service represents private-home B&Bs in homes, man-' sions, yachts, and houseboats in San Francisco, Marin County, Monterey, Carmel, and the Wine Country.

*Fees:* One-time inspection fee of $50, no annual fee

*Commission:* 25 percent

*Directors:* Richard and Susan Kreibich

*Member:* No membership

## COLORADO

### Bed & Breakfast Agency of Colorado at Vail
PO Box 491
Vail, CO 81658
(970) 9490-1212 or (800) 748-2666

This service covers over 100 homes and inns throughout Colorado. Each home needs to be inspected, carry all the necessary insurance, have a valid business and/or tax license, clearly state their pet, smoking, and child policy, and follow reservation service policy.

*Annual fee:* $50–$75

*Commission:* 10–25 percent

*Director:* Kathy Fagen
*Member:* Worldwide

## CONNECTICUT

### Nutmeg Bed & Breakfast Agency
PO Box 1117
West Hartford, CT 06127
(203) 236-6698    Fax: (203) 232-7680

Nutmeg is Connecticut's oldest reservation service, the only one that is statewide. They are affiliated with the National Network. They visit all their B&Bs and act as a total "front desk" for your B&B.

*Annual fee:* $50
*Commission:* 15–25 percent depending on number of rooms
*Contact:* Michelle Souza
*Member:* TNN

## DISTRICT OF COLUMBIA

### Bed & Breakfast League/Sweet Dreams and Toast
PO Box 9490
Washington, DC 20016-9490
(202) 363-7767

This service covers Washington, DC, and Bethesda, MD. All homes must be in good, safe areas with good access to public transportation.

*Annual fee:* None
*Commission:* 25 percent
*Director:* Millie Groobey
*Member:* Worldwide

### Bed & Breakfast Accommodations, Ltd.
PO Box 12011
Washington, DC 20005
(202) 328-3510    Fax: (202) 332-3885

This service covers Washington, DC, and nearby Maryland and Virginia, and specializes in historic properties decorated with antiques.

*Inspection fee:* $25
*Commission:* 20 percent if exclusive
*Director:* Jacqueline Reed
*Member:* TNN and Worldwide

See also **Maryland,** Amanda's Bed & Breakfast
Reservation Service

*DELAWARE*

**Bed & Breakfast of Delaware**
Box 177
3650 Silverside Rd.
Wilmington, DE 19810
(302) 479-9500, phone or fax

This service is statewide and also covers the Brandywine region of Pennsylvania and the Chesapeake area of Maryland.

*Annual fee:* None
*Commission:* 20 percent
*Director:* Millie Alford
*Member:* Worldwide

See also **Maryland,** Amanda's Bed & Breakfast
Reservation Service

*GEORGIA*

**R.S.V.P GRITS, Inc.**
**(Great Reservations in the South)**
541 Londonbery Rd., NW
Atlanta, GA 30327
(404) 843-3933 or (800) 823-7787
Fax: (404) 252-8886

This service covers an area within a 100-mile radius of Atlanta and the North Georgia Mountains, as well as Huntsville, Montgomery, Birmingham (Alabama), and Chattanooga (Tennessee). It specializes in small B&B inns, carriage houses, and guest quarters with two or more bedrooms. All are inspected each year and must conform to all local, state, and national laws.

*Annual fee:* $50
*Commission:* 15 percent
*Director:* Marty Barnes
*Member:* Worldwide

*IDAHO*

See **Montana,** B&B Western Adventure

*LOUISIANA*

**Bed & Breakfast, Inc., New Orleans**
1021 Moss St., Box 52257
New Orleans, LA 70152-2257
(504) 488-4640 or (800) 729-4740
Fax: (504) 488-4639

This service represents exclusively historic B&Bs of one to five rooms in New Orleans. Every staff member visits each property. Each B&B is inspected and rated annually. Free listings available.

*Annual fee:* Yes, depending on room rates.

*Commission:* 20 percent

*Contact:* Hazel Boyce

*Member:* Worldwide

*MAINE*

**B&B of Maine at Quaker Tavern Bed & Breakfast**
377 Gray Rd.
Falmouth, ME 04105
(207) 797-5540     Fax: (207) 797-7599

This service accepts hosts throughout the state of Maine. Each must meet high standards of cleanliness, ambiance, and goodwill ambassadorship.

*Annual fee:* None

*Commission:* 10 percent

*Director:* Donna Little

*Member:* Worldwide

*MARYLAND*

**Amanda's Bed & Breakfast Reservation Service**
1428 Park Ave.
Baltimore, MD 21217
(410) 225-0001     Fax: (410) 728-8957

This service represents B&Bs in private homes, small inns, and on yachts throughout Maryland and selected locations in Pennsylvania, Virginia, West Virginia, Delaware, New Jersey, and Washington, DC.

*Annual fee:* $60

*Commission:* 20 percent

*Director:* Betsy Grater

*Member:* Worldwide

**Bed & Breakfast of Maryland/Traveler in Maryland**
PO Box 2277
Annapolis, MD 21404-2277
(410) 269-6232
Fax: (410) 263-4841

This service covers the state of Maryland. Hosts must meet high quality and assurance standards, and local insurance and licensing requirements.

*Annual fee:* $80

*Commission:* 20 percent

*Director:* Greg Page

*Member:* TNN and Worldwide

See also **Virginia,** Blue Ridge Bed & Breakfast

*MASSACHUSETTS*

**Bed & Breakfast Bay Colony, Ltd.**
PO Box 57166
Babson Park
Boston, MA 02157-0166
(617) 449-5302 or (800) 347-5088
Fax: (617) 449-5958

Established in 1981, this service covers central Boston, the North Shore, South Shore, Cape Cod, Martha's Vineyard, Nantucket, and suburban towns within 40 miles of Boston.

*Annual fee:* Yes, varies by location

*Commission:* Yes

*Directors:* Marilyn Mitchell and Arlene Kardasis

*Member:* TNN

**Folkstone Bed & Breakfast Reservation Service**
51 Sears Rd
Southboro, MA 01772
(800) 762-2751

This service covers central Massachusetts from the Amherst area to Concord and also the northeast corner of Connecticut near Sturbridge.

*Annual fee:* $50

*Commission:* 20 percent

*DIrector:* Abigail Miller

*Member:* Worldwide

See also **New York State,** the American Country Collection

## MISSISSIPPI

See **Alabama,** Lincoln, Ltd.

## MISSOURI

**Ozark Mountain Country B&B Service**
PO Box 295
Branson, MO 65615
(417) 334-4720 or (800) 895-1546
Fax: (417) 335-8134

This service covers southwest Missouri and northwest Arkansas. All host homes must be inspected and meet standards of quality and cleanliness.

*Annual fee:* $25
*Commission:* 20 percent
*Director:* Kay Cameron
*Member:* Worldwide

## MONTANA

**Bed & Breakfast Western Adventure**
PO Box 4308
Bozeman, MT 59772
(406) 585-0557     Fax: (406) 585-2869

This service covers the Glacier and Yellowstone National Park sections of Montana, Wyoming, and Idaho. All B&Bs are inspected.

*Annual fee:* $75
*Commission:* 15–20 percent
*Director:* Paula Deigert
*Member:* TNN and Worldwide

## NEW HAMPSHIRE

See **New York State,** the American Country Collection

## NEW JERSEY

**Bed & Breakfast Adventure**
2310 Central Ave., Suite 132
North Wildwood, NJ 08260
(609) 522-4000     Fax: (609) 522-6125

This service covers all of New Jersey and eastern Pennsylvania from Lancaster to the New York border (excluding Philadelphia). The owners teach adult education classes and run seminars about how to operate a B&B. Private consulting is also available.

*Annual fee:* $100

*Commission:* 15 percent

*Directors:* Diane and Paul Buscham di Filippo

*Member:* TNN and Worldwide

### Amanda's Bed & Breakfast Reservation Service
21 S. Woodland Ave.
E. Brunswick, NJ 08816
(908) 249-4944    Fax: (908) 246-1961

See **Maryland,** Amanda's Bed & Breakfast
Reservation Services, for details.

### NEW MEXICO

### Bed & Breakfast of New Mexico
PO Box 2805
Santa Fe, NM 87504
(505) 982-3332

This service covers B&Bs throughout New Mexico.

*Annual fee:* None

*Commission:* 25 percent

*Director:* Debbie Bennet

*Member:* TNN and Worldwide

### NEW YORK

### The American Country Collection of Bed & Breakfast
1353 Union St.
Schenectady, NY 12308
(518) 370-4948

This service covers eastern and central New York State, western Massachusetts, all of Vermont, western New Hampshire, and the island of St. Thomas in the U.S. Virgin Islands. Inspection is required prior to membership.

*Annual fee:* $50 the first year, then sliding scale fee relative to business activity

*Commission:* 20 percent

*Director:* Carol Matos

*Member:* TNN and Worldwide

### At Home in New York
PO Box 407
New York, NY 10185
(212) 956-3125    Fax: (212) 247-3294

This service represents more than 300 B&Bs and private pied-à-terre in New York City, the Hamptons, and Westchester. Listings in several European cities are also offered.

*Annual fee:* None
*Commission:* 25 percent
*Director:* Lois Rookes
*Member:* Worldwide

## PENNSYLVANIA

### Rest and Repast
PO Box 126
Pine Grove Mills, PA 16868
(814) 238-1484    Fax: (914) 234-9890

This service represents B&Bs in central Pennsylvania and near Penn State University.

*Member:* Worldwide

See also **Maryland,** Amanda's Bed & Breakfast
Reservation Services, and **Virginia,**
Blue Ridge Bed & Breakfast.

## RHODE ISLAND

### Anna'a Victorian Connection
5 Fowler Ave.
Newport, RI 03840
(401) 849-2489    Fax: (401) 847-7309

This service represents over 200 inns, private homes, and self-catered lodgings in Rhode Island and southeastern Massachusetts. All are inspected.

*Annual fee:* $35
*Commission:* 20 percent
*Director:* Susan Collis White
*Member:* TNN and Worldwide

## TENNESSEE

### Bed & Breakfast about Tennessee
PO Box 110227
Nashville, TN 37222-0227
(615) 331-5244    Fax: (615) 833-7701

This service covers Tennessee statewide.
*Annual fee:* $25
*Commission:* 25 percent
*Director:* Fredda Odom
*Member:* TNN and Worldwide

## TEXAS

### Bed & Breakfast Texas Style
4224 W. Red Bird Lane
Dallas, TX 75237
(214) 298-8586    Fax: (214) 298-7118

This service covers Texas statewide.
*Annual fee:* $50
*Commission:* 20 percent
*Director:* Ruth Wilson
*Member:* TNN and Worldwide

### Gasthaus Schmidt Reservation Service
231 W. Main St.
Fredericksburg, TX 78624
(210) 997-5612    Fax: (210) 997-8282

This service covers Gillespic County of greater Fredericksburg and focuses on romantic and historic homes with quality antiques.
*Annual fee:* $60
*Commission:* 21 percent
*Director:* Donna Mittel
*Member:* Worldwide

## VERMONT

### Vermont Center Point
PO Box 8513
Essex, VT 05451
(800) 449-2745    Fax: (802) 872-2745

This service covers the state of Vermont only. The B&Bs must be licensed by the state of Vermont. Hosts must live in the home and meet all standards of quality set by the reservation service.
*Annual fee:* $200
*Commission:* 20 percent
*Director:* Denise Perraudin
*Member:* Worldwide

See also **New York State,** the American Country Collection

## VIRGINIA

### Guesthouses Bed & Breakfast, Inc.
PO Box 5737
Charlottesville, VA 22905
(804) 979-7264     Fax: (804) 293-7791

This service covers central Virginia around Albemarle County and Charlottesville.

*Annual fee:* None

*Commission:* 25 percent

*Director:* Mary Hill Caperton

*Member:* TNN and Worldwide

### Blue Ridge Bed & Breakfast
Rye 2, Rocks and Rills, Box 3895
Berryville, VA 22611
(703) 955-1246     Fax: (703) 955-1246

This service covers Virginia, West Virginia, and portions of Pennsylvania and Maryland. Inns are inspected every year.

*Annual fee:* None

*Commission:* 20 percent

*Director:* Rita Duncan

*Member:* Worldwide

See also **Maryland,** Amanda's Bed & Breakfast
Reservation Services

## WASHINGTON STATE

### A Pacific Reservation Service
701 NW 60th St.
Seattle, WASHINGTON 98107
(206) 784-0539     Fax: (206) 782-4036

This service covers Seattle, Washington State, and Vancouver and Victoria in British Columbia. The staff can book several locations or plan a guest's whole trip.

*Annual fee:* None

*Commission:* 20 percent

*Director:* Irmgard Castleberry

*Member:* TNN and Worldwide

*WEST VIRGINIA*

See **Maryland,** Amanda's Bed & Breakfast Reservation Services, and **Virginia,** Blue Ridge Bed & Breakfast

*WYOMING*

See **Montana,** Bed & Breakfast Western Adventure

# CANADA

*BRITISH COLUMBIA*

**All Seasons B&B Agency**
PO Box 5511, Stn. B
Victoria, BC V8R 6S4
(604) 655-7173
Fax: (604) 652-2117

This service covers Victoria and Vancouver Island, British Columbia.
*Annual fee:* $75
*Commission:* 20 percent
*Director:* Kate Catterill
*Member:* No membership

See also **Washington State,** A Pacific Reservation Service

# EUROPE

See **New York,** At Home in New York, for Bed & Breakfasts in Paris, Rome, Naples, Florence, and London

# Appendix B

# The Guidebooks

**G**uidebooks are presented alphabetically by title in the table on the following pages. Inclusion in any book is ultimately at the discretion of the author or editor. There have been a number of very regional books printed, but only the most popular, mostly national guides with definite plans to do another edition in the future, have been included. For an extensive list of over 250 guidebooks, contact: PAII, PO Box 90710, Santa Barbara, CA 93190, (805) 569-1853.

| Name, Author, and Address | Phone | Frequency | Cost | Requirements | Inspection | Editions |
|---|---|---|---|---|---|---|
| *AAA Tourbooks* AAA Approved Accommodations Dept. 1000 AAA Drive Heathrow, FL 32746 | (407) 444-8370 | Annual | No | 24-hour coverage of your inn | Yes | National |
| *America's Wonderful Little Hotels & Inns* by Sandra Soule PO Box 150 Riverside, CT 06878 | (203) 637-7642 | Biannual | No | Recommended by guests | No | New England, National (includes Canada), Mid-Atlantic, Midwest, South, Rocky Mountains/ Southwest, West |
| *Annual Directory of American & Canadian Bed & Breakfasts* Ed. by the editors of Rutledge Hill Press 211 Seventh Ave. N. Nashville, TN 37219-1823 | (615) 244-2700 Fax: (615) 244-2978 | Annual | $25, deadline June 1 | None | No | National, Canada, Puerto Rico, Virgin Islands |
| *B&B Homes Directory, West Coast* Ed. George Winsley PO Box 1281 Jacksonville, OR 97530 | (503) 899-1868 | Next edition planned for 1998 | Annual fee based on rates | Brochure, <6 rooms, owner-occupied, breakfast included | Yes | California, Oregon, Washington, and British Columbia |
| *B&B in the Mid-Atlantic States* by Bernice Chesler PO Box 363 Newton Highlands, MA 02161-0003 | No phone | Biannual | $50-$150 | Maximum of 10 rooms, breakfast included, owner-occupied, common room, no bar, no restaurant | No | Delaware, District of Columbia, Maryland, New Jersey, New York, North Carolina, Pennsylvania, Virginia, and West Virginia |

| Name, Author, and Address | Phone | Frequency | Cost | Requirements | Inspection | Editions |
|---|---|---|---|---|---|---|
| E&B in New England by Bernice Chesler [See B&B in the Mid-Atlantic States] | No phone | Biannual | $50–$150 | Same as above | No | Connecticut, Massachusetts, Maine, New Hampshire, Rhode Island, Vermont |
| B&B Southern California by Charles Smith Automobile Club of Southern California PO Box 2800, Terminal Annex Los Angeles, CA 90051-0890 | (213) 741-4052 | Annual | No | Inn atmosphere | No | Southern California |
| B&B USA by Betty Rundback & Peggy Ackerman Tourist House Association of America RD2, Box 355A Greentown, PA 18426 | (717) 676-3222 | Annual | $35, includes copy of book | Under 15 rooms, submit photos, breakfast included | No | National |
| Bed & Breakfast Guest Houses & Inns of America by Marie R. Brindza PO Box 38929 Memphis, TN 38183-3829 Published exclusively for travel agents.* | (901) 755-9613 Fax: (901) 758-0816 | 3 times a year | $130 | Under 30 rooms | No | Canada, West Coast, New England, mid-America, South (includes Caribbean) |

*CD-ROM version: text plus up to 14 photos ($50 per picture over 1), updated quarterly. On-line service for travel agents, corporate travel departments, and libraries. Inn travel club for guests where they earn free lodging, a quality assurance program for innkeepers. The Bed & Breakfast collection offers discount program to innkeepers. You must be in their books or a recognized state association.

| Name, Author, and Address | Phone | Frequency | Cost | Requirements | Inspection | Editions |
|---|---|---|---|---|---|---|
| *Birnbaum's Country Inns and Back Roads, North America* Contact: Lois Spritzer, Editorial Director HarperCollins 10 E. 53rd St. New York, NY 10022 | No phone | Annual, deadline: June | No | None | Yes | National, Canada |
| *Christian Bed & Breakfast Directory* PO Box 718 1819 Barbour Drive Uhrichville, OH 44683 | (614) 922-6045 Fax: (614) 992-5948 | Annual | $25 | None | No | U.S. and Canada |
| *Complete Guide to B&Bs, Inns, and Guesthouses\** by Pamela Lanier PO D Petaluma, CA 94952 | (707) 763-0271 | Annual | $85, includes spring and fall newsletter | None | No | U.S., Canada, and worldwide |
| *Fodor's Short Escapes from NYC* by Nicola Coddington Beachscape Publishing 145 Palisade St. Dobbs Ferry, NY 10522 | (914) 674-9283 | Every two years | No | Near historic or architectural interest or convenient & charming | Yes | New York |
| *Great American Travel Guide* by Anne and Colin Pottinger Annlin Publications PO Box 1562 Santa Clara, CA 91386 | (805) 252-1238 | Ongoing | $19.50/year | None | No | National |

\*Guide on-line on CompuServe, World Wide Web/Internet, and Geosystems (R. R. Donnelly). Send SASE to Pamela for a free list of B&B resources.

| Name, Author, and Address | Phone | Frequency | Cost | Requirements | Inspection | Editions |
|---|---|---|---|---|---|---|
| Inn Review Yellow Pages Inn Business Review PO Box 1789 Kankakee, IL 60901 (Informational resources for innkeepers) | (815) 939-3509 | Annual | Cost of ad | Subscribe to Inn Business Review | No | National |
| Inspected, Rated, & Approved Bed & Breakfasts and Country Inns ABBA, PO Box 1387 Midlothian, VA 23113-1387 | (804) 379-2222 Fax: (804) 379-3627 | Annual | $350 membership | Many | Yes | USA and Canada |
| Mobil Travel Guide 4709 W. Gulf Rd., Suite 803 Skokie, Il 60076 | (708) 329-1140 | Annual | No | Cleanliness, stars depend on evaluation | Yes | Regional |
| National Trust Guide to Historic B&Bs, Inns and Small Hotels by Barbara Sturni & Suzanne Dana National Trust for Historic Preservation 1785 Massachusetts Ave., NW Washington, DC 20036 | (202) 673-4099 | Every 1½ years | $85-295 | At least 50 years old, preserves historic ambiance | No | National |
| Official Airline Guides (OAG)* 2000 Clearwater Dr. Oak Brook, IL 60521-8806 | (708) 574-6000 Fax: (708) 574-6667 | Annual | Range of cost | None | No | National |

*Often called the OAG Travel Planner, most used by travel agents (electronic version available).

| Name, Author, and Address | Phone | Frequency | Cost | Requirements | Inspection | Editions |
|---|---|---|---|---|---|---|
| *The Official Bed & Breakfast Guide for the US, Canada, and the Caribbean* by Phyliss Featherston and Barbara F. Ostler PO Box 332 Norwalk, CT 06852 | (203) 847-6196 Fax: (203) 847-0469 | Biannual | $100 for 2 years, includes picture and 200-word description | <30 rooms, breakfast included | No | National |
| *Official Guide to American Historic Inns* by Deborah & Tim Sakach American Historic Inns PO Box 336 Dana Point, CA 92629 | (714) 496-6953 | Annual | $48, includes copy of book and newsletter | B&B built 1939 or earlier | No | National |
| *On the Road Again with Man's Best Friend* by Dawn and Robert Habgood Dawbert Press PO Box 2758 Duxbury, MA 02331 | (617) 934-7202 Fax: (617) 934-2945 | Annual | No | Must accept dogs | No | National, New England, West Connecticut, Mid-Atlantic, Southeast, 8 regional guides expected by 1997. |

# Appendix C

# State Bed and Breakfast Associations

This information was fact-checked in 1995 and should be accurate into 1996. Because most officers of state associations are volunteers and their terms end every year or two, key people will change. The contact information that follows should get you to a past president even if officers have changed. He or she will be able to pass you on to the correct contact person. As this book will not be revised again for a few years, dues and member benefits may change.

*ARIZONA*

**Arizona Association of B&B Inns**
PO Box 7186, Phoenix, AZ 85011
(602) 277-0775

*Members:* 19
*Annual dues:* $175.
*Member benefits:* Networking, annual brochure, approved inspection, business meeting in January, educational conference in August or October, group buying, participation in state brochure.

*CALIFORNIA*

**California Association of B&B Inns**
2715 Porter Sq., Soquel, CA 95073
(408) 462-9191
Fax: (408) 462-0402

*Members:* 250

*Annual dues:* $200 plus $10 a room with a cap of $300

*Member benefits:* Group credit card program, liability insurance and workers compensation, annual trade show, networking and inclusion in the state guide (a basic listing, larger ads done at an additional charge). The association inspects each B&B and certifies that each meets all requirements.

## COLORADO

### Bed & Breakfast Innkeepers of Colorado Association
PO Box 38416
Colorado Springs, CO 80937-8416
(719) 687-6784

*Members:* 122

*Annual dues:* $150 plus $20 a room

*Member benefits:* Newsletter, statewide directory, conference, inspection, credit card discount, and subscription discounts on industry newsletters.

## FLORIDA

### Inn Route

### The Association of Smaller and Historic Lodging Properties of Florida
PO Box 9792
Palm Harbor, FL
(813) 786-9792, fax or phone

*Members:* 100

*Annual dues:* $20 a room with a minimum of $225 and a maximum of $500

*Member benefits:* Aggressive marketing, 50,000 brochures distributed annually, 800 number, press releases, cooperative advertising, and yearly conference. Members must be licensed.

## GEORGIA

### Georgia B&B Council
600 W. Peachtree St., Suite 1500
Atlanta, GA 30308
(404) 873-4482

*Members:* 200

*Annual dues:* $153.75

*Member benefits:* Annual brochure, part of state promotional literature.

*HAWAII*

**B&B Homestay Proprietors Association of Hawaii**
1277 Mokulua Dr.
Kailua, HI 96734
(808) 261-1059

*Members:* 32

*Annual dues:* N/A

*Member benefits:* Annual brochure. Once you are inspected and approved, you can access any of the B&B's through *Travel Life.*

*ILLINOIS*

**Illinois Bed & Breakfast Association**
Corner of Main and Mill
Macytown, IL 62256
(618) 458-6660 for consumers or (800) 342-3100 for brochure

*Members:* 108

*Annual dues:* $75 base + inspection fees

*Member benefits:* Marketing statewide, direct mail of brochure, lobbying in department of tourism, and bank card services.

*INDIANA*

**Indiana Bed & Breakfast Association**
Box 1127
Goshen, IN 46526
(219) 926-5781

*Members:* 135

*Annual dues:* Range from $110 to $235 depending on number of rooms

*Member benefits:* Quality review inspection, brochure, workshops, newsletter, networking, leadership classes, speakers bureau.

*IOWA*

**Iowa B&B Innkeepers Association**
629 1st Ave. E
Newton, IA 50208
(515) 792-6833 or (800) 743-4692

*Members:* 62

*Annual dues:* $89 and $1 a room, plus $45 for brochure

*Member benefits:* Brochure and conference, networking.

## KANSAS

**Kansas B&B Association**
Rte. 1, Box 93, Wakeeney, KS 67672

*Members:* 85

*Annual dues:* $75 + $10 a room

*Member benefits:* Annual publication, inspections, meetings

## KENTUCKY

**B&Bs of Kentucky**
Sue Richards
RidgeRunner B&B
208 Arthur Hts.
Middleborough, KY 40965
(606) 248-4299

*Members:* 100

*Annual dues:* $100

*Member benefits:* Automatic membership in the Kentucky Tourism Council, network through them, inspection every two years, annual two-day conference, quarterly newsletter, cookbook, and association advertising.

## LOUISIANA

**Louisiana B&B Association**
PO Box 4003
Baton Rouge, Louisiana 70821
(318) 896-6529

**Louisiana Travel & Promotion Associations**
(504) 346-1857     Fax: (504) 336-4154

*Members:* 136

*Annual dues:* $180

*Member benefits:* Inclusion in the Louisiana Tour guide ($60 more gives you a photo, too), Louisiana Tourism Association membership, annual conference, inspection program, advertising, networking, education, and awards.

## MAINE

**Maine Innkeepers Association**
305 Commercial St.
Portland, ME 04101-4641
(207) 773-7670

*Members:* 525 (includes hotels)

*Annual dues:* Varies from $90 to $300 depending on number of rooms

*Member benefits:* Monthly newsletter, insurance program, health and dental benefits, full-time lobbyists, statewide directory listing (display ads extra), annual meetings, scholarships (hotel/motel or culinary), educational meetings for employees.

## MARYLAND

### The Maryland Bed & Breakfast Association
PO Box 23324
Baltimore, MD 21203
(301) 831-4455

*Members:* 50

*Annual dues:*   $50 per member plus $50 a room

*Member benefits:* Group buying program, medical insurance and retirement plan, fire insurance, one or two newsletters a year, annual conference, 800 number sponsored by the State Tourism Council, statewide brochure listing.

## MICHIGAN

### Lake to Lake Association
19271 S. Lakeside Rd.
New Buffalo, MI 49117
(616) 756-3445     Fax: (616) 756-3480

*Members:* 280

*Annual dues:* $130-$160 depending on number of rooms, $75 review fee to cover inspection (first year only), $85 directory listing fee (changes every year)

*Member benefits:* Telephone consultation, quarterly newsletter, annual conference, work with Michigan travel bureau, cookbook, room trades with participating members, discount on long-distance telephone service, member discount to PAII, credit card service.

## MINNESOTA

### Minnesota Bed & Breakfast Guild
1161 Bluff Creek Drive
Chaska, MN 55318
(612) 433-5248

*Members:* 70

*Annual dues:* $50

*Member benefits:* Set standards and review B&Bs, twice-a-year seminars for new innkeepers, newsletter.

### Minnesota Historic B&B Association
17500 St. Croix Trail North
Marine on St. Croix, MN 55047

*Members:* 12

*Annual dues:* $30

*Member benefits:* Newsletter, networking.

## *MONTANA*

### Montana B&B Association
480 Bad Rock Dr.
Columbia Falls, MT 59912
(800) 453-8870

*Members:* 41

*Annual dues:* $75 plus 10 a room

*Member benefits:* Joint advertising, which for most members brings 80 percent of their business, phone co-op, 800 number for last-minute reservations (operated by a different member each month), inspections.

## *NEBRASKA*

### Nebraska Association of Bed & Breakfast
RR 2 Box 17
Elgin, NE 68636-9301
(402) 843-2287

*Members:* 56

*Annual dues:* $100

*Member benefits:* 25,000+ brochures, cooperative advertising, picture files that are distributed at key points, how-to packet for future members ($5), two general meetings yearly at which there are workshops and seminars.

## *NEW HAMPSHIRE*

### New England B&B Association (covers 6 states)
PO Box 1089
North Hampton, NH 03862
(603) 964-6689    Fax: (603) 964-6792

*Members:* 350

*Annual dues:* $150-$650 depending on size

*Member benefits:* Educational seminars twice a year, resource center for B&Bs, co-op advertising, networking.

## *NEW JERSEY*

### B&B Innkeepers Association of New Jersey, Inc.
PO Box 108
Spring Lake, NJ 07762
(908) 449-3535

*Members:* 80

*Annual dues:* $150 plus $6 a room

*Member benefits:* Distribution of 50,000 wonderful, full-color, brochures; helped change the state fire code; meetings, networking, cooperative advertising with the state of New Jersey.

## NEW YORK

### BBANYS (B&B Association of New York State)
B&B Wellington
707 Danforth St.
Syracuse, NY 13208-1611
(315) 474-3641     Fax: (315) 474-2557

*Members:* 126

*Annual dues:* $70 for under five rooms; $90 for over five rooms. Statewide brochure extra

*Member benefits:* Standards setting, newsletter, annual conference with educational workshops and aspiring innkeeper classes, brochure.

## NORTH CAROLINA

### North Carolina B&B Inns
318 W. Queen St.
Hillsborough, NC 27278

## OHIO

### Ohio B&B Association
4211 Donlyn Ct.
Columbus, OH 43232
(614) 868-5567     Fax: (614) 868-1177

*Members:* 200

*Annual dues:* $100 for up to six rooms; $5 a room for additional rooms. Special rate for aspiring innkeepers of $50.

*Member benefits:* Standards review every three years, statewide directory mailed through 1-800-BUCKEYE (the state tourism number), inns listed on-line through CompuServe.

## OKLAHOMA

### Oklahoma B&B Association
766 DeBarr
Norman, OK 73069
(405) 321-6221

*Members:* 30

*Annual dues:* $100 plus $5 a room. Optional co-op ad program

*Member benefits:* Inspections, brochure at all state information centers, conferences twice a year.

*OREGON*

**Oregon Bed & Breakfast Guild**
PO Box 3187
Ashland, OR 97520
(503) 482-8707

*PENNSYLVANIA*

**Pennsylvania Travel Council**
Bed and Breakfast Division
902 N. Second St.
Harrisburg, PA 17102
(717) 232-8880

**Bed & Breakfast Inns of Bucks and Hunterdon Counties**
PO Box 215
New Hope, PA 18938

*SOUTH CAROLINA*

**Bed & Breakfast of South Carolina**
278-K Harbison Blvd., Suite 120
Columbia, SC 29212
(803) 869-2535

*SOUTH DAKOTA*

**Bed and Breakfast Innkeepers of South Dakota**
PO Box 7682
Rapid City, SD 57709
(605) 456-2836

*Members:* 34

*Annual dues:* $150 for five rooms or less, $175 for over five rooms

*Member benefits:* Inspection uniform standards (inspectors are not innkeepers but volunteer couples who stay at all inns and then rate them), PAII membership, creative promotions, legislative watchdog, wide variety of listings from Victorian homes to sheep farms to cabins.

*TENNESSEE*

**Tennessee B&B Association**
PO Box 120428
Nashville, TN 37212
(800) 820-8144

*Members:* 110

*Annual dues:* $75-$125

*Member benefits:* 800 number, mail association brochure on request, marketed nationally, joint marketing and advertising, buying discounts, two educational conferences a year for all levels and aspects, mentor program for first-year inn-keepers, and three yearly aspiring innkeeper workshops.

## TEXAS

### B&B Society of Texas
1200 Southmoore Blvd
Houston, TX 77004
(713) 523-1114

No state association. This is a statewide reservation service.
*Members:* 70
*Annual dues:* $50 to start up, no yearly dues
*Member benefits:* Inspection, marketing, and reservations.

## UTAH

### B&B Inns of Utah
PO Box 3066
Park City, Utah 84060
(801) 595-0332

*Members:* 30
*Annual dues:* $200 first year plus $10 a room, then drops to $100 plus $10 a room in subsequent years
*Member benefits:* Logo, inspection to meet standards, credit union, meeting.

## VERMONT

### Vermont Chamber of Commerce
Box 37
Montpelier, VT 05601
(802) 223-3443

*Members:* 1,600 travel-related properties. Not limited to B&Bs, but can perform many of the functions of a state as-sociation.

## VIRGINIA

### Bed & Breakfast Association of Virginia
PO Box 791
Orange, VA 22960
(703) 672-0870

*Members:* 183
*Annual dues:* $200 plus $25 a room, for a maximum of $400
*Member benefits:* Quarterly newsletter, color brochure (80,000 copies in 1995), state association guidebook (also available on CD-ROM), cookbook, commercials, and gift certificate program.

## WASHINGTON STATE

**Washington B&B Guild**
PO Box 2442
NW Market Street
Seattle, WA 98107
(800) 647-2918

*Members:* 106

*Annual dues:* Starts at $100, depending on size

*Member benefits:* Members must be licensed, inspected, and approved by state. Works as a group on state issues.

## WEST VIRGINIA

**West Virginia Division of Tourism**
Attn: B&B's
State Capital Complex
Charleston, WV 25305
(304) 558-2286

*Members:* 50

*Annual dues:* $50 for six rooms, $10 for each additional room

*Member benefits:* No formal state B&B association. Above address is a state-run tourism association that accepts B&Bs.

## WISCONSIN

**Wisconsin B&B Homes & Historic Inns Association**
108 S. Cleveland St.
Merrill, WI 54452
(715) 536-2507 or (800) 432-TRIP

*Members:* 254

*Annual dues:* $150 plus $15 a room

*Member benefits:* Wonderful color brochure including pictures, annual convention, joint marketing and advertising.

## WYOMING

**Wyoming Homestay & Outdoor Adventure (WHOA)**
1031 Steinley Rd
Douglas, WY 82633
(307) 358-2380

*Members:* 80

*Annual dues:* $75, plus $10 a room over three rooms

*Member benefits:* Brochure (40,000 printed), networking, joint marketing, co-op advertising, two meetings a year.

# Appendix D

# Sources

## FOOD

**Favorite Products**
PO Box 581067
Minneapolis, MN 55458-1067
(800) 721-8639

They sell ten flavors of Land O'Lakes®, Cocoa Classics®, Hot Cocoa Mix; gourmet coffees and teas; and other food-related products. Call to be on their mailing list.

## HARDWARE AND HOME

**Antique Hardware & Home**
1C Mathews Court
Hilton Head, SC 29926
(800) 422-9982    Fax: (803) 681-9790

Their free catalogue offers a complete line of old-style hardware and housewares. Order direct to save big money.

## INSURANCE

**James W. Wolf Insurance**
PO Box 510
Ellicott City, MD 21041
(800) 488-1135    Fax: (410) 750-0322

Jim and Christy Wolf have developed insurance coverage offering specific policies for the inn, the innkeeper, and the guest. This is one of the most comprehensive packages on the market.

**Potter, Leonard, & Cahan, Inc.**
6161 Northeast 175th St., Suite 205
Seattle, WA 98155
(206) 486-4334 or (800) 548-8857
Fax: (206) 486-4681

Potter, Leonard, & Cahan, Inc., has been specializing in Bed and Breakfast insurance since 1986. They offer a policy tailored to the needs of B&B owners and insure over 500 inns across the country.

# LINENS

**The Linen Source**
5401 Hanger Court
Tampa, FL 33634
(800) 431-2620
Fax: (813) 882-4605

Their free catalogue offers a wide selection of bedding and linen items at very good prices with the convenience of mail-order shopping.

# PRINTING AND PROMOTION

**French Creek Trading Co.**
PO Box 822
Kimberton, PA 19442
(800) 216-8057

Send for a free catalogue describing the wide range of custom-printed promotional items sold by this company. They produce a beautiful guest register, as well as pens, note pads, flags, sportswear, amenities, and so on.

# Index